THE LETTERS
OF JOHN

THE NIV
APPLICATION
COMMENTARY

From biblical text . . . to contemporary life

THE LETTERS
OF JOHN

THE NIV
APPLICATION
COMMENTARY

From biblical text . . . to contemporary life

GARY M. BURGE

ZONDERVAN.com/
AUTHORTRACKER
follow your favorite authors

To Donald Mitchell
and LeRoy King
Wise elders in the faith
who guided me through
two important doors.

ZONDERVAN

The NIV Application Commentary: The Letters of John
Copyright © 1996 by Gary M. Burge

Requests for information should be addressed to:

Zondervan, *Grand Rapids, Michigan* 49530

Library of Congress Cataloging-in-Publication Data

Burge, Gary M.
  The letters of John / Gary M. Burge.
    p. cm.—(NIV application commentary)
  Includes bibliographical references and index.
  ISBN 978-0-310-48620-6
   1. Bible. N.T. Epistles of John—Commentaries. I. Bible. N.T. Epistles of John. English.
  New International. 1996. II. Title. III. Series.
  BS2805.3.B884 1996
  227'.94077—cd20   95-47530

Edited by Verlyn D. Verbrugge

Printed in the United States of America

14 · 35 34 33 32 31 30 29 28 27 26 25 24 23 22 21 20 19

Table of Contents

The NIV Application Commentary Series

When complete, the NIV Application Commentary
will include the following volumes:

To see which titles are available,
visit our web site at www.zondervan.com

NIV Application Commentary
Series Introduction

THE NIV APPLICATION COMMENTARY SERIES is unique. Most commentaries help us make the journey from the twentieth century back to the first century. They enable us to cross the barriers of time, culture, language, and geography that separate us from the biblical world. Yet they only offer a one-way ticket to the past and assume that we can somehow make the return journey on our own. Once they have explained the *original meaning* of a book or passage, these commentaries give us little or no help in exploring its *contemporary significance*. The information they offer is valuable, but the job is only half done.

Recently, a few commentaries have included some contemporary application as *one* of their goals. Yet that application is often sketchy or moralistic, and some volumes sound more like printed sermons than commentaries.

The primary goal of The NIV Application Commentary Series is to help you with the difficult but vital task of bringing an ancient message into a modern context. The series not only focuses on application as a finished product but also helps you think through the *process* of moving from the original meaning of a passage to its contemporary significance. These are commentaries, not popular expositions. They are works of reference, not devotional literature.

The format of the series is designed to achieve the goals of the series. Each passage is treated in three sections: *Original Meaning, Bridging Contexts*, and *Contemporary Significance*.

THIS SECTION HELPS you understand the meaning of the biblical text in its first-century context. All of the elements of traditional exegesis—in concise form—are discussed here. These include the historical, literary, and cultural context of the passage. The authors discuss matters related to grammar and syntax, and the meaning of biblical words. They also seek to explore the main ideas of the passage and how the biblical author develops those ideas.

After reading this section, you will understand the problems, questions, and concerns of the *original audience* and how the biblical author addressed those issues. This understanding is foundational to any legitimate application of the text today.

THIS SECTION BUILDS a bridge between the world of the Bible and the world of today, between the original context and the contemporary context, by focusing on both the timely and timeless aspects of the text.

God's Word is *timely*. The authors of Scripture spoke to specific situations, problems, and questions. Paul warned the Galatians about the consequences of circumcision and the dangers of trying to be justified by law (Gal. 5:2–5). The author of Hebrews tried to convince his readers that Christ is superior to Moses, the Aaronic priests, and the Old Testament sacrifices. John urged his readers to "test the spirits" of those who taught a form of incipient Gnosticism (1 John 4:1–6). In each of these cases, the timely nature of Scripture enables us to hear God's Word in situations that were *concrete* rather than abstract.

Yet the timely nature of Scripture also creates problems. Our situations, difficulties, and questions are not always directly related to those faced by the people in the Bible. Therefore, God's word to them does not always seem relevant to us. For example, when was the last time someone urged you to be circumcised, claiming that it was a necessary part of justification? How many people today care whether Christ is superior to the Aaronic priests? And how can a "test" designed to expose incipient Gnosticism be of any value in a modern culture?

Fortunately, Scripture is not only timely but *timeless*. Just as God spoke to the original audience, so he still speaks to us through the pages of Scripture. Because we share a common humanity with the people of the Bible, we discover a *universal dimension* in the problems they faced and the solutions God gave them. The timeless nature of Scripture enables it to speak with power in every time and in every culture.

Those who fail to recognize that Scripture is both timely and timeless run into a host of problems. For example, those who are intimidated by timely books such as Hebrews or Galatians might avoid reading them because they seem meaningless today. At the other extreme, those who are convinced of the timeless nature of Scripture, but who fail to discern its timely element, may "wax eloquent" about the Melchizedekian priesthood to a sleeping congregation.

The purpose of this section, therefore, is to help you discern what is timeless in the timely pages of the New Testament—and what is not. For example, if Paul's primary concern is not circumcision (as he tells us in Gal. 5:6), what *is* he concerned about? If discussions about the Aaronic priesthood or Melchizedek seem irrelevant today, what is of abiding value in these passages? If people try to "test the spirits" today with a test designed for a specific first-century heresy, what other biblical test might be more appropriate?

Yet this section does not merely uncover that which is timeless in a passage but also helps you to see *how* it is uncovered. The author of the commentary seeks to take what is implicit in the text and make it explicit, to take a process that normally is intuitive and explain it in a logical, orderly fashion. How do we know that circumcision is not Paul's primary concern? What clues in the text or its context help us realize that Paul's real concern is at a deeper level?

Of course, those passages in which the historical distance between us and the original readers is greatest require a longer treatment. Conversely, those passages in which the historical distance is smaller or seemingly nonexistent require less attention.

One final clarification. Because this section prepares the way for discussing the contemporary significance of the passage, there is not always a sharp distinction or a clear break between this section and the one that follows. Yet when both sections are read together, you should have a strong sense of moving from the world of the Bible to the world of today.

THIS SECTION ALLOWS the biblical message to speak with as much power today as it did when it was first written. How can you apply what you learned about Jerusalem, Ephesus, or Corinth to our present-day needs in Chicago, Los Angeles, or London? How can you take a message originally spoken in Greek and

Aramaic and communicate it clearly in our own language? How can you take the eternal truths originally spoken in a different time and culture and apply them to the similar-yet-different needs of our culture?

In order to achieve these goals, this section gives you help in several key areas.

First, it helps you identify contemporary situations, problems, or questions that are truly comparable to those faced by the original audience. Because contemporary situations are seldom identical to those faced in the first century, you must seek situations that are analogous if your applications are to be relevant.

Second, this section explores a variety of contexts in which the passage might be applied today. You will look at personal applications, but you will also be encouraged to think beyond private concerns to the society and culture at large.

Third, this section will alert you to any problems or difficulties you might encounter in seeking to apply the passage. And if there are several legitimate ways to apply a passage (areas in which Christians disagree), the author will bring these to your attention and help you think through the issues involved.

In seeking to achieve these goals, the contributors to this series attempt to avoid two extremes. They avoid making such specific applications that the commentary might quickly become dated. They also avoid discussing the significance of the passage in such a general way that it fails to engage contemporary life and culture.

Above all, contributors to this series have made a diligent effort not to sound moralistic or preachy. The NIV Application Commentary Series does not seek to provide ready-made sermon materials but rather tools, ideas, and insights that will help you communicate God's Word with power. If we help you to achieve that goal, then we have fulfilled the purpose for this series.

The Editors

General Editor's Preface

WE LIVE IN AN AGE in which discernment has never been more important: Christian discernment; theological discernment; discernment based on biblical standards; discernment that will show us the narrow way between excess and stinginess, license and legalism, innovation and sterility. In the face of a culture bombarding us with the pop wisdom that the difference between true and false is an outdated remnant of Western dualism, Christians must never relinquish the need to proclaim the difference between right and wrong. The Johannine letters teach just such discernment.

As Professor Burge shows in this commentary, the Johannine community was struggling with internal theological threats that can only be called heretical. "Threats that were once external"—believers in secret esoteric wisdom, incorrect views of Jesus, immoral behavior—"were now found within the ranks of the fellowship itself." John, the author of these letters, demands that the Christians reading these words realize that they have a responsibility to discern between the true and the false, between Christian behavior and un-Christian behavior. The Johannine letters are a clear call to stand firm in the historic revelation of Jesus Christ and the Incarnation.

We need discernment every bit as much as did the first readers of 1 John, 2 John, and 3 John, but the need takes a different form these days. We are living in a time between worldviews, a vacant, interim period between a consensual, orthodox championing of a single theological system and an as yet unknown approach to truth that will come to grips with (and finally defeat) that powerful conviction that there is no single gospel truth. Into this vacuum have rushed a flood of theological experiments, each attempting to reconcile the eternal, unchanging nature of God with the constantly shifting focus of everyday life.

Make no mistake. This vacuum is real. It is a vacuum that will produce a new, gospel-honoring approach to theology, a theology that will reflect unchanging scriptural truth. But in the meantime a thousand theologies will bloom and have their day in the sun. Like wildflowers dotting today's theological wilderness, they will each display a raw if temporary beauty. We must judge which will last.

Each of these wildflower theologies has some value. They are like the short-term flora and fauna that spring up in ecological systems ravaged by disasters like forest fires. They hold the ground in place until the larger, more stable plants get a chance to grow back. When a building is bulldozed to an empty lot, weeds and wildflowers spring up before the return of more lasting species. Wildflower theology can serve a similar purpose, but in the end their true nature as opportunistic mistakes emerges, and they drift away.

They wither away, that is, if we as the true church are doing our job, the job of theological discernment, a job that in its essence has not changed from John's day. John taught that the measuring sticks of true discernment will never change: the truth revealed in the historical coming of Jesus Christ and everything which that glorious event revealed, and in the powerful theological traditions that have grown up around that event. Those are our measuring sticks, too.

In the end a theology will prevail, a theology that picks up the threat of truth that goes back to creation itself. But that theology will not come without hard work and some risk. Gary M. Burge shows us how the Johannine letters can play a crucial role in the task of discerning truth.

Terry C. Muck

Author's Preface

FEW WRITINGS IN THE NEW TESTAMENT fascinate us like the writings of John. Commentaries on the Fourth Gospel, like commentaries on Romans, draw surprising interest among scholars and teachers of the Scriptures. In some fashion we sense that John has probed the center of Christian belief and practice, that he is describing a depth of insight and experience unmatched by many other writers. It is not surprising that at the early church councils of Nicea and Chalcedon, theologians looked to John's writings for guidance as they discerned the contours of Christ's relation to the Father and the meaning of the Incarnation.

I have been intrigued with the Johannine literature from the early 1980s when I wrote a dissertation on John's theology of the Holy Spirit (published in 1987 as *The Anointed Community: The Holy Spirit in the Johannine Tradition*). Since that time Johannine scholars have come to appreciate how John's Gospel and letters spring from a living community of Christians who were working to live and express their faith in a world that was not always congenial to them. For some scholars, this means compromising the historical character of John's Gospel; but for others, it means discovering a second depth of meaning to words and stories we have read for many years.

The letters of John have traditionally received limited attention. For some Christians, 1 John is a brief, familiar collection of favorite verses to which we turn when seeking encouragement; it is a patchwork of memorable lines that speak to us about forgiveness, truth, and particularly love. John's other two letters, sadly, have been escorted to the periphery of the New Testament writings. Their brevity and highly personal character have given them uncertain value to the average Christian.

This commentary has unveiled to me the value of John's letters because they disclose something of the history of early Christianity. When we reconstruct the world of John's churches (uniting the Fourth Gospel with his letters) and begin to locate these letters in that world, an entirely new vista opens before us. This is not a church setting of leisure and calm; rather, this is a church that is struggling with the intellectual milieu of its day as well as with matters of internal leadership and thought. John is writing because problems have arisen—because certain people have either challenged his leadership or upended traditional teachings about Jesus. And these issues must be addressed.

It is reassuring to see that we can and should lay to rest the fantasy of a pristine, harmonious early Christianity. The church—John's church and our church—is both a *divine* creation and a *human* institution. And the extent to which we can appreciate John's struggles and victories, we will learn how to cope with and overcome the human struggles in our own Christian communities.

The Christian communities in which I live have contributed to many of the thoughts found in the commentary. Wheaton College, with its intellectual rigor and its spiritual zeal, reflects many of the high ideals that the Johannine community held dear. Its students and faculty never cease to be examples to me of men and women who passionately desire to "walk in the light" as John envisioned it (1 John 1:7). Glen Ellyn Covenant Church is another community for me that holds aloft a vision for Christian life, delicately joining together the Johannine themes of obedience and love (3:18–24). David and Judy Smith, Lee and Ken Phillips, Kaye and Wally Filkin, my wife, Carol, and I all formed our own community in a small group that studied John's letters for one year. Our shared thoughts and experiences appear throughout the application sections of the book.

The editorial staff at Zondervan and the general editors of this series have provided invaluable help. Jack Kuhatschek gave generous advice and encouragement at critical moments, and Verlyn Verbrugge's expert editorial skill improved the manuscript on every page. Marianne Meye Thompson and Terry Muck each read the manuscript carefully and suggested insightful, percipient improvements. And special thanks is due to Meredith Omland, who prepared the Scripture index.

Finally, a word of explanation about the dedication. In 1981 Donald Mitchell was the president of King College in Bristol, Tennessee. At what must have seemed a significant gamble, he offered a job to one freshly minted Ph.D. For his trust and confidence I will always be grateful. LeRoy King continues to serve Tennessee as a representative of Eerdmans Publishing Company, a true renaissance man with a love for literature and Christian theology. I am grateful for his efforts and encouragement to publish my first manuscript. Dr. Mitchell and Mr. King opened doors I could not open myself and became friends whom I grew to admire deeply. The writer of Hebrews may well have had such men in mind when he wrote, in Hebrews 13:7:

> Remember your leaders, who spoke the word of God to you. Consider the outcome of their way of life and imitate their faith.

Gary M. Burge
Autumn 1995

Abbreviations

AB	Anchor Bible
BTB	*Bibilical Theology Bulletin*
Gk	Greek
ICC	International Critical Commentary
IVPNTC	InterVaristy Press New Testament Commentary
JSOT	Journal for the Study of the Old Testament
LXX	Septuagint
MNTC	Moffatt New Testament Commentary
NICNT	New International Commentary on the New Testament
NIV	New International Version
NRSV	New Revised Standard Version
NTS	*New Testament Studies*
RevExp	*Review and Expositor*
RSV	Revised Standard Version
TDNT	*Theological Dictionary of the New Testament*
WBC	Word Biblical Commentary

Introduction

CHURCHES OFTEN STRUGGLE. Even good churches. What seems to be an ideal and harmonious situation on the surface may disguise a congregation wrestling at a profound level with questions of mission, belief, and leadership. Sometimes there is outright conflict.

Unfortunately we often idealize the New Testament era and its churches. We fantasize about how life must have been then. We think, for instance, that the congregations of Paul generally found their conflicts to be *external* to their congregational life. A synagogue, perhaps, much like those in Antioch of Pisidia or Iconium (Acts 13–14), gave Paul's followers trouble. Or perhaps it was a rival body of believers, another "denomination," like the Judaizers who dogged his churches in Galatia. But rarely do we accept the notion that some of these churches struggled *internally*; that they experienced a laity in revolt, or failed leadership, or elders who rivaled the authority of the pastor, or genuine confusion about Christian faith and practice.

Occasionally we are given glimpses of such struggles. The church at Corinth, for instance, certainly had internal problems of leadership and mission. First Corinthians 1:10–17 means at least this much. Likewise, Paul's letter to Philippi was occasioned not simply by the persecutions of those hostile to Christ (Phil. 1:27–30), but also by reports that members of the church itself were at each other's throats, living selfishly, arguing aggressively, and barely exhibiting the character of Christ (2:1–18). Simply put, Paul had churches that were engaged in seriously destructive behavior.

I am convinced that the churches led by the apostle John likewise struggled. And the letters of John, particularly 1 John, are documents that lend some insight into difficult years of pastoral leadership. For instance, 1 John 2:18–19 suggests that the church receiving this letter had even split; some members had left the congregation in an uproar. John even uses the term "antichrist" to describe their behavior. But the trouble didn't stop there. These disgruntled former members still held a pull on the church.[1] They were playing heavy-handed politics. They were cajoling John's faithful members to come away and join the revolt (2:26). John spares no words in criticizing these people. He calls them "children of the devil" (3:10).

This commentary is committed to "bridging" the contexts of the biblical text and the context in which we live today. In the past I have valued the letters of John as sources of personal encouragement and exhortation. I still do. Just like the Fourth Gospel, these letters— particularly 1 John—are filled with memorable thoughts that seem timeless. However, recent years have done much to reconstruct the likely setting of these letters and unveil the circumstances that brought them to life. Discovering that original context has, for me, given them a relevance for the modern church that is unparalleled. *In other words, the Johannine context can be bridged because its setting is utterly germane to our world today.*

Recently I attended a men's retreat, thinking that most of the participants would be laymen of our church. But sitting across from me the first morning was a minister from a mainline denomination—an ex-minister I should say—who had been "run out of his church" (to use his words). A circle of elders claiming inspiration in the Spirit had challenged his authority and demolished his ministry. They claimed to know new things about the Lord and the Spirit, and their persuasive abilities had won over the bulk of the congregation. The pastor had become a casualty of the many lethal skirmishes that went on weekly.

The letters of John know conflict and struggle. They were born in the midst of intense controversy. In their pages John works to give guidance; in doing so, he draws a sweeping panorama of what should be normal Christian thought and behavior when congregational life gets tough. But this hardly means that we have to be in crisis to appreciate the words of these letters. *While the original context may have been conflictual, still, the substance of John's response to this conflict has value for many other situations.* Life in community is often challenging and sometimes difficult. John provides us with guidelines that help us assess the quality of our life together as we try to build the type of Christian communities John no doubt envisioned.

---

1. It is difficult for us to know if the letters of John represent his comments to a single congregation or to a cluster of churches planted by the apostle. I am inclined to agree with the latter view.

John's Timeless Questions

UNFORTUNATELY MANY COMMENTARIES on these letters attempt to reconstruct the questions of antiquity without sincerely bringing their concerns into our own generation. I am convinced that these letters have a great deal to say when we lift their concerns from the first century and bring them into our own. Many come to mind immediately:

Handling conflict. Are there limits to dissent in a congregation? What does leadership do when members decide that the usual course of church life is no longer satisfying? Or what if the usual course of theological orthodoxy is deemed archaic? What happens when dissent becomes so acerbic and biting that it inevitably splits the congregation? What is a pastor supposed to do? John found himself in this very predicament.

Charismatic tensions. When debate is fueled by people claiming new experiences and revelations in God's Spirit, conflicts become that much more intense. *How do we confront wrong teaching when it is buttressed by claims of spiritual authority?* How can we spiritually equip sincere believers so that they will not fall prey to people who irresponsibly undermine pastoral authority? John's opponents were claiming to be filled with the Spirit, and this inspiration was the basis of their complaints.

Testing true faith. Many people claim to be Christians today and even embrace a faith that says, "Jesus is the Son of God." But what happens when doctrinal compromises seem to change what it is these people actually believe? Does the Christian faith bear a content—not just an experience or feeling—about which there is no compromising? What is doctrinally *essential* for Christian faith? Today we live in a world of competing religious truth-claims, and "heresy" is a noun few of us are comfortable using anymore. John's opponents would readily say that they were Christians; but they had put a spin on Christian doctrine that the apostle found utterly abhorrent. Should we be as intolerant—even abrasive—as John seems to be when confronting these views?

Testing Christian conduct. What happens when people with crystalline orthodoxy pursue a lifestyle that makes you wonder if the Christian faith has even touched their personal lives? What if their behavior, their attitudes, or their ethical decisions are utterly foreign to discipleship in Christ? *Does Christian faith require Christian conduct for it to be valid?* Or better still, is it appropriate to weigh the sincerity of someone's faith by looking at the way he or she behaves in community and in the world? John's opponents were threatening his congregation. Did their behavior invalidate their claim to be Christians? If so, how do we identify such behavior without becoming legalists?

Is love the most important value? Everyone knows that 1 John again and again affirms the importance of love and acceptance in a Christian community. But a more perplexing question has arisen today: *Should love and tolerance be the litmus test of acceptable theology today?* Is there no longer room for serious (or severe) doctrinal disagreements? My Presbyterian colleagues are wrestling with this as I write. For instance, those who take a "literal" reading of the Bible want to claim that homosexuality is an unacceptable lifestyle and that those who are self-affirming and active in the gay community should not be ordained. Others in the PCUSA call this "gay bashing" and a "gross distortion of Christian teaching and logic" that denies the scriptural command to love and respect the differences among God's children.[2] Does loving one another mean that we dare not be inflexible about some theological positions?

The History of John's Church

SCHOLARS TODAY RARELY view the Johannine literature[3] as the product of an author without a historical context. In fact, elaborate theories have attempted to reconstruct the precise setting of the Christians who owned this literature in order to help us better understand their convictions. Such a history for Paul's churches has been helped no doubt by Luke, who penned Acts, thereby giving us a chronological framework in which to place Paul and his letters. Thus, for example, reading Acts 15 helps us immeasurably to understand the depth of Paul's feeling in Galatians.

---

2. A. E. Crouch, R. A Crouch, and P. D. Crouch, "Silence Would Mean Betrayal," *Monday Morning* ([published by the Church Vocations Unit, The Presbyterian Church, U.S.A.], March 22, 1993), 11.

3. By *Johannine literature* I refer to the Gospel of John and the three letters: 1, 2, and 3 John. Many scholars also include the book of Revelation in this list. That the same author penned the Gospel and the three letters seems to me beyond question.

The Johannine literature owns no such chronology. Nevertheless, we can safely assume that it did not surface in a vacuum, but that Christians in living congregations read and venerated these documents. It is also not far-fetched to assume that John himself—John the apostle, son of Zebedee, one of the Twelve—was a pastor/evangelist who built churches in the Mediterranean world and was a custodian of traditions about Jesus.[4] If this is the case, then we may wonder if the literature that survives this community, the biblical documents we possess today, do not bear some evidence of the character of these Christians. All literature tells us something about its author and its recipients.[5] And sometimes when pieces of this literature are compared carefully, we learn more: They tell us something of the development of thought among John followers, along with their passions, their wars, and even their history.

John's Fledgling Community[6]

EARLY TRADITIONS INDICATE that John planted churches in Ephesus. Eusebius, the fourth-century historian, quotes Irenaeus (A.D. 130–200), bishop of Lyons (France), who tells us that John was a leading ecclesiastical figure in Asia Minor (present-day western Turkey). Clergy from throughout the area traveled to Ephesus just to learn from John and hear his stories about Jesus. How did Irenaeus know all this? He says it was confirmed to him by Polycarp, the bishop of Smyrna, who *in his younger years was instructed by John.*[7] Similarly, Eusebius also preserves for us a letter by the bishop of Ephesus itself (Polycrates), in which the Ephesian bishop tells us that John, who reclined near the Lord at the Last Supper (John 13:25), was buried in Ephesus. Today two

---

4. The link between John the apostle and the Johannine literature is complex, but it would not serve our purposes to elaborate on it here Elsewhere I have demonstrated that the integrity of this ancient tradition is not unreasonable. See G. M Burge, *Interpreting the Gospel of John* (Grand Rapids: Baker, 1992), 37–54.

5. Even modern literature (including films, books, and magazines) unveils the values and the culture of its users.

6. A variety of scholars have attempted to reconstruct the history of John's church, using the documents of the New Testament. See R. E. Brown, *The Community of the Beloved Disciple* (New York: Paulist, 1979); J. L. Martyn, *History and Theology in the Fourth Gospel*, 2d ed. (Nashville: Abingdon, 1979); O. Cullmann, *The Johannine Circle* (Philadelphia: Westminster, 1975). Brown's views have been revised in his commentary *The Epistles of John* (AB 30; New York: Doubleday, 1982), 69–115

7. The full text of Irenaeus is cited in G M Burge, *Interpreting the Gospel of John*, 46–50.

tombs still exist in this ancient city, both claiming to be the burial place of John.

While the early church was well known for its fanciful traditions about the apostles, many scholars do not count this story about John among them.[8] John was a pastor, a leading pastor, whose memory of Jesus and whose recollection of his teachings gave him unique prowess in antiquity.

John's community of believers lived on the frontiers of Judaism. His church was heterogeneous: Jews who had moved into the Greek world lived alongside Greeks who knew nothing of the Old Testament.[9] Their common bond was a firm allegiance to Jesus, their Messiah, and John was their leader. And yet because John himself and his "Christian message" were rooted in Judaism, it was natural that this community would live in close proximity to the synagogues of his city. In fact it is here, in this relationship with the synagogue, that the Johannine community's "story" was forged.

The Fourth Gospel

THE GOSPEL OF John is a by-product of John's ministry. That is why it repeatedly anchors its message in John's "eyewitness" testimony (John 19:35; 20:24). Its text tells us about Jesus, to be sure; but more than that, the way its message is framed tells us about its author and his audience. This explains, for instance, why again and again the Gospel refers to "the Jews" as if they were the opponents of the church (neither Paul nor Luke write with this same tone).[10] Even though some have criticized the New Testament and especially the Fourth Gospel as anti-Semitic, such a view misrepresents the cultural and historical framework unique to these writings. In its earliest days, John's congregation felt that it was under siege: External enemies particularly

---

8 Other fictional accounts do exist, such as the third-century apocryphal *Acts of John* and the unusual Syriac *History of John*. Both of these fictionalize the life of the apostle. Some debate, however, if even Eusebius's record is reliable. Another writer, Papias, mentions an "elder John," and it is disputed if this is the same as John the apostle or another "John" in the ancient church

9. It is difficult to know if we should understand that the Johannine community consisted of a single house church or a number of related fellowships under John's direction Given the wide distribution of Paul's churches, I am inclined to think that the latter is correct

10 The Fourth Gospel refers to "the Jews" sixty-four times; Matthew refers to them four times, Mark and Luke, each five times

from the synagogue were in debate with them. This also explains the importance of John's lengthy story in John 9, where the blind man's expulsion from the synagogue may have meant a lot to John's Jewish followers who themselves were being expelled.

At its earliest stages, this community was cultivating an outlook of division: The world outside the church was a place of darkness, persecution, and turmoil. In Jesus' prayer (John 17) there is not even a record of Jesus praying for the world; he simply prays for the survival and success of his followers. Above all, stories that held deep meaning for the community ended up in the Johannine archive about Jesus: fights with Jewish leaders (see John 5, 8, 9, and 10), the continuing relevance of Jewish festivals like Passover (see John 6), and the ongoing importance of John the Baptist (see 1:35–51; 3:22–36), to name a few. We know, for example, that Ephesus had a community of people who were followers of John the Baptist but not of Jesus (see Acts 19:1–7). Did these groups debate? Did a story like John 1:35–51 encourage many of them to join the followers of Jesus?

In these earliest days the Fourth Gospel may have been a loose collection of stories preached by John. It may have even concluded without chapter 21 (notice that chap. 20 has a natural ending). Likewise, this early Gospel may have lacked its unique prologue (1:1–18), thus giving it a starting point like Mark, where John the Baptist is the introductory character. These were the formative years of the community, when prized stories about Jesus were being preserved and polished, and when a collection of John's best memories and personal accounts were being written down.

To be sure, this was a Gospel to be proud of. It elevated Jesus to a lofty status and showed how he surpassed the efforts of Moses (for Jewish debaters) and fulfilled in abundance the various Jewish festivals like Tabernacles, Passover, and Sabbath, dramatically replacing them. The Gospel of John even gave generous amounts of teaching from Jesus—teachings that predicted the sort of persecution the church was having and yet promised an intimacy with Christ that made such suffering immaterial. This was a Gospel that described the Holy Spirit in detail, talking about conversion in terms like "rebirth," "drinking living water," and "eating the bread of life." This was a Gospel that encouraged a profound relationship with God and could inspire the fantasies of those believers prone to mystical experiences of the faith.

Indeed, the Gospel of John was an *empowering Gospel* that shaped this Christian community so that it would expect dynamic spiritual experiences. Jesus and the Father were dwelling inside these spiritually reborn believers (John 14:23)! *No other gospel speaks like this!* The Holy Spirit promised to provide them with incredible powers: power to recall Jesus' very words (14:26), power to work miracles greater than those of Jesus (14:12), power to have prayer answered (14:13–14), and power to confront a hostile world (16:7). They even had the power to forgive sin (20:23). Above all, the Spirit gave them the power of *prophecy*, to continue speaking with Jesus' voice, revealing *new things* not recorded in Scripture (16:13).

John's Gospel suggests that his community was a *pneumatic community*. Today we might call it a *charismatic community*. This is not to say that the Johannine literature provides a detailed working-out of the spiritual gifts as, for example, Paul does in 1 Corinthians 12–14. There is no evidence that the Johannine Christians spoke in tongues (though it is not implausible). Rather, the Johannine literature evidences a community alert to the centrality of the Spirit and ready to experience the Spirit in its fullness. In short, Johannine theology laid the context in which a pneumatic/charismatic Christianity would flourish.

Chaos and Conflict

BUT WE CAN only speculate that something serious happened at a later stage of the church's life. The once-unified congregation began to tear apart from within. Threats that were once external now were found within the ranks of the fellowship itself. For John, it must have been a crisis beyond belief. In 1 John 2:18 he even says that it is "the last hour" for the community.

Who were these dissenters? In a moment we will outline their beliefs and speculate who they were. But for now, we need to sketch the role they played. Essentially, these were a select group of Johannine Christians who knew the Fourth Gospel well, claimed to be inspired by the Spirit, and challenged John's understanding of Jesus Christ's personhood and work.[11] And apparently they were succeeding. The com-

---

11. Theories abound that identify these opponents in other ways. Some have argued that they were Jews who opposed the messiahship of Jesus (like the Jewish adversaries in the Gospel of John). Others have argued that they were lapsed Jewish Christians and that the

munity was splitting, harsh words were being exchanged, and the vocabulary once reserved in the Fourth Gospel for those in "the world" was now being aimed at fellow Christians within the church.

Our evidence for this division is found in John's response to the crisis: the first letter of John. In its pages we have evidence of severe social conflict: the painful departure of the group (1 John 2:19–26) and warnings about "deceivers" and "liars" who twist the truth of Christ (2:22; 2 John 7). In addition, severe theological debates (1 John 5:5–8) were being fought among teachers claiming to be filled with the inspiration of the Holy Spirit (2:20–21; 4:1–6). The letter's repeated emphasis on love hints at the severity and desperation of the situation.

The Johannine scholar Raymond Brown believes that at this point the Fourth Gospel may have gone through a revision to correct some of these misunderstandings.[12] The Gospel, for instance, gained its prologue (John 1:1–18), which emphasizes Jesus' full incarnation (v. 14). These introductory verses have an uncanny resemblance to the opening verses of John's first letter (see 1 John 1:1–4). It is possible that the event that inspired this "writing up" of the Gospel was John's death. John 21 implies that the apostle has died, even though his community thought he would survive till Christ's second coming (see John 21:20–25). In fact, when John's disciples stitched together their leader's story of Christ, they gave him a title of veneration that would make him famous: the beloved disciple (13:23; 19:26; 20:2; 21:7, 20). John did not call himself this; rather, his followers gave him this name.

Therefore, we might view the literary sequence in this way: (1) An early draft of the Fourth Gospel circulates widely and is subject to misinterpretation. (2) John pens his letters and writes a prologue for the Gospel. (3) John dies, and his followers publish the final form of the Gospel (including the prologue and chap. 21), as well as organize and preserve his letters.

In other words, we can say that in some respects John's letters are a response written in debate with those who may be interpreting an early draft of the Fourth Gospel. For some the letters serve as a sort of commentary on the Gospel. Still others would describe them as an

---

letters are continuing the polemic of the Gospel of John For an outline of scholarly views, see Brown, *The Epistles of John,* 49–55

12 See Brown, *The Community of the Beloved Disciple, The Epistles of John,* 73–86

"epilogue" to the Gospel, designed to circulate with it so that erroneous interpretations would not be reached. Stephen Smalley prefers to describe John's first letter as a *paper* that

> sets out to expound Johannine teaching and ideas, now preserved in the tradition and theology of the Fourth Gospel, for the benefit of heterodox members of John's community who were also indebted to the teaching of the gospel but who were understanding it differently and, indeed, erroneously.[13]

The Fate of the Church

BUT THE JOHANNINE church was not to survive the conflict. The church split, with strong leaders taking the fellowship down the road of Gnosticism and Docetism while John's own disciples remained in communion with the other New Testament churches of Paul and the apostles. The earliest commentaries on John (e.g., Heracleon) were written by Gnostics, which shows how the Fourth Gospel was embraced in these heretical circles. And the orthodox church (the "Great Church," as Brown labels it) only embraced the Fourth Gospel reluctantly. The church's Gnostic enemies were using it—or a form of it. *As many scholars believe, it was the letters of John—1 John in particular—that redeemed the Fourth Gospel for the New Testament we possess today.*

Was John a Successful Pastor?

THIS IS AN intriguing question. By modern standards, if this above historical reconstruction is accurate, John failed to build the kind of church we esteem today. His congregation did not thrive, grow, and prosper. Paul and Barnabas's church in Antioch became a mega-church. It was large, wealthy, and influential, sending missionaries throughout the Mediterranean. Even famous biblical scholars in later centuries (such as Diodore and Lucian) hailed from this church. For six hundred years (until the conquests of the Ummayad Muslims) Antioch gave theological and pastoral leadership to the Christian world.

But no such claim can be made for John's career. The Johannine community disappears into history. No heritage. No records. No fame.

---

13 S S Smalley, *1,2,3 John* (WBC 51; Waco, Tex . Word, 1984), xxvii. Smalley points to numerous parallels between 1 John and the Gospel's farewell discourse (John 14–17).

Controversy swirled around his writings as they were being twisted by his opponents. And so the question remains: *Was John a successful pastor?*

John was a *faithful pastor.* He was a pastor who found himself navigating his congregation through an impossible storm. And as his community was being battered, he distinguished his leadership with discretion and good judgment. With the aid of the Spirit and deep study he cultivated sound theological instincts, which served him well in battle. He knew which issues were utterly essential to the faith. He knew where there could be no compromise. He also possessed keen insight into what made for a vital Christian community. John did not want a church that was orthodox but unloving, any more than he wanted a church that misrepresented Jesus Christ. He wanted both—sound doctrine and vibrant community—and he refused to settle for less.

John was faithful because he knew how to stand firm in what was essential. His compassion for his congregation burned as intensely as his anger against those who were making them prey. In one breath he could speak of "his little children" and then chastise his opponents as "the children of the devil."

John's Opponents

WHO WERE THESE opponents whom John confronted? What issues did they debate? It is virtually impossible to name them specifically or label their "movement" (although some scholars have attempted to do so). What we can do is outline their beliefs, using the refutation that John has given us in his letters. But let me say at the outset that this is a difficult endeavor. Writers rarely give a complete hearing to their opponents' views, and we have no firsthand information from John's adversaries. *None of their writings have survived.* Moreover, sometimes John opposes things in his letters that may not be on the agenda of his opponents. For instance, in 1 John 4:18 he says there is no fear in love because perfect love casts out fear. John may be taking an opportunity to chastise his followers, not *necessarily* addressing anyone else.

But it is important that we do our best to discover the context that forced John to pen the letters we possess today. If we are careful, we can then take the hints given to us in these letters and compare them with doctrinal distortions we know existed in antiquity. By understanding his opponents, we can better understand John himself and reflect on his themes.

This was a difficult period of Christian history, when the boundaries between orthodoxy and heresy were unclear. There were no creeds or church councils. There was not even a collection of books called "The New Testament" that could be used to arbitrate theological disputes. But John returns to two major subjects repeatedly as he writes: Christology and ethical behavior.[14] And it is likely (as we shall see) that the two are intimately connected. The secessionists had embraced an aberrant form of Christology that led them to make wrong judgments about Christian living.

Christology

WHAT SOMEONE THINKS about Jesus often lies at the heart of most theological disputes. John says that his opponents hold the following beliefs:

- they deny the Son (1 John 2:23)
- they deny that Jesus Christ has come in the flesh (4:2; 2 John 7)
- they deny that Jesus is the Christ (1 John 2:22)

These statements may be compared with affirmations in the letters that buttress John's own Christology. It is likely that these verses are also connected to the opponent's Christological error.

- *Jesus* is the Christ (5:1)
- Jesus Christ has come in the flesh (4:2)
- *Jesus* is the Son (2:23; 3:23; 5:11) or the Son of God (1:3, 7; 3:8, 23; 4: 9, 10, 15, etc.)
- Jesus Christ came "by water and blood" (5:6)

From these statements a composite image of John's opponents begins to emerge. They are no doubt Christians who have begun to deviate

---

14. These two major themes have led some, such as S. Smalley, "What About 1 John?" *Papers on Paul and Other New Testament Authors*, ed. E. A. Livingstone (JSOT Supp Series 3, Sheffield· JSOT, 1980), 337–43; and J Painter, *John Witness and Theologian* (London SPCK, 1978), to speculate that John is actually opposing two different groups in his letter But such theories today have found little acceptance. See I H. Marshall, *The Epistles of John* (Grand Rapids Eerdmans, 1978), 16–17

from the traditionally received understanding of Jesus Christ. They affirm the idea of Christ, but doubt whether Christ became flesh and whether the man Jesus was indeed the incarnation of God.

Today many scholars have concluded that John's opponents embraced a "high Christology" that elevated Christ's divinity at the expense of his humanity. The Hellenistic world commonly affirmed a cosmos populated by numerous deities. Elevating Christ into their company was easy, given the tolerant and syncretistic outlook of the day. And yet this same Hellenistic world was predisposed to reject that such divinities ever materially entered our world. Using a dualistic outlook, Christ was separated from the world, set apart with the divinities of heaven, and there left to rule. One Christian variety of this view said that Christ may have "seemed" (Gk. *dokeo;* hence, Docetism) to appear in the flesh but in actuality did not. To them, the notion that Christ would appear "in flesh" was ridiculous if not abhorrent.[15]

If the earthly life of Jesus Christ was now irrelevant, these people still claimed to have immediate access to God. In their view they had moved beyond the basic, elementary orthodox teachings of Christianity and, inspired by the Spirit, could know God directly. I. Howard Marshall describes them well: "They were like men kicking away the ladder on which they have climbed to the heights and leaving themselves without any visible means of support."[16] The very gospel that had given birth to their faith was being jettisoned. Second John 9 says it nicely: They are not abiding in the teaching of Christ *but are going beyond it.*[17]

This tendency to divide the world along dualistic lines that separated reality into opposing forces (light/darkness, above/below, spirit/flesh, etc.) was common in the first century. Furthermore, the notion of immediate revelation through divine knowledge (known as Gnosticism) was just coming to life.[18] But the application of these principles to a Christian Christology was something new.

---

15. Note the strong emphasis of John 1:14 in this context. Its emphasis on an incarnational Christology suggests that it was penned in the context of the present debate.

16. Marshall, *The Epistles of John,* 21.

17. This is the effective rendering of *pas ho proagon kai me menon en tei didachei tou Christou,* as translated in the NRSV.

18. It has not been proven that Gnosticism as a formal, organized system of belief had been developed by John's time. However, the tendencies that later flowered in the second and third centuries were certainly in place. See E. Yamauchi, *Pre-Christian Gnosticism: A Survey of the Proposed Evidences* (Grand Rapids: Eerdmans, 1973).

One of the first teachers to do so was Cerinthus. What we know about him is contained in the records of his opponents, particularly, Irenaeus. In Irenaeus's work *Against Heresies* (c. A.D. 180), we find an important story, reported by Polycarp, that brings Cerinthus and John together. Apparently once when John was in the public baths at Ephesus, he discovered Cerinthus there and cried out, "Let us save ourselves; the bath house may fall down, for inside is Cerinthus, the enemy of the truth." Irenaeus goes on to say that John proclaimed his gospel in order to refute the errors of Cerinthus.[19]

Irenaeus carefully outlines Cerinthus's theology. He was one of the first to distinguish carefully *Jesus* and *Christ*. He argued that *Jesus* was the earthly man of Nazareth, well known for his piety and wisdom. *Christ* was a heavenly deity, who descended on Jesus at his baptism and departed before the crucifixion. Thus, the man Jesus died on the cross, not the Son of God. When we therefore read in 1 John 2:22, "Who is the liar? It is the man who denies that *Jesus* is the Christ,"[20] many commentators wonder if it is just this sort of distinction that John has in mind (see also 5:1, 11, etc.). Someone was saying that the man Jesus is not the Christ.

It is notoriously difficult to confirm Polycarp's bathhouse story or build any kind of chronology for Cerinthus. But even if he lived after the time of John, incipient ideas like his, ideas shaped by the dualistic environment of Hellenism, were likely present in Asia Minor.

In summary, we have cautiously rebuilt the Christological context from which John's opponents were working. The incarnate Jesus Christ was no longer occupying the central place in Christian faith. At best, the secessionists had a nominal interest in the Jesus of history and tradition and instead were looking to inspired spiritual experiences that lifted them above the conventional views of John.

Ethics

JOHN'S LETTERS ALSO evidence a sustained critique of the moral disposition of certain persons. This is not like the usual exhortations we

---

19. See Irenaeus's *Against Heresies*, 3 3.4 and 3.11 1. A full record of the ancient evidence available to us on Cerinthus is conveniently supplied by Brown, *The Epistles of John*, Appendix 2, 766–71

20. In fact John employs the term for liar (Gk. *pseustes*) seven times, but this is the only time a definite article is used. This is generally an indication that the writer has a particular individual in mind.

find in Paul's writings, where believers are warned against catalogues of sins (1 Cor. 6) or dispositions of the heart (Gal. 5). In the Johannine context a theological rationale had formed that made ethical behavior of no consequence for the Christian life. John mentions his opponents' views in a number of places:

- they boast that they are "without sin" (1 John 1:8, 10)
- they boast that they "have fellowship" with God but walk in the darkness (1:6)
- they boast that they know God but nevertheless are disobedient (2:4)
- they boast that they "love God" but hate their brothers and sisters (4:20)
- they boast that they are "in the light" but hate their fellow Christians (2:9)

John also repeats a number of affirmations that shed light on the nature of the secessionist's ethical position:

- to abide in God is to obey him—it is to walk as Jesus walked (1 John 2:6)
- to sin willfully shows that one has not known God (3:3–6; 5:18)
- whoever acts sinfully belongs to the devil (3:7–10)
- we should love one another (3:11–12, 17–18)
- refusing to love one's brother or sister means that one has not inherited eternal life (3:14–15)
- God is love—and to know him is to love (4:8–10)

While I believe that Christology was the main battleground in the community, the tangible expression of these disagreements came in the form of open conflict and hostility. In other words, faulty Christology spilled into unethical conduct.

What does John mean when he says that these people are not obedient? There is no evidence that they were living immoral lives; 1 John 2:15–16 is likely a general exhortation for the church not to be worldly. Instead, these people were not following the conventional authoritative teachings of the church. Since they denied the significance of Christ's incarnation, it stands to reason that they would deny the significance of his earthly teachings. As a result, they did not heed Jesus' words written in the Gospel. Likewise, if they denied their own sinfulness, they would feel no need for Christ's atoning death on the cross. Theirs was a "deeper" religion, a mystical faith, fueled by non-traditional insights gleaned from the Spirit (2:20–23; 4:1). They refused to conform to traditional teachings and consequently refused to submit to the leadership that bore those teachings.

The secessionists were not simply indifferent to those who disagreed with them; they were intolerant. This explains the repeated reference of John to "hating" fellow Christians. Conflict resulted from their superior spirituality. *These people had become elitist in their view of themselves.* And those who sought to exhort them, who could not catalogue similar experiences for themselves, had no credibility.

We must not, however, read John's words about community love as applying merely to his opponents. Too often we have characterized these unorthodox Christians as difficult, haughty, and unremitting in their attitudes toward the church. John *also* exhorts his own followers to exhibit love because they were responding to the secessionists with equal hostility. And just because their theology was right by no means says their angry attitudes were justified. Defenders of good traditions cannot defend their own misconduct because they are correct.

This disposition to spiritualize the earthly career of Christ, giving it no great salvific importance, and to deny the spiritual importance of one's own physical, moral life had some currency in antiquity. Gnostic systems of religious thought were in intense debate with Christianity from about A.D. 150–300, years after John's death, yet the framework that would lead to these systems was already in place. This later literature speaks of a religion of enlightenment and of special knowledge, preserved only for the initiated. Believers were "reborn," creating a unique union with God that literally brought about a state of sinless perfection. "Sin" belongs to another nature, our material nature, which no longer mattered in God's economy. Hence, enlightened spiritual experiences validated spirituality while at the same time practical questions of moral conduct were deemed irrelevant.

Scholars who have compared the Johannine literature with second- and third-century Gnostic writings find striking similarities of language and tone. For instance, when 1 John 3:9 talks about God's "seed" remaining in one born of God, this echoes the teaching of the Valentinian Gnostics, who were great opponents to the orthodox church. In the nineteenth century this even led some to conclude that John was directly in debate with a fully developed Gnostic religious system (and hence his writings were to be dated much later than the first century). But this is not necessary. The predisposition to divide the world along material and spiritual lines (dualism), to seek spiritual enlightenment (mysticism), and to deny personal moral responsibility were well established. Colossians and the Pastoral Letters, for example, bear similar witness to Christians with Christological deviations, who disregarded the value of practical moral conduct.

John's Secondary Concerns

A NUMBER OF secondary themes are found throughout these letters. In some sense these appear by accident because they are a part of the refutation the author is making against his opponents. In most cases these are intimately connected with the two primary subjects under debate in his church: Christology and ethics.

The Holy Spirit. If study of the Fourth Gospel was central to this community's spiritual formation, as I have suggested, it comes as no surprise that the Spirit played a pivotal role in discipleship. No Gospel places as much emphasis on the Spirit as John's Gospel.[21] In fact, the indwelling of Christ and the transformation of the believer are both framed in terms of Spirit-experience in this literature (John 3:1–8; 14:23–24). Even the Lord's Supper is defined as an assimilation of Christ in Spirit (6:52–63). This is why I suggested above that John's community had strong pneumatic or ecstatic tendencies. His followers were confident of their "anointing," and in his polemic against the secessionists, he must take this pneumatic context into consideration.

In 1 John 4:13 John reassures his followers that possessing the Spirit is characteristic of those who "abide in God." Such abiding is not simply a matter of orthodox confession (4:15) or loving conduct (4:16), although these are important. Abiding in God is *experiential*, it is a personal experience with the Holy Spirit. Therefore John's opponents (the false teachers) must buttress their authority with some pneumatic experience, some evidence that they have the Spirit too. This explains

---

21. Various studies have examined the role of the Spirit in the theology of the Fourth Gospel. See G. M. Burge, *The Anointed Community The Holy Spirit in the Johannine Tradition* (Grand Rapids· Eerdmans, 1987)

why in 4:1–3 the church is called to "test the spirits." These opponents are claiming to be prophets (4:1 labels them *false* prophets) who, under the inspiration of the Spirit, are making striking new claims about Christ.

This is a pneumatic context. It is interesting to note what John does not say. He does not employ his apostolic authority as, for example, Paul does in Galatians to refute the Judaizers. He does not leverage pastoral authority, power anchored in a position. Instead, he urges the church to test the spirits to see if they affirm traditional beliefs about Jesus, thereby undercutting the authority of these prophets. His tactic, therefore, is characteristic of those struggling against rival leadership claims in a "charismatic" setting. One cannot deny the Spirit. One must teach *discernment* and urge congregants to weigh claims made in the voice of the Spirit.

But John goes further. If these secessionists are claiming a superior spirituality, John reminds the church that each member has been equally anointed with the Spirit (2:20, 27). In other words, spiritual discernment is the task of *every* person. To be a Christian is to possess the Spirit, and no one may come along claiming exclusive spiritual insight. Thus 2:27 remarks, "As for you, the anointing you received from him remains in you, *and you do not need anyone to teach you.*" Christians must be well grounded and confident in the authenticity of their own spiritual experience and not swayed by the seemingly more compelling experiences of others.

Discernment and tradition. These letters remind us that the church is the custodian of the truth. Foremost among John's concerns is the responsibility of the corporate community to discern false belief and practice, to distinguish between truth and error. While this theme is explicitly mentioned only in 4:1ff., it is assumed throughout 1 John. The church must stand guard against any who would bring distortion or error (cf. 2 John 8).

But this presents a problem. How can we discern truth from falsehood? If a prophet urges something new under the authority of the Spirit, how can it be weighed? In 1 Corinthians 14:29 Paul confronted a similar dilemma. His solution was to have the prophets weigh one another's words, thereby checking individual inspiration in a deliberative corporate body. John nowhere uses that tactic, setting prophet against prophet. Rather, he believes that the church is accountable to the historic revelation given in Jesus Christ and passed down through the apostles. *Individual inspiration, therefore, must be weighed against truth revealed in Scripture and tradition.*

Throughout 1 John the author affirms that what was "from the beginning" should be the anchor for what we believe now (1:1; 2:13, 14; 3:11). In fact, "from the beginning" becomes a virtual refrain as John urges his readers to recall what they first learned and measure everything else by it. "Let what you heard *from the beginning* abide in you. If what you heard *from the beginning* abides in you, then you will abide in the Son and in the Father" (2:24 NRSV). He says that his commandments are not new, but "old [commandments], which you have had *since the beginning*" (2:7; cf. 2 John 5).

John is not merely writing in defense of tradition, as if "older is better" or any innovation is suspect. He is pointing elsewhere. By "the beginning" he refers to the historic coming of Jesus Christ and the preservation of that revelation. What was revealed in the Incarnation must be the litmus test for all new theological insights. Thus in 1 John 1:1–3, John points to what he saw with his eyes and touched with his hands—the incarnate Christ. *Historic Christology must be the touchstone for all Christian belief.* How do we know love? God "sent his one and only Son into the world" (4:9). Curiously, his exhortation in 2:12–14 twice reminds the fathers—those who are older—to rekindle their acquaintance with the ancient teachings, things the younger generation may no longer treasure.

This theological anchor in historic Christology is reminiscent of what we read in the Gospel of John. In his farewell discourse, Jesus talks about the Spirit and the limits of what he will do. As Jesus' words cannot deviate from the Father's words (John 5:19), so too the Spirit will reiterate what Jesus himself has said in history (14:26). The Spirit "will not speak on his own; he will speak only what he hears" (16:13). In Christian faith, Father, Son, and Spirit provide a revelation that is self-consistent and harmonious. No later revelation contradicts what has gone before.

Since John did not possess the Scriptures as we do today, he was forced to elevate "tradition" or historic teaching passed down with apostolic authority. No doubt his own record of Christ—the Gospel of John—served as a reservoir of such traditional teachings. Were John with us today, he would undoubtedly point to Scripture as an apostolic archive of teachings against which our modern teachings should be weighed. And this is how many Christians have generally understood John's view of things. But other more ancient Christian communities (such as the Roman Catholic and Eastern Orthodox Churches) object to such a narrow explanation of "tradition." Tradition means the archive of normative religious truth passed down from one generation to the next, which has an authoritative voice in the present. The most obvious examples for us are the Councils of Nicea (A.D. 325) and Chalcedon (A.D. 451), where orthodox views of the Trinity and incarnational Christology were decided.[22] John is affirming that Christian wisdom and truth—anchored in right Christology—are cumulative and that they are binding. Those who are tradition's heirs are right to defend this heritage.

Love, unity, and fellowship. The letters of John, along with the Gospel of John, place a high premium on the quality of Christian community. Jesus' commands in John 13:34 and 15:12, 17 made clear that love should be the hallmark of his followers. In his prayer in John 17 Jesus prays for harmony and unity among his followers so "that they may be one," on the model of the oneness of the Father and the Son (17:20–23).

No doubt the schism in John's church placed unity and love on the ecclesiastical agenda. He even makes love a command: Christians who love God *must* love their brother or sister in the church (1 John 4:21). This teaching John anchors "from the beginning" as well (3:11; 2 John 5), harking back no doubt to the Gospel. In 1 John 3:23 he almost sums up the Christian life, giving two simple exhortations: believing in Jesus Christ and loving one another.

But John does not give an exhortation without offering some theological ground, since there are indeed times when loving those who are unlovely seems impossible. God first loved us, he says (1 John 4:19). Love, especially in difficult circumstances, cannot be fueled by

---

22. Many of us need at least to acknowledge that much of our heritage is dependent on traditional interpretations of the Scriptures. Decisions about worship, lifestyle, and even music are often driven by tradition. I once spent three years living in Scotland among conservative Scottish Baptists, and though they intensely denied that their world was anchored in anything other than the Bible, still, centuries-old Scottish tradition molded what they perceived to be "Christian." The same is true of American evangelicalism. I now worship among evangelicals with a Swedish heritage (Evangelical Covenant), and tradition there—theological tradition—is tangible and authoritative.

human energy. Love originates from God when we apprehend the depth of *his* love for us (4:7a) and when we are born anew by *his* Spirit (4:7b). For John, intimate knowledge of God is the same as enjoying the intimate reciprocity of God's love: He loves us, we love him, and this love spills over to those near us. In harsher terms, *not to love* is evidence, severe evidence, that someone does not know God and has failed to experience him fully (4:8).

If we are uncertain about God's profound desire for us, we need only look to God's love shown to us in Christ. Christ is the material expression of God's tangible love and so once again, John is making a claim for the value of historic, incarnational Christology to address issues of ethics. Because Christ laid down his life for us, so too we ought to do the same for one another (1 John 3:16). John puts it succinctly in 4:10: "This is love: not that we loved God, but that he loved us and sent his Son as an atoning sacrifice for our sins."

John describes living in God's love, knowing him, and obeying his commands as "walking in the light." This is one more metaphor for normative Christian discipleship. Therefore in 1:7 he affirms that when people walk in the light together, when *corporately* they experience God's love, unity and fellowship result. Vibrant community is the natural outgrowth of people who genuinely live in God's presence. But the reverse is also true. When people exhibit hostility and division, when they "hate" (to use John's term), they prove that their lives are being lived "in the darkness" (2:9–11) or even "in death" (3:14). Such so-called Christians are "liars" and hypocrites (4:20). John spares no words for people who claim to know God but fail to exhibit genuine godliness.

There is an important nuance to John's teaching that we dare not miss. To anchor our love in God's affection might inspire passivity. That is, we may wait for God's love to mature and change us, to shape us, before we apply any effort to our own growth. If we cannot feel God's love, John would have us exhibit love toward others as a way to step into God's presence. In 1 John 4:12 he talks about the limits of our experience of God: "No one has ever seen God; *but if we love one another, God lives in us and his love is made complete in us.*" Loving the unlovely or the difficult-to-love is an avenue, a mystical avenue, to discover God in our midst.

A concrete example of how this love might be expressed is in a simple act of charity among God's people. First John 3:17–18 remarks:

"How does God's love abide in anyone who has the world's goods and sees a brother or sister in need and yet refuses help? Little children, let us love, not in word or speech, but in truth and action" (NRSV). In 3 John 10 we are even given a negative example of someone named Diotrephes, who did not know the first thing about Christian charity and hospitality.

Are there limits to love? Of course! John says that we must not love the world (1 John 2:15)—not meaning the people of the world (John 3:16) or God's creation (17:24). This refers instead to everything that is hostile to God and inimical to the truth of the gospel. But in 2 John 10 we have an interesting problem that will require careful attention. John urges his followers not to welcome (better, not to receive into fellowship) anyone who intentionally professes false doctrine. Could John be referring to the secessionists who have divided the church? While participation with the unbelieving world is a necessary facet of Christian discipleship, still, if we are to have integrity, there must be a limit to tolerance. There are lines of personal interaction and public participation that Christians must not cross.

Authorship and Setting

Authorship

WHILE CHRISTIAN TRADITION has attributed these letters to John the apostle, the Johannine letters are anonymous, except that 2 and 3 John call their author "the elder" (2 John 1; 3 John 1). Locating his identity would, of course, solve the mystery. On the one hand, the title may simply refer to a man of high esteem in the community. On the other, good evidence shows us that the apostles themselves were described as "elders" in antiquity.[23]

The situation is sorely complicated by a reference in Eusebius (*Church History*, 3.39.4) to two "Johns," one clearly the apostle and the other possibly an elder who lived later (some have speculated that he was a disciple of the apostle John). Could the elder in our letters be this *second* John? Marshall has shown that this does not necessarily have to be the case and that even if two persons named John lived in this

---

23 See 1 Peter 5 1, Eusebius's citation of Papias in his *Church History*, 3 39 4

period, the attribution of authorship to the later man is purely hypothetical.[24]

While 2 and 3 John appear to come from the same pen, does 1 John originate with this author since he is nowhere described as "the elder"? Exhaustive comparisons of style and content show striking similarities among all three writings and suggest that common authorship is not at all unlikely.[25] A more compelling question is whether the same pen wrote the letters and the Gospel of John. As early as the third century scholars were making this claim based on similarities of content and style, and today the parallels between the Gospel and the Johannine letters is a commonplace in New Testament studies. This is particularly true of 1 John and the Gospel. In fact, careful comparison of 1 John and the Gospel's farewell discourse (John 13–17) shows even more remarkable parallels.[26] As Brown remarks, the parallels in style and content are comparable to those found in Luke and Acts or even Colossians and Ephesians. This has led the vast majority of scholars to affirm common authorship for 1 John and the Gospel.

If the documents have a literary history as I have suggested, we can see John as the source of most of the Johannine materials. (1) John's early draft of his Gospel circulated widely, but its misuse by some required further clarification. (2) John penned his letters as well as the Johannine prologue to correct Christological errors in his community. He may have added other changes to his Gospel (the Farewell Discourse is a strong candidate), but these remain uncertain. (3) When John died, his disciples gathered up his writings—the Gospel (which may have been edited again), a story about the resurrection (now chap. 21 of the Gospel), and John's letters. This then became John's legacy to his community.

But this still fails to solve the mystery completely: Unambiguous objective evidence for apostolic authorship is not at hand for the Gospel *or* the letters. But the absence of such evidence does not make such authorship implausible, and, I would argue, the burden of proof

---

24 Marshall, *Epistles*, 42–48

25 Brown, *Epistles*, 14–35, and particularly Appendix 1, charts 1–2, pp 755–59

26. Brown's parallels are given in Appendix 1, chart 2. Such lists are commonly found in most commentaries. See A. E. Brooke, *A Critical and Exegetical Commentary on the Johannine Epistles* (ICC; Edinburgh T. & T Clark, 1912), i-ix, J Stott, *The Epistles of John* (Grand Rapids: Eerdmans, 1964), 18–19

rests with those who want to dismantle the tradition.[27] I have chosen, therefore, to label the author of the letters as "John," keeping in mind the limits of any historical investigation.

Date

SINCE THE LETTERS have been closely associated with the Fourth Gospel, those who place the Gospel in the late first century locate the letters anywhere from A.D. 90–110.[28] However, arguments for such a late date now must bear the weight of serious criticisms, and increasingly the Gospel has been given an earlier time frame, closer to A.D. 70 or 80.[29] Allowing time for the development of the heresy described in the letters, a date between 70 and 90 is not unreasonable.

Location

THE TRADITIONAL VIEW that the Johannine writings originated from Asia Minor is sound. The heresies addressed in the letters (and perhaps the Gospel) were well established in this area. Furthermore, the Fourth Gospel is traditionally associated with Ephesus. We can also argue by inference. John 1:35–42; 3:22–4:3; and 10:41 suggest that the Johannine community was in a debate with followers of John the Baptist, who had not affirmed the messiahship of Jesus. Acts 19:1–7 describes twelve such followers of the Baptist *in Ephesus,* who found themselves at odds with the Christians in that city.

The Sequence of 1, 2, and 3 John

SINCE LITTLE SUPPLEMENTAL information exists telling us about the circumstances of these letters, we cannot simply assume that they were written in the sequence in which they appear in our New Testament. Scholars have rearranged the three letters in every conceivable con-

---

27 I have shown the credibility of this tradition elsewhere, G. M. Burge, *Interpreting the Gospel of John,* 37–54

28. These dates generally turn on linking the Johannine writings with the early fathers, namely, Ignatius and Polycarp

29. J. A. T. Robinson once argued convincingly that a priori there is nothing in the New Testament that requires that any of its writings be dated after A D 70. See his *Redating the New Testament* (Philadelphia Westminster, 1976)

---

figuration. Some have argued that 2 John precedes 1 John because the tone is quite different: In 2 John the false teachers are addressed mildly (2 John 7–9), while in 1 John the struggles are described more severely (1 John 2:19; 4:1ff.). We can wonder, then, if the problems brought on by the secessionists are just beginning in 2 John (making it earlier) and only later come to blows in 1 John.

On the other hand, the differences in the letters may be explained by geographical locale. That is, 1 John may be addressed to a community setting at the heart of the Johannine world, perhaps the very center where the secessionists had launched their campaign. This would explain the personal nature of the letter as well as its intensity. On the other hand, 2 John may be addressed to outlying house churches not fully embroiled in the controversy. Perhaps this is why 2 John is more formal and detached in the way it addresses its readers (see 2 John 1, 5, 13) and essentially is a warning about what is to come (2 John 8–11).[30]

Another possibility is that 2 John and 3 John were cover letters that were accompanied by the more substantial treatise, 1 John. Some believe that this fits 3 John particularly well since it is addressed to Gaius, and Demetrius (being commended to the church) may have been the letter's courier (3 John 12; cf. 8). But we cannot be confident about any of these theories.

It is no doubt best to view these letters as coming from the same approximate time period and addressing the same general crisis in the church. First John is the author's full broadside against his opponents, while 2 and 3 John are personal notes that either accompanied 1 John or were sent separately to another destination.

Epistolary Structure

SECOND JOHN AND 3 John have all of the usual features of first-century letters: the author and recipient are identified at the beginning, a blessing or prayer follows ("Grace, mercy, and peace ... will be with us," 2 John 3; "I pray that you may enjoy good health and that all may go well with you," 3 John 2), and there is a concluding greeting (2 John

---

30. This is the view defended by Brown, *Epistles*, 29–30.

13; 3 John 14).[31] The letters also contain personal references and allusions that suggest they are intended for a specific, personal situation.

The same cannot be said, however, for 1 John. There is no address and no greeting at the beginning. No conclusion ends the document—5:21 even sounds abrupt, as if the writer's thoughts have been cut off. Furthermore, no personal comments suggest that the author is writing a personal letter. No names appear anywhere. This is highly unusual when we consider the intensely personal character of the crisis in the church. This could be helpfully compared with Galatians, where Paul confronts a theological crisis but writes directly and personally to the recipients.

This absence of form has rightly led many to suggest that 1 John is not a personal letter at all but a general treatise aimed at wide distribution.[32] Some prefer to call it a sermon or an address. Perhaps it is a pamphlet, a brochure, or an encyclical. Kümmel prefers to think of it as a tractate engaged in some sort of polemic, a kind of manifesto that addresses specific theological issues across a general front.[33]

The Structure of 1 John

DISCOVERING A RECOGNIZABLE pattern or structure of thought in 1 John has proven impossible. Most scholars have sought to divide it into either two or three sections.[34] Some commentators, such as Brooke, Dodd, Grayston, Marshall, and Houlden, believe this is pointless and find instead either spirals of cyclical thought or a list of unconnected units. According to this view, John's units link up with each other only casually and are "governed by an association of ideas rather than by a logical plan."[35]

---

31. This pattern can be easily traced among Paul's letters, where early Christians developed their own unique epistolary style. "Grace and peace" were typically Pauline styles (cf. Gal. 1·3; 1 Thess. 1:1)

32. Marshall, on the other hand, points out the close relation between the author and the readers, and the occasional reference to a specific situation (2:19) shows that the author is writing for a specific group so that "the writing is in effect a letter" (*The Epistles of John*, 99).

33. W. G. Kümmel, *Introduction to the New Testament* (Nashville: Abingdon, 1975), 437.

34 Some early medieval scholars attempted to find seven parts, but this has found little modern support.

35 Marshall, *The Epistles of John*, 26

The most famous threefold division belongs to Robert Law, whose 1909 commentary argued that 1 John had three parts, each part offering three "tests of life": righteousness, love, and belief.[36] The secessionists fail to acknowledge the importance of *righteous* behavior, do not *love* fellow Christians, and deny *belief* in Jesus Christ, the Son of God. While such a theory's creativity is attractive, it falls short in many places in the letter, particularly in the third part (4:7–5:13). Nevertheless, a number of current scholars have defended such a three-unit theory: A. E. Brooke,[37] E. Malatesta,[38] P. R. Jones,[39] M. Thompson,[40] and R. Schnackenburg.[41] Those who find a threefold structure appealing generally look for thematic divisions at 2:27/28/29 and at 3:22/24, 4:6, or 4:12.

A twofold or bipartite division has traditionally been less popular but today is commanding renewed attention. Marshall notes that the French scholar A. Feuillet defended this view in 1972,[42] and most recently R. Brown and S. Smalley have become its champion in their 1982 and 1984 commentaries. Two observations argue for this structure. (1) John makes two main declarations about God in his Gospel, which Brown suggests are *keys* to his master plan: "God is light" (1:5) and "God is love" (4:8). (2) The Gospel of John, which enjoys a bipartite form, may therefore be the *structural model* for this second Johannine writing. Similarities between the two writings have often been observed. Each begins with parallel prologues, and the bodies of each writing move from doctrinal truths to practical applications for life.

---

36 R Law, *The Tests of Life A Study of the First Epistle of St John* (Edinburgh: T. & T. Clark, 1909) For a helpful chart examining the various ways 1 John can be divided, see R Brown, *Epistles*, Appendix 1, chart 5, page 764 Law's divisions are: 1:5–2·28, 2:29–4:6; 4.7–5·13.

37. Brooke, *Epistles*

38 E Malatesta, *The Epistles of St John Greek Text and English Translation Schematically Arranged* (Rome. Gregorian University, 1973)

39. P. R. Jones, "A Structural Analysis of 1 John," *RevExp* 67 (1970): 433–44

40. M. M Thompson, *1–3 John* (IVPNTC; Downer's Grove, Ill.. InterVarsity, 1992)

41 R. Schnackenburg, *Die Johannesbriefe* (Freiberg: Herder, 1965) These theories are outlined by Marshall, *The Epistles of John*, 22–25, and Brown, *Epistles*, 116–29

42. A Feuillet, "Étude structurale de la première épître de Saint Jean," in H. Baltensweiler and B. Reicke, eds., *Neues Testament und Geschichte, Festschrift für O Cullmann* (Zürich, 1972), available in English as "The Structure of First John Comparison with the Fourth Gospel," *BTB* 3 (1973): 194–216

If these observations are correct, the symmetry of 1 John and the Gospel of John might look like this:[43]

THE GOSPEL OF JOHN	THE FIRST LETTER OF JOHN
A. Prologue 1:1–18	**A. Prologue** 1:1–4
The entry in the beginning of the word of life into the world.	The revelation of life in Jesus Christ who appeared "in the beginning."
B. The Book of Signs 1:19–12:50	**B. Part One** 1:5–3:10
The light shined in the darkness of Judaism and was rejected.	God is light and like Jesus we must walk in his light.
C. The Book of Glory 13:1–20:29	**C. Part Two** 3:11–5:12
Jesus cares for and nurtures "his own," those who believe in him.	God is love and those who know him must love one another.
D. Epilogue 21	**D. Epilogue** 5:13–21
Final resurrection stories about Jesus and explanation of purpose.	The author explains his purposes.

Smalley prefers to divide the letter between 2:29 and 3:1, which employs a division popularly used by those making a threefold division. Brown's divisions shown here provide proportionally sized halves for the letter and also find parallel introductory lines for 1:5 and 3:11, "This is the message we [you] have heard . . ."

While none of these theories find universal acceptance, we can at best attempt to make some orderly sense of John's progression of thought. I have found Brown's argument for a twofold division convincing, but within these divisions there seems to be a loosely connected series of exhortations reinforcing the themes of the division itself.

---

43. See similarly Brown, *Epistles*, 124.

A. Prologue: 1:1–4
The word of life which we have witnessed among us.

B. Part 1: 1:5–3:10: God is Light—and we should walk accordingly.
"This is the message we have heard from him and declare to you."

- 1:5–7:   Thesis: walking in the light and walking in the darkness
- 1:8–2:2:   First Exhortation: Resist sinfulness
- 2:3–11:   Second Exhortation: Obey God's commands
- 2:12–17:   Third Exhortation: Defy the world and its allure
- 2:18–27:   Fourth Exhortation: Renounce those who distort the truth
- 2:28–3:10:   Fifth Exhortation: Live like God's children

C. Part 2: 3:11–5:12: God is Love—and we should walk accordingly.
"This is the message you heard from the beginning: We should love one another."

- 3:11–24:   Love one another in practical ways.
- 4:1–6:   Beware of false prophets who would deceive you.
- 4:7–21:   Love one another as God loves us in Christ.
- 5:1–4:   Obey God and thereby conquer the world.
- 5:5–12:   Never compromise your testimony.

D. Conclusion: 5:13–21
The boldness and confidence of those who walk in God's light and love.

The Structure of 2 and 3 John

FEW HAVE DISCOVERED a careful literary structure for these brief letters. Like personal letters everywhere, they simply begin with a greeting and proceed developing one theme after another in a casual manner.[44] Each letter is occasioned by the same concern: living the truth. This takes on two dimensions: (1) It means loving those who abide in the family of God; (2) it means chastising those who want to dismantle that family. In each case John warns against community

---

44. As the commentary will note, however, they follow a structure well known to Hellenistic authors.

destroyers—a theme grounded in the concerns about division well
known throughout 1 John.

Second John

- 1–3: Personal Greetings
- 4–6: Loving the Family of God
- 7–11: Protecting the Family of God
- 12–13: Closing

Third John

- 1–2: Personal Greetings
- 3–8: Loving Christ's Emissaries
- 9–12: Exhortations About Diotrephes
- 13–14: Closing

Select Annotated Bibliography

Commentaries on the Letters of John

Barker, G. W. "1 John, 2 John, 3 John." *The Expositor's Bible Commentary*, vol. 12. Grand Rapids: Zondervan, 1981. A spiritually penetrating study of John's letters by a beloved provost at Fuller Seminary, well known for pastoral wisdom.

Brooke, A. E. *A Critical and Exegetical Commentary on the Johannine Epistles.* ICC. Edinburgh: T. & T. Clark, 1912. This is the classic study of the Greek text in the International Critical Commentary series. Useful particularly for critical text issues.

Brown, R. E. *The Epistles of John.* AB 30. New York: Doubleday, 1982. Written by one of the most famous Johannine scholars, Brown's commentary covers every detail with encyclopaedic depth in 812 pages. An incomparable volume filled with scholarly riches and sound pastoral insight.

Bultmann, R. *The Johannine Epistles.* Hermenia. Philadelphia: Fortress, 1973. A brief though important study in the Hermeneia series, Bultmann's work shows his mastery of the religious currents in the Hellenistic world. Less useful for preaching and exposition.

Dodd, C. H. *The Johannine Epistles.* MNTC. New York: Harper & Row, 1946. Occasionally eccentric, Dodd's commentary always gives a fresh insight or unexpected solution to historical problems. A scholarly work with limited application to the contemporary church.

Marshall, I. H. *The Epistles of John.* NICNT. Grand Rapids: Eerdmans, 1978. An evangelical scholar at Aberdeen University, Scotland, Marshall brings a wealth of pastoral experience to careful exegetical work. An outstanding volume that richly repays careful study.

Smalley, S. *1, 2, 3 John.* WBC 51. Waco, Tex.: Word, 1984. Stephen Smalley is a famous Johannine scholar and here culls the best insights from massive scholarly literature. An essential volume for serious exegetes.

Strecker, Georg. *The Johannine Letters.* Hermenia. Philadelphia: Fortress, 1995. This is a new volume in the Hermenia series, designed to supplement, if not replace, Bultmann's earlier work.

Popular Expositions of the Letters of John

Barclay, W. *The Letters of John*. Philadelphia: Westminster, 1976. While Barclay is found in almost every parish library, he often takes up one view on an issue and fails to let readers know what options are available. Always interesting, but best supplemented with other writers.

Bruce, F. F. *The Epistles of John*. Grand Rapids: Eerdmans, 1970. An easy-to-read commentary by one of the leading scholars of New Testament studies in the twentieth century.

Stott, J. R. W. *The Epistles of John*. Grand Rapids: Eerdmans, 1964. Perhaps one of the best popular commentators, Stott writes passionately about these letters' message for the church today. Always creative, always penetrating.

Thompson, M. M. *1–3 John*. IVPNTC. Downer's Grove, Ill.: InterVarsity, 1992. A professor at Fuller Seminary, Meye Thompson's study gives lively, outstanding illustrations for preaching, based on a wealth of scholarly research.

General Studies in John

Ashton, J. *Understanding the Fourth Gospel*. Oxford: Clarendon, 1991. Perhaps the most comprehensive technical survey of Johannine scholarship to date. Written for the scholar.

Brown, R. E. *The Community of the Beloved Disciple: The Life, Loves, and Hates of an Individual Church in New Testament Times*. New York: Paulist, 1979. An attempt to reconstruct the history of the Johannine community, using the Fourth Gospel and John's letters as windows into community life.

Cullman, O. *The Johannine Circle*. London: SCM, 1976. A provocative study placing the community of John in the wider framework of the New Testament.

Culpepper, R. A. *The Johannine School*. Missoula, Mont.: Scholars, 1975. An important technical study of "schools" or academic/religious "communities" in antiquity and how this relates to the "Johannine community."

Law, R. *The Tests of Life: A Study of the First Epistle of St. John*. Edinburgh: T. & T. Clark, 1914; reprint, Baker, 1968. This famous early study of the letters weds scholarly insight with pastoral wisdom, arranging the contents of the letters topically.

Painter, J. *The Quest for the Messiah: The History, Literature and Theology of the Johannine Community*. Edinburgh: T. & T. Clark, 1993. This thorough scholarly treatment surveys the current research on the literature of the Johannine community and provides outstanding academic background to the study of the Fourth Gospel and the letters of John.

———— *John: Witness and Theologian.* London: SPCK, 1975. A helpful and readable introduction to Johannine studies by students just breaking into the field.

Smalley, S. S. *John: Evangelist and Interpreter.* Exeter: Paternoster, 1978; reissued, 1983. The best introduction for those beginning a critical study of the Johannine literature.

1 John 1:1-4

❦

T HAT WHICH WAS from the beginning, which we
have heard, which we have seen with our eyes,
which we have looked at and our hands have
touched—this we proclaim concerning the Word of life.
²The life appeared; we have seen it and testify to it, and
we proclaim to you the eternal life, which was with the
Father and has appeared to us. ³We proclaim to you
what we have seen and heard, so that you also may have
fellowship with us. And our fellowship is with the Father
and with his Son, Jesus Christ. ⁴We write this to make
our joy complete.

JOHN'S OPENING WORDS serve as an introduction and present us, as C. H. Dodd once
wrote, with a "grammatical tangle," which has
been well disguised by the NIV. Phrases pile
up on one another as John attempts to compress into a single paragraph
ideas whose complexity will be worked out in the letter. Any careful
reader of the Johannine literature will immediately note echoes of the
Fourth Gospel's prologue. In each prologue (the Gospel and 1 John)
the *logos* or Word of God is central, and yet the two paragraphs do not
run parallel to each other. Instead they are complementary.[1] In the
Gospel we learn about the history and work of the Word in creation,
his incarnation into the world, his rejection, and the eternal life he
offered. Now John takes up two themes: the reality of this incarnation
("[that] which we have heard ... seen ... and ... touched") and its
salvific importance ("this we proclaim concerning the Word of life").
John seems to emphasize the centrality of the *incarnate* Word as if controversy swirled around the subject, as if some were disputing whether
or not the Word of God had actually become flesh (complete human

---

1. This, incidentally, suggests that the Gospel in its completed form was written prior
to 1 John and that the present verses are a reflection on the earlier Johannine prologue.

flesh) in Jesus Christ. As we shall see, right thinking about Jesus Christ is the fulcrum on which right theology is balanced.

While this hunch about theological controversy will be borne out in later verses (cf. 4:2–3), we can see in 1:3–4 that John's emphasis is entirely pastoral and practical. His mind is on the fabric of Christian community and how its fellowship and joy are being affected by dispositions concerning Jesus. He assumes that intimate fellowship in the Christian community is only possible when there is consensus about the identity and presence of Jesus.

The Incarnate Word (1:1a)

THE STRAINED GRAMMAR of verses 1–3 underscores John's emphasis on the centrality of the incarnate Word. A literal rendering makes the sense clear:

> [1]What was from the beginning;
> what we have heard;
> what we have seen with our eyes;
> what we beheld and our hands touched
> —*concerning the word of life*—
> ([2]and the life appeared
> and we have seen and testify, and announce to you the
> eternal life which was with the Father and was revealed to
> us);
> [3]What we have seen and heard
> *We* **proclaim** *also to you.*

Placing the main verb of the sentence in verse 3 permits John to stack four relative clauses at the beginning (a fifth is in 3a) and thereby emphasize the object of proclamation (the Word) rather than the act of proclaiming itself. It is also peculiar that the relative pronoun is neuter ("what," Gk. *ho*, rather than "who"). Since "Word" (Gk. *logos*) is masculine, it would seem appropriate and grammatically correct to place the relative pronoun in agreement with its intended subject, Jesus, the incarnate Word.[2] However, using a neuter pronoun can be

---

2. The text would then read, "The one who was in the beginning, whom we have heard and seen with our own eyes. . ."

a way to express "the whole career of Jesus."[3] Neuter pronouns can function "comprehensively to cover the person, words and works."[4] Therefore, John is saying that the whole sweep of Jesus' life bears importance to his subject, not simply particular events or even the abstract appearance of God in history. In Christ, God walked with humankind, and anyone who had contact with that reality, anyone who had heard, seen, and touched that reality, could never make it less than pivotal.

All this is to say that John's singular interest is not some abstract doctrine about Jesus or the importance of preaching about Jesus (though some commentators take it this way); rather, it is the reality of Jesus' personhood—his incarnation or his entry into history. He is described as "the Word," not as if Jesus is an idea preached or message that enlightens. This term rather harks back to the Gospel's prologue, where Jesus is called "the Word" as a personal title of importance to both Greek and Jewish ears. The Word is the creative self-expression of God by which the cosmos was made (Judaism, Gen. 1:1ff.). It is the divine reason that gives the universe coherence and purpose (Hellenism; cf. Philo). Thus in verse 1 John writes that this word was "from the beginning" (cf. John 1:1, "In the beginning was the Word, and the Word was with God"). This does not refer necessarily to the beginning of Jesus' life on earth (though some have argued for this). It instead sets out the marvelous tension of Christian thought: He who existed from limitless eternity has entered time and space and taken up residence here on earth.

Thus, of critical importance is the relationship of this Word to human history. John's present verses serve as a reflection, an expansion perhaps, on the Gospel prologue's primary verse, John 1:14: "The Word became flesh and made his dwelling among us. We have seen his glory." To dispel any suggestion that this appearing in history was imagined or partial, John speaks graphically of the sensory confirmation (hearing/seeing/touching) that accompanied this revelation.

---

3 Brown, *The Epistles of John,* 154.

4. Ibid Brown cites examples in John 3:6; 6:39, 17·2, 7, 24, and 1 John 5·4 Typically see John 6.37, "All *that* the Father gives to me will come to me. . ."

The Word of Life (1:1b–2)

HOWEVER, THIS IS not simply any Word. Nor is this a Word "about life," as if it were a message that explained the meaning of living. The final phrase of verse 1 is pivotal because it explains the importance of this revelation. Once again the Fourth Gospel's prologue in John 1:4 gives us our clue. There we learn that this incarnate Word is the source of life: "In him was life."[5] "Concerning the Word of life" is almost an awkward parenthesis inserted into the paragraph to make absolutely certain that the eternal life described here is grounded in the historical events of Jesus' life. In other words, eternal life is not the by-product of some enlightenment or knowledge acquired mystically. Eternal life is historically anchored in what we may call *the scandal of particularity* unique to Christianity. The life of God has been channeled to us through a historical event, an event that John says has been verified by people who saw it.

It is interesting that in verse 2 the authority behind John's affirmation is not merely some tradition or doctrinal convention. It springs from experience. It would be one thing for John to defend the particularity of the Incarnation as a logical requirement of some theological system. And no doubt he could do this. The repeated emphasis on personal experience—seeing and testifying what was revealed to us— is not just a way to shore up his defense of the Incarnation. John's authority rests in what he knows to be true *because he has touched it*. He is making a compelling appeal; he is offering a testimony, not just to coherent, orthodox theology, but to a living Word, Jesus Christ, whose reality is the principal reference point of his life. In the earliest Christian community when the apostolic replacement for the deceased Judas Iscariot was sought, the chief criterion for nomination was possessing this experience of the incarnate Lord. Matthias was a candidate because he had *seen and heard and touched* Jesus Christ, "beginning from John's baptism to the time when Jesus was taken up from us" (Acts 1:22).

The Word and Fellowship (1:3–4)

EMBRACING THIS WORD, experiencing this life, gaining this reference point—these are all prerequisites for Christian community. The pur-

---

5 See also John 11:25 and 14 6, where Jesus says that he is life The NIV supports this interpretation by printing "Word" with a capital W in verse 1

pose of John's letter is fellowship, "so that you also may have fellowship with us" (v. 3a). The Greek word translated "fellowship" in the NIV is *koinonia*, which means to have something in common. *Koinonia* may describe a shared labor (such as the fishing of James, John, and Simon, Luke 5:10) or the common enjoyment of some gift or experience (such as the grace of God, Phil. 1:7; the blessings of the gospel, 1 Cor. 9:23; or the Holy Spirit, 2 Cor. 13:14).

This is the crux of John's thought and the purpose of his writing. Christian community is not some passing association of people who share common sympathies for a cause. Nor is it an academy where an intellectual consensus about God is discovered. It cannot be so superficial. Christian community is partnership in experience; it is the common living of people who have a shared experience of Jesus Christ. They talk about this experience, they urge each other to grow more deeply in it, and they discover that through it, they begin to build a life together unlike any shared life in the world.

But Christian community is not merely horizontal; it is not just a social phenomenon. John asserts that this fellowship is also "with the Father and with his Son, Jesus Christ" (v. 3b). This puts one more dimension to the meaning of community. Fellowship is not just the coincidence of a shared experience of God, where we compare our private spiritual walks; it is living and experiencing the Father and the Son *together* as believers. Christian fellowship is triangular: my life in fellowship with Christ, your life in fellowship with Christ, and my life in fellowship with yours. The mystical union I enjoy with Christ becomes the substance that binds the church together. In verse 4 John adds that the net result of such a community will be joy—"to make our[6] joy complete." This is a benefit, a by-product, of a genuinely Christ-centered fellowship.

The themes seen here find a close parallel in Jesus' teaching in John 15. Abiding in Christ, the vine, is the way to becoming Jesus' disciple (15:8) and experiencing his joy (15:11). Moreover, our union with the vine is the prerequisite for loving one another (15:12–17). Christian community once again grows from a matured relationship with God

---

6. Some ancient texts read "your joy" instead of "our joy." Evidence for this alternate reading is considerable (hence its appearance in the NIV footnote), and the similarity of the two words in Greek (*humon, hemon*) makes a scribal confusion understandable. The alternate reading may have been influenced by the appearance of "your joy" in John 15:11 and 16:24

in his Son, Jesus Christ. And no doubt where this relationship with Christ is absent, such community is an impossibility.

FROM MY OVERALL study of the Johannine literature (see the introduction) and from what I discern here in these verses, John's emphasis tells me that he is writing to a community where there is considerable disunity. Factions have broken out and severe theological disagreements have undercut the church's vitality. From 1:1–4 and 4:1–3 it is clear that the Incarnation is under siege. We speculated in the introduction that these opponents may well have been early Gnostics who, if they affirmed the divinity of Jesus at all, could hardly agree that he was genuinely physical in any manner. To them, physical properties could not share anything with a divine realm. Therefore, in this diverse community Christians were trying to discern what was *essential for Christian identity*. It is not a far-fetched speculation to imagine debaters insisting that any "doctrine that divides" be set aside so that none will be offended.

In addition, John has on his mind the quality and character of Christian fellowship that should accompany Christian life. John's repeated emphasis on love throughout his letter suggests the harsh tone of the debates. Christians were at each other's throats, trying to figure out how to live in an environment where there was such diversity. Therefore, even here in 1:1–4 his urgency springs from a desire to restore fellowship and joy in an otherwise divided community.

Curiously, however, his approach is not simply ethical. John does not merely catalogue what behaviors are unbecoming to Christians and then list appropriate virtues, such as Paul does in Galatians 5:16–26 and Colossians 3:5–17. John unites the themes of Christology and community as he exhorts the church that a right understanding of Jesus should inform how we live together. Jesus' incarnation is the central doctrine of Christian faith. Embracing this historical Jesus and continuing to bear witness to him (seeing/touching/hearing) should be at the center of our lives together. Jesus Christ as God-in-flesh cannot be marginalized.

As an interpreter I understand that this precise context, complete with proto-Gnostic heretics, is barely a part of my world. Some trends, especially among those who seek to forge a new unity among all religious movements, may come close in how they dispense with the centrality of Christ as a first order of business. Some New Age religions likewise try to inherit the "center" of Jesus' teaching, leaving his personhood behind.

On the other hand, I must look for themes that bridge John's context and mine. I must seek to distill what is *contextually transferable* to bring this passage to life. Two themes come to mind. (1) John is wrestling with *the essence of Christian identity*. What is the essential core of belief that distinguishes the Christian? What is the watershed doctrine at the heart of our faith? We will return to this again and again as we see that incarnational theology is for John the crux issue of thought. (2) John is describing the *basis of Christian fellowship*. Within the church the quality of our life together is an essential datum in fulfilling our mandate as God's people. However, should we pursue this harmony and unity of purpose at all costs?

 WE LIVE IN a culture that is eager for religious experience. George Barna reports that in the United States over 90 percent of the population believes in a God or gods that have power over the universe.[7] As a result, religious tolerance and experimentation are commonplace. Furthermore, when asked if all of the world's religions essentially prayed to the same God, 64 percent of the adult public agreed. In the Christian church, among those who called themselves evangelicals, 46 percent agreed, and among those who labeled themselves "born again," 48 percent agreed. Among adults who simply called themselves "regular church attendees," fully 62 percent said that they believed all religions essentially prayed to the same God.[8] This is astonishing. Within the pews of America's churches, two-thirds of the people do not believe in the *exclusive* character of the Christian message, and almost half of all evangelicals say the same.

In light of these tendencies both inside and outside of the church, how will we define our life together as Christians? What will be the

---

7 G. Barna, *What Americans Believe An Annual Survey of Values and Religious Views in the United States* (Ventura, Calif.. Regal, 1991), 174
8. Ibid., 212.

essential character of Christian thought and community? John's first words to his churches force us to ask penetrating questions about our own Christian identity.

(1) *What does it mean to hold to "the scandal of the Incarnation"?* John sets before us the particularity of Christian thought. At the center of our faith is the entrance of Jesus Christ into history as a *definitive revelation of God.* This is an event that cannot be jettisoned. It cannot be redefined as a myth or compared with the religious revelations offered by others (Mohammed, Joseph Smith, New Age prophets, etc.). Jesus Christ is definitive.

Throughout the world Christians are often tempted to forge new alliances in order to achieve noble ends. This is particularly true in countries where multiple faiths coexist side by side. For instance, I have been privileged to become acquainted with the Palestinian Christian community and to learn of its fight for survival in Israel. In the hills of the West Bank, moderate Palestinian Muslims and Palestinian Christians ask what sort of unity they might build in order to construct a unified front for justice.[9]

The same questions are with us here in the Western world. The difficulty becomes acute when we find ourselves in interfaith dialogues that try to build unity particularly for commendable social programs. I recall attending one such attempt in Skokie, Illinois. This was a meeting of Jewish rabbis and Christian pastors who, for the sake of Chicago's northern suburbs, agreed that a united front was needed against crime and drugs. As the discussion progressed, all sides pressed for a "common theological denominator" that would be the basis of prayer, worship, and ethics. It goes without saying that Christological emphases had to be set aside.

I have also spent a number of years in the United States Navy as a chaplain. The military chaplaincy succeeds miraculously to protect the distinctives of each faith tradition so that each worshiping community need not compromise what is essential to its beliefs. And yet the exercise of public, interfaith religion puts unique demands on the chaplain. I recall leading a prayer at an officers' school near the Navy War College in Newport, Rhode Island. I was reminded gently by the

---

9 See further, G. Burge, *Who Are God's People in the Middle East? What Christians Are Not Being Told About Israel and the Palestinians* (Grand Rapids: Zondervan, 1993).

commanding officer not to include anything offensive, such as any reference to Jesus Christ. Imagine wearing a cross as your collar device in the military and not referring to Jesus! Is this appropriate theological conduct? I was once with the Marines at Camp Pendleton, California, and one night in the field stood watch from midnight till 4:00 A.M. with a Mormon chaplain. After three hours together, it was clear that if Jesus remained central, we would have severe limits on our fellowship together.

Is it possible to conduct ourselves as Christians and exclude the place of Jesus Christ? Should we abstain from any such involvements? Or should we cease to call them "Christian" encounters? If Christ is offensive to some, do we continue on in ministry and deny the central event of our faith? Or do we hold fast to the scandal of what we affirm? John would quickly say that there is no Christianity if Jesus Christ is not at the center.

But perhaps there is a more nuanced problem here for us—the more pressing question of whether it is appropriate for Christians to have a "strategic" silence about Jesus when meeting people of other faiths and persuasions. When the time is right, when trust is secure, then the central theme of our faith, Jesus, will be heard. Wheaton College chose this option recently when our Center for Islamic Studies hosted a dialogue with a circle of Islamic leaders. (Things were particularly unusual when they dismissed themselves so that they could go out into the hall and pray toward Mecca!) The difficulty, of course, arises when that strategic silence is no strategy at all but a quiet concession to pluralism and tolerance.

(2) *Should theological distinctives be set aside for the unity of the church?* The issue of pluralism becomes even more problematic when the dialogue takes place within the church itself. Evangelicals often find themselves living and working in mainline denominations or local congregations where adherence to particular orthodox doctrines brings tension. Charismatic Christians feel the same when they try to share the preciousness of their experiences and yet discover that their presence risks bringing disunity. In my own Presbyterian Church, U.S.A., the limits of pluralism are often stretched to a breaking point. In order to maintain unity, a theological "lowest common denominator" is sought—a minimalist doctrinal umbrella that excludes no one. At what point does right belief become more important than church unity?

First John 1:1—4 suggests that at least one doctrine, one conviction, cannot be dismissed lightly. Any minister, any Christian, who does not embrace the reality of God-in-history, any believer who can be cavalier about the definitive event in salvation history, namely, Jesus Christ as God-among-us, has departed significantly from the faith of the early church.

I recognize this opens up a whole variety of other questions. Are there other essential beliefs that define Christian identity? The virgin birth, for instance, is a corollary of incarnational theology, but is it essential for Christian identity? What about less directly connected doctrines, such as Scripture, charismatic gifts, the sacraments, universalism, women's ordination, and the saints? Should the church sanction within its ranks diversity on these issues for the sake of a larger unity? Whatever we make of these, at least John would have our starting point be the Incarnation. Jesus-in-history is the touchstone from which all other doctrines emerge.

A friend of mine once told a remarkable true story about Harvard Divinity School. Upon learning that one of her professors there was agnostic, she inquired about the range of theological diversity on the seminary campus. "Anything goes," came the reply. My friend pursued the point: "You mean no belief or absence of belief would keep one from being hired to teach theology?" "Only one," came the clarification, "the refusal to endorse women's ordination." Regardless of how one feels on this subject, John would anchor the starting point (or litmus test) of Christian theology elsewhere. The absence of a sound Christology is John's test. The same confusion rests in evangelicalism. The Evangelical Theological Society, an academic fellowship of hundreds of evangelical professors and pastors, has only one doctrinal affirmation that every member must sign: the inerrancy of Scripture. A faithful Mormon could join easily. Both concerns in my illustration—the ordination of women and inerrancy—are legitimate and important. But they are not central. John reminds us that Christology is at the center of our theological identity.

Many theologians who are in dialogue with modern theological trends see this clearly. The intramural theological debates of the church often lose sight of the larger question of Christology on the border between the church and the world. In his generation Dietrich Bonhoeffer's lectures on Christology, *Christ the Center,* sound this challenge clearly.[10] The same call needs to be sounded today. The particularity of Jesus Christ is the scandal of Christianity that sets us apart from the world. Christology is the one theme that we cannot jettison, no matter what the benefit or what the temptation.

(3) *What does it mean to see/touch/hear Jesus today?* It seems clear to me that John is trying to describe a compelling experience for himself and the first generation of believers. But it is less clear what that means for believers who live even one generation removed from Jesus' ascension. Of course we might say that this compelling experience belonged only to one generation and that all subsequent generations must live with reference to that experience, a "touching" from afar, as it were.

But I believe that John wants more than this. The Fourth Gospel, for instance, suggests that there will be a continuity of "Jesus experience" for all generations and not just the first. In John 14 Jesus promises that he will never leave his followers "orphans" (14:18) and that those who love him and are obedient will become Christ's new dwelling place (14:23). In other words, Johannine theology does not see the Ascension as a terminus of Christ's presence. Christ's Spirit given to his followers (John 20:22) is indeed his own Spirit. First John 3:24 says clearly, "And this is how we know that he lives in us: We know it by the Spirit he gave us." And 4:13 adds, "We know that we live in him and he in us, because he has given us of his Spirit." Therefore, a necessary dimension of Christian discipleship is the ongoing communion of the believer with the Lord.

Is this a mystical experience? An ecstatic or charismatic experience? How do we commune with the Lord in a way that corresponds to John's experience? At least we can say what it is not. It is not just doing Christian things (although obedience to his word is a part of it, see 1 John 2:5). It is not just giving intellectual assent to a set of doctrines (although believing right things is a part of it too, see 4:2–3). *Christian discipleship must be experiential.* It must be personal in the sense that the person of Jesus indwells our life and makes himself known. Using John's terms in 1:3, the believer has fellowship with the Father and the Son in a manner not dissimilar to having fellowship with other Christians.

This is why John knows that true Christian community is hinged to true experiences of Jesus. In this letter he desires a sort of intimacy

---

10. D. Bonhoeffer, *Christ the Center* (New York. Harper and Row, 1960).

that unites spiritual realities with life together. On the other hand, when church members meet together and no one can speak of the way Christ is penetrating and healing and leading the chief areas of life, it is doubtful we should call this fellowship at all. Furthermore, such experiences of Jesus form the basis of Christian authenticity. John writes with authority because he knows what he says is true—not because of reason, but because of experience. Today the authenticity of our faith is likewise linked to the vitality of Jesus' life within us. If Jesus is a doctrine, our testimony will be hollow. If Jesus is a person, our testimony will be potent.

In an age that places religious experience above doctrine and ethics, however, one caution must be sounded. Indeed, the present reality of Jesus may be mystically seen in prayer and powerful encounters of Christ-in-Spirit. Yet there are other ways that Christ should be seen. I remember the first time a friend placed a copy of Jim Wallis' *Agenda for a Biblical People* in my hand.[11] Wallis wrote a stirring, compelling argument for transformed communities that bear Christlike qualities in our cities. Christ is more than conversion, salvation, and private renewal. He is about the transformation of the world. He calls us to bring his kingdom to bear upon the powers of this world. In a similar way, Stanley Grenz has reviewed the failed attempts of evangelical theology to fire the imagination of the modern world.[12] He argues for "the kingdom of God" as the new organizing center of what we say and do. In a world of fractured communities, Christ has come to bring a new vision of life, to give a "transcendent vantage point for life in the present," and to give "a qualitative meaning to life, time and space, persons and groups."[13] This forging of radical community is likewise the work of Christ—the presence of Christ—which John would no doubt champion as well.

---

11. J Wallis, *Agenda for a Biblical People* (New York: Harper and Row, 1984)

12. S Grenz, *Revisioning Evangelical Theology A Fresh Agenda for the 21st Century* (Downer's Grove, Ill.: InterVarsity, 1993).

13. Ibid., 155

1 John 1:5-7

THIS IS THE message we have heard from him and declare to you: God is light; in him there is no darkness at all. ⁶If we claim to have fellowship with him yet walk in the darkness, we lie and do not live by the truth. ⁷But if we walk in the light, as he is in the light, we have fellowship with one another, and the blood of Jesus, his Son, purifies us from all sin.

Original Meaning

THE PREVIOUS SECTION, 1 John 1:1–4, serves as the prologue, launching the twin themes that will occupy the interest of the letter. In the introduction I discussed the various ways in which this letter can be divided; I have chosen a two-part division, finding natural divisions introduced by 1:5 and 3:11. The common phrase, "This is the message [Gk. *angelia*] we [you , 3:11] have heard," signals a new transition in each case to one of John's two concerns introduced in the prologue.[1] On the one hand, right thinking about God ("God is light") is a necessary prerequisite for life in the Christian community. This will be the subject of the first section of John's letter, 1:5–3:10, and is introduced in the prologue with John's firm words about the Incarnation. On the other hand, right living within the community ("God is love"), living honestly and in love, is also on John's mind. This will be the subject of the second section, 3:11–5:12. In the prologue hints of this concern come through in John's desire for fellowship and joy as hallmarks of Christian life together.[2]

However, as I mentioned in the introduction, there is little agreement among scholars concerning the organization of 1 John. Thus I am reluctant to defend the present division as definitive. John's ideas

---

1. The text of the NIV is confusing at this point. The phrase, "This old command *is the message you have heard*," also appears in 2:7, but in this case the Greek word is not *angelia* but *logos*, "word, communication." The NRSV translates 2:7, "the old commandment is the *word that you have heard*." *Angelia* appears only twice in 1 John—1:5 and 3:11.

2 For further details about the organization of the letter, see the introduction, pp. 41–45.

spill from one category to another; theological correctness and ethics intermingle again and again, echoing back and forth in these chapters and playing havoc on those of us who like to find clean-cut, tightly organized divisions.

The internal organization of 1:5–3:10 begins with a thesis statement ("God is light") and proceeds to build a list of expectations that attend to those who walk in this light. We will see that John's discussion is peppered with quotations that must have had some currency in his community. He cites these and then gives a careful rebuttal. After John's thesis statement in 1:5–7, I have broken down the remaining verses into five units, each of which is an exhortation engaging some debate or heretical theme that formed part of the controversy in John's church. In each case, to deny the truth of John's words is to step out of the light and break with fellowship among God's people. (1) We must resist sinfulness, 1:8–2:2; (2) we must obey God's commands, 2:3–11; (3) we must defy the world and its allure, 2:12–17; (4) we must renounce those who distort the truth; and (5) we must live like God's children, not children of the devil, 2:28–3:10.

The present section, 1 John 1:5–7, is closely linked with the prologue in that it carries forward themes already announced there. The message is anchored in what was heard, and all along a plural subject is maintained ("we have heard," "we claim," "we walk"), suggesting that John is engaged in some sort of debate in which he is addressing a community of people whose ideas are opposed to the message of the gospel.[3] However, in this case John's interest (even through 3:10) is practical and moral: Truly acknowledging the reality of God results in changed living. John engages in no esoteric theological debate. His point initially is not to dispute doctrine. Instead, he wants to cultivate discipleship that knows how to "live by the truth."

Many have pointed out that the structure of 1:5–7 has a quasi-poetic form that is too precise to be an accident and likely recalls Semitic habits of parallelism. Lines mirror one another in an inverted

---

3. It is interesting to compare the verse that follows the prologue in the Gospel of John (John 1:19) with 1 John 1:5. Just as the vocabulary of the two prologues match, so too 1 John 1:5 ("this is the message [*angelia*]") echoes John 1:19 ("this is the testimony [*martyria*]"). Similarly, just as 1 John 1·5 is drawn from the epistolary prologue, so too John 1:19 is drawn from John 1:6. See Brown, *Epistles of John*, 225

fashion (called a *chiasmus*); this is often symbolized by the symbols A B B' A'.[4] Rewriting these verses makes its organization evident:

A   God is *Light*
   B   No *Darkness* in God
   B'   Walking in the *Darkness*
A'   Walking in the *Light*

It is immediately clear that John's interest turns on determining the meaning of the light/darkness metaphor and applying it ethically to Christian living.

God Is Light (1:5)

IN VERSE 5 John narrows his thought to give the essence of the message[5] he has brought to his readers. But note again, as in the prologue, that John appeals to historic revelation as the *anchor* of what he believes. "In him" (though ambiguous in Greek) no doubt refers to Jesus. John's reflex is to build everything he says theologically on the revelation, the historic revelation, he witnessed in the life of Jesus Christ (cf. 1:1–3). It is fair to ask why he does this. In 2:20–21 we will see how the problems in the church are essentially pneumatic. They stem from prophets who, under the alleged inspiration of the Spirit, are teaching false things. John's first response when faced with such teachings is to train his followers that theology must be anchored objectively or else it will be shaped by any whim or inspiration. Theology must always begin with recitation in which we examine and state clearly what God has already said in history. This *special revelation*, then, becomes the check on our inspirations and our speculations.

When John affirms that God is light, he is recalling an idea whose lineage begins in the Old Testament. In Exodus 3 Moses experiences God as fire. In 13:21 God's presence as fire illumines the way the Israelites travel in the desert (cf. Num. 9). Thus when the tabernacle

---

4. A simple and well-known chiasmus in the Gospels is· **A** The Sabbath / **B** is made for man / **B'** not man /**A'** for the Sabbath The term *chiasmus* comes from the Greek letter *chi* (written **X**), which is made when the AB/B'A' is written on two lines and the corresponding letters are connected

5 The Greek word John employs here, *angelia*, appears nowhere else in the New Testament except in 1 John 3:11. It is related to *apangelein* ("announce, proclaim") in 1·2–3 But since John never uses the usual word for "gospel" (Gk *euangelion*), it may be that *angelia* is a synonym.

is erected, God's presence is signaled with fire in the golden lampstands (8:1–4). Fire brings light, and so similarly God is described as light. Hence Psalm 104:2 says, "[God] wraps himself in light as with a garment," and the psalmist appeals to him, "Let the light of your face shine upon us, O LORD" (4:6). God's working among people is consistently described as the bringing of light that eliminates darkness (Ex. 13:21; 2 Sam. 22:29; Ezra 9:8; Pss. 13:3; 18:28; 19:7–8).

John also appeals to the coming of Jesus that is described in the Gospels as the revelation of light. When the baby Jesus is presented at the temple, Simeon celebrates his coming as a "light for revelation" (Luke 2:32). Matthew sums up Jesus' early ministry citing Isaiah to describe Jesus' messiahship in terms of a great light to those in darkness (Matt. 4:16). But it is unlikely that John had these Synoptic texts in front of him. If we are correct that the Johannine community possessed an early draft of the Fourth Gospel as its unique record of Jesus' life, John may likely be appealing to passages such as John 1:5 ("The light shines in the darkness") or 1:9 ("The true light that gives light to every man was coming into the world"). This is particularly likely since we have already observed the heavy dependence of the present verses on the Johannine prologue. Furthermore, in John 3:19–21 the Baptist uses the light metaphor for Jesus, and in 8:12 Jesus actually says, "I am the light of the world" (also see 9:5; 12:35, 46). In fact, in the Gospel of John itself some variation on the word "light" (either as noun or verb) occurs over forty times.[6]

The implication for Johannine theology is simple. Since God is light, Jesus in bringing God to us has likewise brought light, divine light. But there is something curious at work in the present verse. Of the many uses of "light" in the Johannine literature, the vast bulk refer to Jesus as the light (in the Gospel, nineteen of twenty-three uses refer to Jesus). While John's emphasis usually is Christological, in the present verse he makes a stark *theological* assertion not in keeping with his usual tendency. John generally places Christ, not God, in sharp relief. His writings make only three absolute affirmations about God: God is Spirit (John 4:24), God is light (1 John 1:5), and God is love (4:8). Why has John not gone on here to urge that Jesus is the light?

---

6. The popularity of light imagery for this period is also evidenced at Qumran, where followers were called the "sons of light" and light/darkness metaphors were commonly used to describe the world. See 1QS 1:9–10, 5:19–20.

The importance of this theological image for 1 John should not be missed. John seems to be appealing to a slogan used by his opponents, since in the next five verses he will cite them precisely. Among Gnostics light was a premier metaphor for God, for Gnosticism promoted a religion of mystic enlightenment. As C. H. Dodd writes on these verses, "Anyone who speaks in this way is at home in the religious world of first-century Hellenism."[7] As early as Plato, light imagery formed the conceptual basis of Near Eastern dualism. Even Philo, who merged Hellenism with Judaism, affirms, "God is light, and not light only, but the archetype of every other light, or rather, more ancient and higher than any archetype (*De Somniis*, 1.75)."[8] Thus John may be staking out some common ground, laying a framework from which to assault the error at hand.

Indeed, John says, God is light. He is pure, perfect, and utterly righteous. And above all, light is revealing. Light unveils our spiritual identity—whether we abide in the Son—and it identifies boldly those who live in darkness. Therefore light also has a judging function, for it unveils. This is not an idle theological speculation for John. God stands in contrast to darkness, to evil, to error, to imperfection. Implicit in this notion, therefore, is a challenge: Do we live in God's light or are we exposed, discovered to be in the darkness?

Life in the Darkness (1:6)

ALTHOUGH THE GREEK text of verse 6 uses indirect discourse, it is helpful to convert verses 6, 8, and 10 into direct discourse to see that John is confronting three false ideas, possibly three slogans well known in this church. Six "if" clauses (Gk. *ean* clauses) appear in 1:6–2:1; three are negative and three are positive.

1:6 If we say, "We have fellowship with him," yet walk in the darkness	1:7	But if we walk in the light as he is in the light . . .
1:8 If we say, "We have no sin"	1:9	But if we confess our sins . .
1:10 If we say, "We have not sinned"	2:1	But if anybody does sin . . .

---

7 C H. Dodd, *Johannine Epistles*, 18.

8. Ibid., 19, see further, R Bultmann, *Johannine Epistles*, 16

Each of these statements, paraded out so carefully for us, is a subtle variation on the same theme. Individuals in John's church were claiming that they had an intimate walk with God, that their lives were unstained with sin, and that they had done no wrong. The issue was not some disagreement over specific acts of purported wrongdoing. They were not refusing to acknowledge some sin for which John is rebuking them. The problem lay deeper; verse 6 hints that these Christians were living a double life. Many people in John's day believed that God was detached from the material world, that his holiness and purity set him above the common stuff of our existence. This explains, for instance, why his opponents had such a difficult time with incarnational theology (1:1–4; 4:2). God is ineffable light, pure and perfect. He cannot enter into the banal stuff of human history.

But there is an important ethical corollary here. If God is utterly removed from our world, if his existence is unaffected by earthly, material concerns, then behavior outside the spiritual context is unimportant. Earthly things and heavenly things exist in different spheres. In fact, a spiritual appraisal and a moral appraisal of one's life can be quite distinct. These Christians were claiming that sin is unimportant— they were not of the world—and that God only looks on the inward condition of a man's or a woman's soul.

John says that no such division is possible. A good God expects good people. A God of light expects lives that are permeated by such light. In verse 6 John describes this moral conduct as "walking" (Gk. *peripateo*) in darkness. This is a Semitic idiom akin to the Jewish term *halakah*. The religious life is not merely a matter of spiritual reflection or intellectual persuasion, rather, it is comprehensive. It is a habit of walking, a way of living (cf. Prov. 8:20; Isa. 2:5; Eph. 5:2). These opponents were not just *in darkness*, they were living lives of darkness (conveyed by the present tense of *peripateo*). They were persistent, dogged, and tenacious in the habits they had chosen. Smalley translates the verb "living habitually in darkness" and says it "implies a determination to choose sin (darkness) rather than God (light) as one's constant sphere of existence."[9]

This sort of spirituality is a lie. Again, John draws on dramatic verbs to uncover this religious falsehood. While the NIV translates

---

9. S. Smalley, *1,2,3 John*, 22.

that such people fail to "live" by truth, the Greek text employs another Semitic idiom that is much more dynamic. People living this lie do not "do" (Gk. *poieo*) the truth.[10] Truth is an essential concept for John. Nearly half of all its uses in the New Testament appear in John (of 109 uses, 25 are in John's Gospel and 20 in his letters). Truth describes not only the reality of God's existence shown to us in Christ (hence doctrinal truth) but also the genuineness of pure religion, true religion, true personal conduct that coheres with the essence of God's character.[11] John's opponents were not just ignorant of some fact about God— they were hostile. They had not simply overlooked something about God; they were lying and self-deceiving in their conduct. John 3:21 provides a parallel critique: "But whoever *does the truth* comes into the light, so that it may be revealed that what he has done has been done through God" (pers. tr.; cf. 8:44). Such conduct prefers to remain in darkness because living in the presence of God's light would expose its error.

Life in the Light (1:7)

IN CONTRAST, JOHN urges in verse 7 that we "walk" in the light (Gk. *ean de* makes the contrast explicit). As in verse 6, this is a habitual, consistent response that should be characteristic of those who know God. There is a way of living that harmonizes every facet of life with the presence of God. But how do we know if someone is in God's light? That they are walking as they ought? John does not say that such walking is evidenced by doctrinal purity, not yet anyway. Instead, two things result: Genuine fellowship is possible and sins are forgiven.

John sees an intrinsic connection (as we saw in 1:3–4) between our relationship with each other and our relationship with God. One is not possible without the other. It is curious that instead of saying that those who walk in the light "have fellowship with God" (as his opponents argued in v. 6), John says that fellowship *with each other* is the most obvious consequence. Again, we have to keep the Johannine

---

10. The phrase "doing the truth" appears in the Old Testament twice: 2 Chronicles 31.20 and Nehemiah 9.33.

11 Scholars debate whether John's notion of truth is essentially Greek (that is, adherence to some esoteric, heavenly reality) or Hebrew (the saving revelation of God on earth). I have chosen the latter but acknowledge that John's opponents may well be operating with the former

controversy in mind. John is confronting spiritually elitist Christians who not only exhibited erroneous beliefs, but in their delusions destroyed the fabric of Christian community. Perhaps they were promoting a "superior" spirituality that looked down on others who remained uninitiated. Perhaps they were unconscious of their separatist demeanor. Either way, dishonest spirituality led to fractured communities.

The theme of dishonest spirituality deserves careful treatment since John is one of the few New Testament writers to draw the connection between our spiritual integrity and the quality of the communities we create. It goes far beyond the presence of false believers or spiritual elitism. When participation in the body of Christ is motivated by interests other than the worship of God; when the foundation of our spirituality is not built on a candid assessment of sin and a healing experience of forgiveness; when the center of spiritual life, Jesus Christ, is gone—then churches cannot build the transforming, forgiving, generous communities they desire. Walking in the light is the *only* way we can genuinely walk with each other.

While some have viewed the last phrase of verse 7 as an artificial editorial insertion, which, as Bultmann wrote, "is disturbing to the content" of the verse,[12] the inherent logic of thought is clear. Walking in the light brings a penetrating revelation of who we are. The way forward for communities wracked by spiritual elitism and insincerity is confession and forgiveness. And this is achieved only by the sacrificial blood of Jesus. It is through Jesus' forgiveness—it is at the foot of the cross—that communities that have a chance of surviving must be built. And this is not simply for us to embrace the doctrine of sacrifice or some mere dogma. It is to know the cross and to experience its work and power.

John's purpose in mentioning Jesus' death is important when we reflect on the views of his opponents. If material realities are bypassed, an incarnate Jesus with a salvific earthly death would have little meaning. Furthermore, if the Fourth Gospel was the document that had forged the faith of John's churches, some may have been reading this

---

12 Bultmann, *Johannine Epistles*, 20 Bultmann also argued (wrongly, I think) that the phrase disturbs the poetic balance of the *ean* clauses There is no manuscript evidence for Bultmann's suggestion

Gospel as if it promoted a salvation that had little emphasis on sacrificial redemption.[13] But this is not the case. John's Gospel not only assumes sacrificial imagery (John 3:14) but employs it directly (1:29; 6:53; 10:11; 11:50; etc.). Nevertheless, John's corrective here (and in 1 John 5:6) suggests that he must reaffirm something missing or neglected among his readers.

To sum up, John's church had fallen on erroneous beliefs, and these led to shortfalls in their community life. Many were living in darkness—not in the sense of disbelief or heinous sins, but rather within a religious context in which they used their beliefs to redefine their need for forgiveness and to separate themselves from others. According to the apostle, *they must be cleansed.* John's word for cleansing (NIV purify; Gk. *katharizo*) does not simply imply forgiveness. It suggests the removal of defilement, the elimination of some stain so that the consequences of that condition no longer have ongoing effects. Cleansing has the future in mind so that the repairs wrought by God will have permanent results.

Bridging Contexts

THE ORIGINAL CONTEXT of these verses is governed by the imagined opponents John paraphrases in verse 5. People were claiming to have intimate fellowship with God and were arguing that they had achieved some sort of religious perfection (see 1:8–10). They were enlightened. John has the difficult pastoral task of telling them that they are in darkness, not in light. His words even seem harsh when he refers to their life as a "lie" that fails to "live by the truth." No doubt we need to keep an eye on the larger setting beyond the scope of these few verses to see the problem more clearly. These people were denying essential ideas within the Christian faith, ideas that have consequences for both belief and living.

John's initial impulse parallels what he did in the prologue. His message originated with the one whom he has heard, seen, and touched. His message is anchored in the historic life of Jesus Christ. This is no doubt to be contrasted with others making theological

---

13. This has been suggested by many commentators. See particularly E. Käsemann, *The Testament of Jesus According to John 17* (Philadelphia. Fortress, 1968)

claims that are not so anchored. John's opponents may well be inspired teacher/prophets who are working outside the historic traditions, and John is here recalling the church to its traditional moorings.

I can only speculate how his historic appeal may have worked. His community did not possess the Scriptures as we do. We cannot even be certain if they owned any of the Synoptic Gospels or any of Paul's letters. Thus when John reminds them of *historic revelation*, to what does he refer? Some see here an appeal to the Fourth Gospel. This is attractive particularly since there are so many parallels between 1 John and the Fourth Gospel. Perhaps the interpretation of the Fourth Gospel had become a battleground in this church. Perhaps there was uncertainty about just what this historic revelation meant! This is especially true in a pneumatic/charismatic setting, where teachers under the presumed guidance of the Spirit may have been deriving new meanings out of the text. If John's community was pneumatic/charismatic as we explained in the introduction, he himself is practicing this sort of "inspired exegesis." The Fourth Gospel nowhere says "God is light— in him there is no darkness at all." And yet John has deduced this from the many things the Scriptures do say. Here is the point: If John can do this, why not his opponents? In a pneumatic/charismatic environment, the weapons of the heretics often come from the pastor's own arsenal.[14] If John himself and his church experienced the revelatory Spirit—as John 16:12–13 warrants—it is no surprise to find the secessionists doing the same.

First, then, there is this claim to intimate spiritual fellowship with God that shows us that John's controversy is an "in-house" matter. These are individuals who are living in proximity to the church, who are claiming to be Christians, and John must use utter candor to tell them they are in error. The original context clearly describes people with a bent toward Gnostic dualism. Second, John suggests that one by-product of living in the light is shared fellowship. Perhaps we might reverse this truth. Any pursuit of spirituality that fractures the community, that cultivates a religious elitism, must surely be a faith lived in darkness. And third, most surprising of all, such community is predicated on forgiveness—not one Christian forgiving another, but God

---

14. See further Brown's reflections on the Spirit and exegesis in the Johannine community, *The Epistles of John*, 226–28

purifying his people of a condition of the heart from which they need rescue. If John's opponents were claiming some religious perfection, this exhortation to be forgiven implies *imperfection*. Anyone in a religious setting who no longer feels humbled by the need for God's mercy will show little mercy to others.

As I work to bridge contexts, three themes therefore emerge as crucial to the meaning of the passage: (1) the pastoral task of exhortation; (2) the quality of our Christian fellowship; and (3) our experience of forgiveness. However, in all candor, bridging these themes to our world is not as easy as it may seem. We will take them one at a time.

(1) We live in a world that is hardly open to public—much less private—exhortation. To import the Johannine dualism (above/below; light/dark; right/wrong) into today's church invites criticism of intolerance. "You're being judgmental!" "You're laying a guilt trip on us!" Nevertheless, John demands that we be equipped to identify and confront those who are in error. Once when I directed the adult education program in a large church, I was forced to confront an eager, popular teacher who wanted to volunteer to teach adult education courses. And yet we all knew he professed some seriously deficient beliefs. "But he wants to serve; he cares about the church." Saying no to him was a costly decision for our entire staff.

(2) The second theme is also challenging. If religious passion, if spiritual zeal sets apart people from the mainstream of the church, should it be stopped? John's community was fragile, and these secessionists no doubt were ruining the corporate body. *But do we not want passion?* John almost sounds as if the unity of the whole must dictate to the freedom of the part. Must the few members "on fire" wait patiently for the lethargic majority? To carry this principle to an extreme is a prescription for church paralysis. I once observed a pastor trying to negotiate between "the mainstream" and "the passionate" over the renewal of the worship service. "You'll have to be patient," he said to the few year after year until they finally lost interest. Some remained in their discouragement. Others found a new church home.

(3) The third theme—forgiveness—is something we talk about frequently. Naturally, therefore, modern audiences are used to it. But our impulse is to repair brokenness, to rebuild esteem, to affirm grace. John's impulse is to remind people that they must be humble. He concentrates on the prerequisite for forgiveness—sin and imperfection. We

concentrate on the consequences of forgiveness—healing and grace. Are candid discussions of sinfulness lost in the church today?

TWO OF MY grandparents were articulate, devoted members of Christian Science. I have strong memories from my youth of summer afternoons in California speaking with them about Mary Baker Eddy's *Science and Health* and questioning what it meant for her to reinterpret the Bible. While I was in college they gave me my own copy of *Science and Health*, and it was then that I began to see that the book promoted breathtaking departures from Christianity. I once marked the margin of a few particularly troubling pages and brought my questions to their home. For example, Mary Baker Eddy had written the following on the atonement:

> Wisdom and love may require many sacrifices of self to save us from sin. One sacrifice, however great, is insufficient to pay the debt of sin. The atonement requires constant self-immolation on the sinner's part. That God's wrath should be vented upon His beloved Son, is divinely unnatural.[15]

Does not this contradict the clear New Testament teaching about Christ's death? Had Eddy never read Hebrews? Or Romans? Later the book talked about sin:

> To get rid of sin through Science, is to divest sin of any supposed mind or reality, and never to admit that sin can have intelligence or power, pain or pleasure. You conquer error by denying its verity.[16]

Does not this denial of sin's reality contradict a basic New Testament teaching too? If sin is not real, then I have no need of a genuine Savior. Of course the explanations of these passages came to me in lengthy, turgid paragraphs, most of which I could not understand. But I remember one moment clearly. When I pointed out what seemed to be a contradiction between *Science and Health* and the plain sense of one

---

15. M. B. Eddy, *Science and Health* (Boston: Trustees under the Will of Mary Baker Eddy, 1906), ch. 2, 23:1–6
16. Ibid., ch. 10, sec. xxxii. p. 339 (lines 28–32)

Bible passage, my grandmother's answer was clear, "Your lack of under-standing simply means you're too immature. The deeper things are beyond your reach." And that was that! End of discussion! I was unini-tiated, an outsider, an unbeliever—and so the depths of *Science and Health* were inaccessible to me.[17] As I think back on it today, I marvel at how this outlook mirrors that of the opponents of 1 John.

It is easy enough to spot this sort of phenomenon in a religious movement that has broken with the mainstream of Christian ortho-doxy. Such new scriptures and new interpretations of the Bible produce a religious mysticism with its own coded theology. But this passage leads me to ask something more difficult: To what extent do such reli-gious substrata exist in the church? Or to use John's language, are there Christians in our churches who are walking in darkness and still claim to have a profound intimacy with God? These are not fallen Christians. These are keenly articulate religious people whose spiritual zeal is impressive but whose instinct for truth is sorely damaged.

(1) *Are we taking "the darkness" seriously?* That is, are we ready to admit that our congregations may well contain men and women whose lives have been swamped by some dubious religious experience? Is it pos-sible that they have departed from the faith, even slipped into apos-tasy? This is the full scope of John's notion of darkness, and he is serious about it. On the other hand, do we look the other way? I am impressed with the boldness and courage John shows in these verses, for he was willing to risk warning his fellow believers.

Risk is inherent in any such warning because those who enjoy these experiences or who have embraced unorthodox theological ideas usu-ally argue that they are spiritually enriching. I recall serving once as an interim pastor in a Tennessee Presbyterian church where most of the men of the congregation were active Masons. Secrecy and quasi-religious rituals were in abundance, and worse yet, I feared, most of the decisions about the church were being made at the Masonic Hall next door.[18] But to mention *anything* critical of the Masons or to fail to incorporate Masonic life into the church's calendar brought serious

---

17 I have often thought that the theological system worked out in Christian Science comes quite near to that in ancient Gnosticism.

18. One deacon took me into the hall one night and gave me a detailed tour of the Masonic rituals and religious (or cultic) artifacts There is no doubt in my mind that this was a religious setting for my congregants

complaints. What would John do? I am convinced John would have addressed such situations head-on. Here there was syncretism at work, blending the Christian faith with breathtaking superstitions. John would have named the darkness, diagnosed the problem, and sought a remedy.

I have witnessed other tragic examples of the darkness as well. In one congregation, a local evangelist in the Pentecostal tradition was planting a new church and encouraging people to take out second mortgages to finance the buildings. His preaching was powerful and members of our church felt renewed in ways they could barely describe. When this pastor disappeared one week with $65,000, the faith of many was crushed beyond repair. In another congregation an influential evangelist came to town with a prophetic ministry; services were conducted to "recall prayers and vows" uttered without thinking. Somehow such prayers were echoing around in heaven and could have a troubling effect on lives if not "exorcised" from "heavenly courts." I still remember the heavy-handed, manipulative ministry of this preacher as he enticed families into his web.

As Christian leaders we are called to protect our sheep, and this means calling the darkness what it is. Religious darkness is all the more insidious because it clothes itself in a piety that cannot always be recognized by its victims. As I write, a new cult group has arrived in Wheaton and is "evangelizing" our students. Its advocates are well-dressed and pious, and they carry Bibles. But they undermine the truth of the gospel. *The Way International* has a deficient understanding of Christ (which is utterly Arian), a hostile view of the local church, and an aggressive system of folding new followers into its small groups. We must mobilize to identify it and defend our sheep against it.

(2) *Does spiritual righteousness lead to separation?* That is, if we are mature in Christ, if we enjoy a holy, excellent walk with the Lord, if we have been powerfully immersed in the Spirit, should this lead us to separate ourselves from other Christians? I am not here concerned with our obligation to remain separate from the world. Here I have in mind mature Christians who have cultivated an elitist view of their place in the body of Christ.

When I was a graduate student in Aberdeen, Scotland, I met a wonderful teacher/pastor who was also working on a Ph.D. in New Testament. As we became good friends, I learned that he belonged to a branch of the Church of Christ. I was utterly astonished to learn how we could not share the Lord's Table together. He was forbidden even to attend our Scottish church but had to drive hours each Sunday to Inverness to find a small band of like-minded souls. Theologically these people believed that they were the *only* true body of Christ. And their exclusive fellowship could not be compromised with outsiders like Baptists and Presbyterians.

This is a tragic example that puts in bold relief realities that take place on a more subtle level each Sunday in our churches. Spiritual elitism stalks congregational life regularly. But John's test is sure: Those who draw near to Christ, who walk in the light, work hard to cultivate the fellowship of the body. Sometimes charismatic Christians are the ones who separate themselves by trying to form a circle of people with similar experiences. Sometimes it is Christians who have discovered a dynamic leader with a new message within the congregation, and their identity is now being shaped by him or her. Sometimes it is young couples eager for community who form their own clique as they try to cultivate *koinonia* with no regard for the larger community. Sometimes it is Christians like us who become a bit too sure of their understanding of Christian faith.

(3) *Is the forgiveness of God in Christ at the center of our fellowship?* One of the chief problems of spiritual elitism is its self-diagnosis: It has few needs; it is complete; it has arrived. It is conscious of who is "in" and who is "out." And left unchecked, it develops into spiritual arrogance.

Those who walk in the light have an ongoing sense of needing forgiveness and being forgiven. When purity is a gift, when the mercy and grace of God are foremost in our experience, spiritual elitism dies. We cannot criticize those whose growth is less than ours because were it not for God's graciousness, we would be immature too. When community is forged in the context of grace, generosity and mercy become commonplace.

Perhaps one of the most stunning examples of this came from a friend of mine who had recently experienced the power of the Holy Spirit. Since I had often spoken up in defense of charismatic renewal movements, he confided in me about his experience, his relation to our church, and his disdain for the character of its leadership. For him, life in our congregation was a *mission*. It was a chance for him to help the pastor discover God's power and to aid less fortunate men and women meet the Spirit. He formed around himself a clique of spiritually keen people—a "Bible study," they called it—that operated outside the network of small groups in the church. In reality it was a ministry that aimed to compensate for the deficiencies of the church's pastors.

What troubled me the most about this man and his friends was that they were singularly unteachable. They *possessed* the Spirit, and therefore their spiritual authority was to be unquestioned. God's light could not penetrate them *because they were walking in the darkness, and yet they argued that they were in the light.* Either the church had to change to their way of thinking or they threatened to leave.

Each of these issues—living blinded by the darkness, spiritual elitism that damages fellowship, the absence of a need for forgiveness—are connected. They spring from a religious experience that cultivates our pride. We have arrived in the inner sanctum, and all others must either join us or be excluded. Perhaps the most sinister side of this pride is that sincere Christians can genuinely deceive themselves. The darkness can take many forms, but like wolves posing as sheep, darkness covers its victims in false light. They are confident that they are divinely illumined, confident that all else is darkness. But they are wrong.

In some cases, it is prideful Christians who deceive themselves that they can flirt with things that cannot harm them. Their tenure in the church, their theological degrees, and/or their prominence and recognition convince them that they are stronger than the darkness. Their misplaced pride brings ruin. I recently read *Sins of the Body* and was profoundly sobered by the book's description of sexual sin among Christian leaders.[19] The deception we live with and the rationalizations we accept build a harrowing picture of the darkness of sin.

Perhaps it is good to give darkness a closer definition. Of course it includes wrong doctrine. But it also includes the power of the evil one and his demons. It also includes sin in its many sophisticated forms. Generally speaking, darkness is an atmosphere that denies the truth of God and forbids his light to enter. It is like fog on a sunny morning that is so thick it obscures the way we are driving and makes us wonder if the sun is out at all. Darkness is where God's glory cannot be found.

---

19. T. Muck, ed , *Sins of the Body Ministry in a Sexual Society* (Dallas: Word, 1989)

To be sure, Satan creates darkness and is its prince. But we also are capable of doing the same through our fallen choices, our deception, and our sinfulness. And before long, we become so accustomed to darkness that we forget what true light really is.

John is looking for a model of Christian life that is like a circle of light on a stage, perhaps a spotlight in a darkened theater. At once the darkness around it is most prominent. A boundary is evident. And yet the circle is created by God's penetrating light. It is a light that is pure, hard, revealing, and guiding. And those who walk in this light discover lives that are knit together by God's forgiveness and redemption. To walk in this light is ultimately humbling. But at the same time it is also healing, renewing, and invigorating.

1 John 1:8–2:2

IF WE CLAIM to be without sin, we deceive ourselves and the truth is not in us. ⁹If we confess our sins, he is faithful and just and will forgive us our sins and purify us from all unrighteousness. ¹⁰If we claim we have not sinned, we make him out to be a liar and his word has no place in our lives.

2 ¹My dear children, I write this to you so that you will not sin. But if anybody does sin, we have one who speaks to the Father in our defense—Jesus Christ, the Righteous One. ²He is the atoning sacrifice for our sins, and not only for ours but also for the sins of the whole world.

Original Meaning

JOHN DEVELOPS FURTHER his objections against those who claimed to be in the light and to have an intimate relation with God, but who all the while really lived in the darkness. As we noted earlier (see on 1:5–7), three citations built around three positive and three negative "if" clauses (Gk. *ean* clauses) outline the erroneous beliefs of these opponents.[1] Now we discover that the seriousness of John's accusations has increased considerably. These people not only lived in the darkness (1:6) but they claimed to be without sin (1:8). Moreover, they claimed that they had no specific sins for which they needed cleansing (1:9). Previously the consequences of these errors only fell on their perpetrators, in that they lied and failed to know the truth (1:6). Now we learn that their deeds made *God a liar* and forbade a place for his word in their lives (1:10).

John's answer to these difficulties rests in the work of Jesus Christ. Forgiveness and purity from these wrongdoings can only come through the sacrifice of Jesus (1:7; 2:2), who makes the forgiveness of God

---

1. A formula is used to make explicit that John is citing his opponents, *ean eipomen hoti* . . . (see vv. 6, 8, 10). I prefer to translate these in direct discourse in order to place the citation in high relief

possible. The response to each cited error notes that a divine work of restoration and cleansing is necessary for anyone to continue "walking in the light."

Sin and Confession (1:8–9)

THE CLAIM TO be "without sin" (v. 8) is the second formula expression we encounter. John's firm rebuttal must mean that the same people described in verses 5–7 would hear John's thoughts about purity in verse 7 and then make the claim that no such purifying was needed. The Greek literally says, "We do not have sin" (*hamartian ouk exomen*) and no doubt should be carefully distinguished from verse 10, where another citation reads, "We have not sinned." In the first case, sin is described as a quality, "an active principle in us."[2] In the second case, the verb employs a perfect tense verb, suggesting a reference to specific sins that spring from a preexisting condition of sinfulness.

While some interpreters are uncertain whether verses 8 and 10 can be distinguished so neatly, Brooke, Brown, and more recently Smalley have made a convincing case that a difference can be discerned if we follow John's vocabulary carefully. In the Johannine literature, the verb "to have" is frequently followed by an abstract noun to represent a general quality: to have fellowship (1 John 1:3, 6–7), joy (John 17:13; 3 John 4), confidence (John 2:28; 3:21; 4:17), hope (3:3), and life (3:15; 5:12–13). In the entire New Testament, "to have sin" appears only in the present verse and in John 9:41; 15:22, 24; 19:11. For instance, in John 15 the Jewish leadership is told that "they have sin," not because of some deed they have done but because Jesus has spoken to them. Their inherent status has changed. Yet deeds are not always separated from a state of being. In John 19 Judas Iscariot "has the greater sin" because he handed Jesus over to Pilate. Thus in 1 John 1:8, "to have sin" likely refers to a quality of personhood, an active principle at work in someone's life. It is a disposition of heart that lives in rebellion and constantly exhibits evil deeds (see further on 1:10).

John's opponents were therefore saying, "We have no sin" (1:8). Who could possibly deny such a truth? Who would urge that a sinful quality was absent in their lives, or that counting sinfulness makes no difference? Once again we meet the error introduced in 1:5–7. John

---

2. Brooke, *Johannine Epistles*, 17

is in debate, not necessarily with those who trivialized sin, but with those who philosophically questioned the relevance of sin as something that can impede our relationship with God. If spirituality is isolated from the commonplace events of everyday living, if the material things of the world are irrelevant to God, spiritual enlightenment might ignore mundane issues such as morality.

John's words are unremitting. Such an attitude is deliberately deceptive, for it denies the reality of sin.[3] It is not ignorance, it is a cover-up (cf. John 7:12, 47; Rev. 2:20). Worse still, it proves something of the character of the claimant: Not only do they fail to live by the truth (1 John 1:6), but now we learn that "the truth is not in them." "To be in," just like "to remain in," is a favorite Johannine expression for the interior life (cf. 2:5; 5:20). Truth is not something abstract, like a moral code, that has been neglected. Truth describes God himself. Truth is personal—Jesus Christ himself *is* truth (John 14:6)—and those who "do the truth" enjoy living in God's light (3:21). In his Gospel John even describes the Spirit as "the Spirit of truth" (14:17; 15:26; 16:13). Therefore people who do not have the truth "in them" are lacking an essential characteristic of God's presence within their inmost being. When Pilate asks, "What is truth?" in John 18:38, he is uncovering his utter alienation from the things of God.

John gives a stern warning that these people may be dubious Christians. They may not even be Christians at all! They are in greater jeopardy than they think. And their only recourse is confession. The appeal to confession in verse 9 balances the citation of verse 8 with another "if" clause. Yet it is not intended to be a mere condition; it is an exhortation, a warning, perhaps even a command.[4] Sinfulness is inherent in our lives, and confession must be the Christian's heartfelt reflex.[5]

Confession is successful (and this is critical to John's argument) because of the character of God. His forgiveness is not an act of mercy, as if he were setting aside some usual disposition in response to a religious act of penitence. *God's character is to be faithful and just* (cf. Deut. 32:4; Ps. 89:1–4; Rom. 3:25; Heb. 10:23). It is essential not to oppose

---

3. The Greek construction here, *heautous planomen*, rather than the simple verb *planometha*, is emphatic.

4. I. H Marshall, *The Epistles of John*, 113.

5. For the practice of confession in the Bible, see Lev. 16·21; Ps. 32:5; Prov. 28:13; Dan. 9:20; Matt. 3:6; Acts 19·18.

these two ideas, as if God's loving-kindness or faithfulness (Gk. *pistos*) and his justice or righteousness (Gk. *dikaios*) were at odds. His faithfulness to us has prompted him to make a way for our purification and thereby satisfy his demand for righteousness.

Confession enjoys the good character of God and is empowered by it. Two consequences necessarily follow: forgiveness and purification. To forgive (Gk. *aphiemi*) really means "to let go" (as a debt, cf. Luke 7:43), and so John indicates that our sins are removed from God's accounting. To purify (cf. 1:7) carries a different nuance and suggests the removal of the residual effects of sin, consequences that linger (such as a stain). Therefore there is hope. The past and its errors as well as the future and its propensity toward sinfulness are both addressed.

Sin and Jesus' Advocacy (1:10–2:1)

VERSE 10 INTRODUCES us to the third presentation of the error (see vv. 6, 8), and it is the most explicit yet. John's opponents now say, "We have not sinned." In his imagined debate, is John anticipating an objection to his exhortation about confession ("What have I done that I need to confess?")? Is he expecting some argument about God's purification ("Purified from what, I ask?")? Perhaps this is one more slogan that is being hurled about by the perfectionists that John must confront. I have already suggested that a case can be made for different nuances here. If verse 8 describes the pitiful sinful condition that plagues us, verse 10 describes specific deeds of sin that spring from that condition. The perfect tense of the verb implies that the debater is now inquiring about specific past deeds. Therefore the nature of the argument has taken a new turn. Can someone claim that they have never committed any sins?

Such a position impugns God's character, making him a liar (v. 10). It maligns the truthfulness of his word, which makes the universal sinfulness of humanity a basic and pivotal tenet (Gen. 3; 1 Kings 8:46; Job 15:14–16; Ps. 14:3; Prov. 20:9; Eccl. 7:20; Isa. 53:6; John 2:24–25; Rom. 3:21–24). If this teaching were not true, God's salvific efforts to save and retrieve his people recorded throughout the Bible would make no sense. But a second, equally severe, consequence follows. As verse 8 says that truth "is not in" someone who believes these things, so verse 10 says that God's word "is not in" them either.[6] "The word" may be a general reference to the Scriptures, which ought to be at the center of the Christian life. Or it may be an intentionally ambiguous reference to Jesus, who in John's writing is called "the Word" (John 1:1–18).[7]

At this point John's logic should introduce the contrasting "if" clause to remedy the problem described in 1:10. We have seen this format at work in 1:6/7 and 1:8/9. However, 2:1a is a parenthesis, a detour in the course of his argument. John is a pastor who dearly loves his people, and therefore he lapses into a brief appeal—his first genuine appeal—that his children, his flock, resist sin. Note that John has shifted audiences here. If formerly he had his opponents in mind, now he is writing to the genuine Christians in his churches, Christians with fragile faith who are being persuaded no doubt to follow erroneous teachings.

The NIV "dear children" is a translation of the Greek *teknia*, which means "little children" (cf. 3 John 4). Pastors in the early church often called their followers "children," taking as a model the metaphorical structure of a family (see 1 Cor. 4:14, 17; Gal. 4:19; 1 Tim. 1:2). John does this frequently. He uses three terms for children: *teknon* (used nine times in his letters), which generally means "child"; *paidion* (1 John 2:14, 18), which literally means "young boy" but was used for little children; the plural form of *teknion* (used here), an endearing variation of *teknon* reserved for very small children.[8] This is a window into John the pastor, whose heartfelt feelings for his followers comes through passionately.

However, what John says to "his dear little children" poses some difficulty. Throughout these verses he has been telling us that sin is inherent to human life. *Everyone does sin.* Now he writes that he does not want us to sin (see also on 3:6–10). Which is it? John does not want his followers to sin, yet in 1:8, 10 he has said that they will sin at times. We will need to give this subject careful attention in our application (see below), but the historical setting may give us some clues. (1) When John talks about avoiding sin, he may be referring specifically to *the error of denying the reality of God's truth about sin.* The course of his opponent's

---

6. The NIV translation, "in our lives," conveys the correct sense of the passage but disguises the Johannine language

7. S. Smalley, *1, 2, 3 John*, 34.

8. Technically, *teknion* is a diminutive form of *teknon*

present thought is strictly sinful. (2) John may also be worrying that some will take his teaching as a license to sin. That is, if sin is endemic to the human condition and if forgiveness is freely available, someone might think that sinfulness can be indulged in generously. Paul had to address this very problem in Romans 6.

Sinfulness has two solutions. Of course, God is eager to forgive, but what is it that makes God's generosity accessible? In 1:7 John wrote that the blood of Jesus effects our cleansing; he will return to this subject in some detail in 2:2. But John's first answer is in 2:1b.[9] Jesus serves with the Father as *our advocate* (NIV, "one who speaks in our defense"). This is a uniquely Johannine term (Gk. *parakletos*), which means one who is called alongside as an aide or counselor, especially in a legal setting.[10] In John's Gospel, it occurs four times (14:16, 26; 15:26; 16:7), describing the Holy Spirit as our counselor/advocate as we confront a hostile world. In this case, Jesus Christ, in his ascended glory, represents us before the Father (cf. Rom. 8:34). This thought parallels the book of Hebrews, in which Jesus now ministers on our behalf in a heavenly setting with God: "The point of what we are saying is this: We do have such a high priest, who sat down at the right hand of the throne of the Majesty in heaven, and who serves in the sanctuary, the true tabernacle set up by the Lord, not by man" (Heb. 8:1–2). Hebrews continues by saying, as John does here, that it is Jesus' sinlessness and purity, his righteousness—identical to the righteousness of God (1 John 1:9; cf. 2:29; 1 Peter 3:18)—that gives him access to God's very presence.

Sin and Jesus' Sacrifice (2:2)

THE SECOND SOLUTION for sinfulness (1:9) is provided in 2:2. The *basis* of Christ's case on our behalf, the power behind his advocacy, comes from his sacrifice on the cross. Here again John uses a technical term, *hilasmos*: Jesus became a *hilasmos* for our sins. In the New Testament this word occurs only here and in 1 John 4:10, although related forms of

---

9. First John 2:1b introduces the sixth and final "if" clause, balancing out the three pairs found in 1 6/7, 1·8/9, and 1 10/2.1b.

10. The word occurs nowhere else in the New Testament except here and in the Fourth Gospel Its meaning and history have all the trappings of a mystery novel. See R. E. Brown, "The Paraclete in the Fourth Gospel," *NTS* 12 (1966–67)· 113–32, and G. Burge, *The Anointed Community The Holy Spirit in the Johannine Tradition* (Grand Rapids: Eerdmans, 1987), 3–31

it appear elsewhere. And controversy surrounds its precise meaning. Its use in extrabiblical literature and the Greek Old Testament (ten times) makes its meaning fairly clear: A *hilasmos* was a sacrifice given to placate someone who was angry. In a religious setting, it was an angry God. By this interpretation God is the object of Jesus' sacrifice, making the sinner acceptable because God's disposition has changed.[11] On the other hand, some have urged that the object is not God, but the sins themselves. The sinner is pleasing to God because the sins are wiped away.[12] Still others think that the two concepts merge and that at the very least, we cannot lose the notion that somehow God's anger has been placated. No doubt the meaning of Christ's sacrifice was forged in Christian thought and was not entirely dependent on sacrificial antecedents outside the Old Testament. There the two thoughts merge clearly: Sins are covered over *and* God's righteous anger is changed.[13] The NIV attempts to catch both emphases with its translation, "atoning sacrifice."

The key, however, is that Jesus does not simply supply a *hilasmos*, he is one himself. Jesus is both *parakletos* and *hilasmos* on our behalf. He has supplied what was needed to effect our pardon. His righteousness made his sacrifice powerful (cf. Heb. 7:26–28) so that it brings benefits not simply to a closed circle of Christian worshipers, but to the whole world.[14] God's interest is not elitist, building a religious clique that excludes some (and this was no doubt one of the problems among John's followers). God's sacrificial work is comprehensive.

SINCE JOHN CONTINUES to cite the arguments of his opponents, the present verses continue to be controlled by their agenda. In 2:1a he lapses into a pastoral exhortation for his true followers, but the bulk of the verses is devoted to a debate about the pervasive character of sin and God's provision for all those who do sin.

---

11 Translators will use the word "propitiation" to convey this meaning

12 Translators will use the word "expiation" to convey this meaning See the RSV

13 See L. Morris, *Apostolic Preaching of the Cross* (Grand Rapids Eerdmans, 1965), D Hill, *Greek Words and Hebrew Meanings* (Cambridge Cambridge Univ Press, 1967)

14 The NIV has added to the Greek text, *"the sins of the whole world "*

Thus far we have listened to three claims and counterclaims that address this problem (1:6, 8, 10). In 1:6 there was a vague hint about what this "darkness" was all about. But in 1:8, 10 the subject becomes explicit. There was a debate about the reality of sin. It was either being denied as if it were unimportant (this is the Gnostic or Docetic thinking we have outlined), or sin was being dismissed as absent from the truly spiritual life (this might be a perfectionist tendency). Either way this had led to a cavalier or arrogant attitude, which had all but torn the Christian community.

John responds by affirming the *fact* of sin; and given this fact, he directs his readers back to the Incarnation. His Christologically centered response is intended not simply to address the Christian's need for forgiveness (Christ as advocate and sacrifice), but to undercut the presupposition that has shaped their outlook in the first place. *A world-denying philosophy has led to a sin-denying theology.* These outlooks naturally jettison all Christology. John urges a different chain of events: affirming the importance of the world, embracing the truth about sin, confessing those sins, and seeking restoration through the work of the incarnate Lord. Thus John anchors the importance of Christ in his function. Affirming the person and work of Jesus is no abstract thing. Jesus is significant because of what he has done before the Father on our behalf.

How do I bridge this historical context to my own? This problem is similar to the one found in 1:5–7. I cannot simply confine the meaning of these verses to a Gnostic debate that died centuries ago. There are themes that transcend this time period altogether, touching on Gnostic attitudes but also speaking directly to our circumstances today. (1) The most important theme is our notion of "sin." Are we convinced that fallenness is characteristic of the human experience? Secular life and religious communities alike struggle with this. Our response will shape our view of society, politics, and even psychology. As I try to bridge John's unequivocating view of sin into my world, I have to wonder if my world is ready for it. John understands that we are captive to sin; we sin compulsively and deliberately. Even though elsewhere he will say that Christians are not prisoners to ongoing sins, here he is saying that just beneath our veneer is a crippling disease, a compulsion waiting to appear. I think, for instance, about Langdon Gilkey's true story of what happened during World War II when the Japanese rounded up the Westerners near Peking/Bejing, China, and placed them in a camp called *The Shantung Compound*.[15] Suddenly the veneer of Christian civility disappeared. Gilkey cites lines from an opera to encapsulate the story:

> For even saintly folk will act like sinners
> Unless they have their customary dinners.

But do we still believe it? Do we see sin as just poor choices, or poor education, or poor childhoods? John is using a theological anthropology that may be foreign to modern audiences. Thus a new bridge must be built before his message can be heard.

(2) There is the opposite error of complacency about sin. In a theological setting where grace is generous and sin is unavoidable, laissez-faire attitudes toward morality grow. I am convinced that this outlook is far more familiar to us today. Particularly in churches where the grace of God is part of a pastoral plan to promote personal health and well-being, the devastating threat of sin—indeed, the warning about sin—is sadly rare. Some in John's audience were complacent. Many in our audiences are complacent too. Therefore John's words bring a needed, provocative word.

(3) John gives us important information about how Jesus Christ accomplishes the salvation we enjoy. His words in 1:5 gave only a fraction of the fuller descriptions here. Yet I cannot help but wonder if sacrifice and atonement as John describes them make any sense today. Churches rarely explain the conceptual framework that informs the biblical world of sacrifice. I recall realizing this once in an adult education class. I digressed for over thirty minutes, explaining how altars, fire sacrifices, and priests all worked together in ancient Israel. And I remember how approximately fifty adults were stunned. Little in our world today directly compares with sacrifice like this (despite stories of heroic sacrifice we might tell).

In order to bridge John's concept of Christ's work on the cross, I must work to rebuild the biblical setting. If I do not, I must be careful lest my modern explanation empties the cross of its true power and meaning. I cannot simply say, "Christ took my place on the cross." He did—but he did more. "God was reconciling the world to himself in

---

15. L. Gilkey, *The Shantung Compound* (San Francisco: Harper, 1966)

Christ" (2 Cor. 5:19). There are deeper mysteries here that a culture lacking a biblical worldview will fail to understand.

While John opens up this important subject of sin, it is unfortunate that he does not explore the subject more fully. Classic theological debates about the pervasive character of sin or the possibility of perfection find only limited attention in these verses. And yet their support is essential. These verses are some of the most important in the New Testament, anchoring the Christian view of the character of humanity and its relation to God.

 SINCE FILMS AND videos are the lifeblood of students today, one of the benefits of working at a college is that the students keep me well informed about current developments at the theater. We often discuss what presuppositions about life, sex, morality, or religion shape the screenplays they all know so well. I once asked them to list films that presuppose that a person is intrinsically fallen and films that presuppose that a person is intrinsically good. I wish I could report that students can figure this out right away, but they do not. However, once they see the pattern and elevate the discussion beyond movies like *Natural Born Killers*, the discussion ignites spontaneously. *Lord of the Flies* is always a favorite since high schools still require the book! In this story good British school boys (complete with starched uniforms) find themselves abandoned on a deserted island and at once turn into savages. The point is that deep within their little hearts resided a monster of untold ferocity. *Mosquito Coast* is another favorite. Harrison Ford leaves the evils of modern America and moves into a Central American jungle, only to learn that those evils were lurking in him all along. He brings the corruption with him.

But these films with their message of inherent fallenness are not the most popular. There is another message that has a growing appeal: Corruption is an option, it is "out there" in society, and still pristine societies and lives may be discovered. Older adults may point to the old Tarzan films (where the boy in the jungle is morally superior). A modern version is *The Emerald Forest*, where an American child gets lost in an Amazon forest and is adopted and raised by natives, who enjoy a morally perfect society (even their lack of clothes symbolizes a life in

Eden before the Fall). A cartoon version of this is available in *Fern Gully*, where again the center of the Amazon is a place without sin, but where the workers burning and cutting the forest bring their own evil with them. Disney's *Pocahontas* and Kevin Costner's *Dances with Wolves* touch on the theme as well.

The essential question at the center of these discussions is our view of humanity. Is there something wrong at our center? Are we broken beyond repair and in need of redemption? Or do we enjoy an optimistic appraisal of the human condition? In *Lord of the Flies*, for instance, redemption comes only when an immaculately dressed British officer arrives on the island to uncover the seriousness of the children's depravity. In other words, salvation comes from *without*—the fallen cannot heal themselves.

I have recently read Stephen Lawhead's trilogy, *The Song of Albion*.[16] Here this popular Christian author depicts a noble Celtic world that has a place for personal, comprehensive evil and yet recognizes that redemption must come from powerful "songs" outside this world's existence. And above all, he acknowledges that no society, no matter how noble, is exempt from such fallenness.

(1) *John would have us take seriously the comprehensive nature of sin.* The biblical and theological teachings here are clear. Paul's memorable phrase in Romans 3:23 sums it up nicely: "For all have sinned and fall short of the glory of God." There are no exceptions. There are no perfect humans and therefore no possibility of a humanly engineered utopia. It does not take long for the average person to admit that something is wrong in our world. We can conceptualize a world that seems better, that eliminates the crime, incurable diseases, starvation, war, and suffering that haunt human society. But few of my students believe "things are going well" on Planet Earth.

However, we live in a therapeutic culture that looks to cures for illness and remedial moral education as a solution to some of our problems. We say that we have the ability to fix what is broken. I am not denying that in some cases such approaches are worthwhile, but they are simply not the principal solution. The Bible insists that we are creatures who are given moral choices for which we are responsible.

---

16. S. Lawhead's trilogy includes *Paradise War* (1991), *The Silver Hand* (1992), and *The Endless Knot* (1993) Each is published by Lion Publishers in Batavia, Illinois

And we consistently choose to rebel against God and his way in our lives. As a result we have ruined the goodness God once gave us. In a word, our entire world is fallen.

I doubt that John reflected on a culture such as ours that rationalizes sin or denies the basis of guilt through a denial of an absolute moral code. The Gnostics saw sin as unimportant (which is a much different idea) because the moral arena of this world was unimportant. However, as I listen to many new religious movements (Eastern mysticism, New Age, etc.), I note a similar phenomenon. Spirituality is being cultivated apart from the course of events in this world and is removed entirely from a rational, moral framework. A religious *mantra*, meditation, or secret mystic rituals transport the believer temporarily into other realms, quite apart from the day-to-day world we know. And *exhaustive value* is given to that other world.

Each year I attend the annual meeting of the American Academy of Religion along with about five thousand other professors. It is interesting to see who shows up. When we met in Boston a number of years ago, I visited the book exhibit of an eccentric publisher in the convention hall. The publisher was selling copies of a lengthy tome presumably written by supernatural beings living on another planet, a planet that had once colonized earth. Secret rituals could link us with the spirits of these creatures and help us disassociate with our own earth, which was simply a shadow of a more real world hidden in outer space. I chuckled until I learned how many of these volumes had already been sold.

This teaching that true religion or spiritual development is unconnected to the day-to-day events of life is growing. It promotes a religious schizophrenia: We have two lives, one spiritual and one physical, and the two have little connection. What I do today is less important than whether I have done my religious exercises.

Nothing could be further from the truth. John affirms that this world is important (hence his incarnational theology) and that the personal God who made it has material expectations for it. Sin is accountability to someone who has set a standard. If either God is denied or if the standard is said not to apply to our world, accountability disappears.

(2) *Comprehensive sinfulness includes Christians.* But does sinfulness, comprehensive fallenness, include those who reside in the church? Here

we enter into considerable controversy. While some say that Christians can reach a level of sinlessness or even perfection, others disagree, saying that sin is an ongoing problem even for the redeemed. Thus in 2:1 John must make an allowance for those *in the faith* who fall. This truth gives some explanation for the downfall of our own moral and spiritual leaders in our own generation; otherwise the sin of someone in prominent Christian leadership is inexplicable.

It is surprising to me how often people in a religious setting can be convinced of their spiritual perfection. When I lived in an orthodox Jewish neighborhood in Chicago, I often found myself talking theology over the back fence. A strict religious woman from the local synagogue told me that Jesus' sacrifice was unnecessary because fulfilling the law—all 613 Old Testament laws by her count—was possible. She and her family had done it. God was happy with her performance.

I cannot help but wonder if some Christians have the same outlook. Their lives have been so transformed by God that they have reached a level of spiritual maturity that excludes the need for ongoing forgiveness. This is particularly the case among those who have experienced profound, genuine renewal—for instance, in the charismatic setting. It is also true for those in more conventional communities whose lives have been saturated by the church and its values for years. In both cases there is limited humility and little recognition that error is a possibility.

This raises a host of practical questions. For church leadership it makes us cautious to invest too much power in any individual—priests, pastors, and elders included. Each one may fall. I have witnessed prominent Christian leaders "in the name of Christ" wield astonishing authority in the pursuit of self-interest or private agendas. And all of it is sin. It also raises questions about church government. If sinfulness is a possibility even among Christians, decision-making must be deliberated in the widest context possible. Leadership must rotate so that the corruption that attends to power will not consume any.

(3) *Comprehensive sinfulness likewise forces us to inquire about confession.* I have always been alarmed by the absence of formal confession in the Protestant tradition. In rejecting the priestly function of mediating forgiveness and promoting the generous gift of God's grace in Christ, we have lost sight of any need to confess. We may have liturgical confessions on Sunday, *but are we personally confessing our sins on a regular basis?*

This year I read Susan Howatch's novel *Glittering Images*.[17] Howatch powerfully describes the demise and restoration of an Anglican priest who knew how to wear a "glittering image" that would conceal his true self. It was only through the intervention of an aggressive spiritual director who understood the absolute necessity of spoken confession that the priest could be saved from himself and the suffocation of his role as a Christian leader.

John affirms that everyone sins—Christians included—and that if we confess our sins, God will forgive (1:9). The pastoral need of this experience is summed up well in Psalm 32:1–5:

> Blessed is he
>> whose transgressions are forgiven,
>> whose sins are covered.
> Blessed is the man
>> whose sin the LORD does not count against him
>> and in whose spirit is no deceit.
> When I kept silent,
>> my bones wasted away
>> through my groaning all day long.
> For day and night
>> your hand was heavy upon me;
> my strength was sapped
>> as in the heat of summer.
> Then I acknowledged my sin to you
>> and did not cover up my iniquity.
> I said, "I will confess
>> my transgressions to the LORD"—
> and you forgave
>> the guilt of my sin.

Unfortunately, John fails to tell us what it means if we do not confess. Is Christ's sacrifice somehow limited to us by our hesitation to confess? Is our maturity in Christ stunted as a result? Furthermore, what sort of confession does he have in mind? Private confession is *at least* necessary, but I imagine that if we listened to church history and experience carefully, we would recognize that more is needed.

---

17. S. Howatch, *Glittering Images* (New York: Ballantine, 1987).

(4) *Christ's work is ongoing.* John's emphasis on the ongoing work of confession is linked directly to the ongoing work of Christ. In 2:2 he speaks of the past work of Christ on the cross not simply for Christians but for the whole world. But we often overlook John's thoughts in 2:1 about the *present function* of Christ.

Viewing Jesus as working on our behalf even now gives an utterly new dimension to spirituality and a new impetus to confess and grow. To be sure, Christ's work on the cross two thousand years ago completed what was necessary for salvation. But more is going on. As we have denied the importance of confession in the liturgical traditions, have we also denied the continuing ministry of Jesus on our behalf?[18] I wonder if the dismissal of priestly ministerial functions that swept away the confessional has likewise lost any recognition that Christ is still at work.

We must recapture some sense of what is happening on our behalf *since* Golgotha. In the Incarnation God passionately embraced our humanity. On the cross Christ in our humanity paid the punishment due us. And in his resurrection/ascension Christ ushered our transformed humanity into heaven, where he stands today representing us before the Father. Therefore the saving work of God in Christ moves from incarnation to ascension; it includes the cross, but it means far more. It means advocacy. But we should not misunderstand this, as if Christ (who bears our humanity) stands at odds with the Father, pleading our case. That *"God was reconciling the world to himself in Christ"* means that Jesus is nothing other than God's own embrace. Jesus is God's mighty overture that draws our humanity to himself. Therefore the success of Christ includes not just what he did on our behalf at Calvary, but what he did in valuing and redeeming our humanity for the Father. The present work of Christ is our inspiration to see spiritual development—complete with confession—as a regular feature of our lives. God did not merely save us two thousand years ago; God continues to embrace us through Christ, who forever resides by his side.

---

18 To what extent, I wonder, is this rejection linked to the Protestant rejection of the Catholic mass and confessional?

1 John 2:3–11

W E KNOW THAT we have come to know him if we obey his commands. ⁴The man who says, "I know him," but does not do what he commands is a liar, and the truth is not in him. ⁵But if anyone obeys his word, God's love is truly made complete in him. This is how we know we are in him: ⁶Whoever claims to live in him must walk as Jesus did.

⁷Dear friends, I am not writing you a new command but an old one, which you have had since the beginning. This old command is the message you have heard. ⁸Yet I am writing you a new command; its truth is seen in him and you, because the darkness is passing and the true light is already shining.

⁹Anyone who claims to be in the light but hates his brother is still in the darkness. ¹⁰Whoever loves his brother lives in the light, and there is nothing in him to make him stumble. ¹¹But whoever hates his brother is in the darkness and walks around in the darkness; he does not know where he is going, because the darkness has blinded him.

IF JOHN'S FIRST exhortation (1:8–2:2) had in mind the secessionists who were making false theological claims about themselves and God, this second exhortation is aimed primarily at the believers in his church, the Christians who have remained under his tutelage but have been influenced by the debates in the congregation. Therefore, even though the tone is somewhat less polemical, it still maintains the rhetorical style of the earlier verses. This time three assertions are listed (2:4, 6, 9), which might be profitably compared with those outlined in 1:6, 8, and 10. However, the chief difference is that in this case, these are assertions that may be affirmed by believers ("I know him," "I live in him," "I am in the light") if they are rightly understood.

These first two exhortations are both concerned with pleasing God. In the first case, John emphasizes pleasing him by renouncing sin. Now the positive fruit of "knowing God" and "living in the light" is raised. Simply put, John underscores *obedience* to God's voice. Theological orthodoxy, no matter how stringent, is hazardous if it is not linked to a living Christian faith. And as John will affirm in these verses, an orthodox faith lived in denial of God's commands will have perilous—even deadly—effects for its possessor as well as those nearby.

The present section is structured with an initial affirmation (2:3), followed by three citation formulas (vv. 4, 6, 9), which the NIV unfortunately obscures.[1] In each case John leads us further in the meaning of obedience, giving it a final application in the third unit.

(1) Whoever says . . .
"I know him"
but does not keep his commands . . .
he is a liar.
(2) Whoever says . . .
"I abide in him"
ought to walk as he walked.
(3) Whoever says . . .
"I am in the light"
but hates his brother . . .
he lives in the darkness.

The three citations are all variations on the same theme. In Johannine thought, *knowing*, *abiding*, and *being* reflect similar meanings, and it is unnecessary to look for a theological progression here. In each case John is acknowledging that men and women might announce their allegiance to Jesus and explain that they have a profoundly intimate relationship with him, and yet there are tests, "tests of life," as Robert Law once called them, that signal the authenticity of spiritual vigor.

---

1. The second and third citations even share a parallel grammatical structure Each citation is introduced with the same participle, *ho logon*, "whoever says," which the NIV has translated three different ways

Obedience and Spiritual Maturity (2:3–5)

EVERYTHING JOHN SAYS in 2:4–11 is hinged to the thesis statement found in 2:3. *Knowing God is evidenced by our heartfelt desire to obey him.* We must be clear that John's choice of words here is not accidental. He is concerned to stress obedience, but also to challenge those who boast in knowing. The Greek term *gnosis* means *knowledge* and describes a religious disposition (hence, Gnosticism) that promoted enlightenment or mystical inspiration as the central feature of faith. No evidence exists that by John's day a formal religion called Gnosticism was known, even though we can confidently say that popular trends in that direction were already beginning and in the second century gave birth to formed religious systems. Thus John's use of the words related to "knowing" (as well as his interest in "light," cf. 1:5ff.) indicates his acquaintance with such trends. Like an infection in the Christian community, this virus urged that the pathway to salvation did not depend on freedom from sin, but rather freedom from ignorance. If esoteric mysticism opened the way to God, then other mundane matters, such as earthly obedience and morality, could easily be swept aside. If we keep in mind the denial of sin and the insensitivity to one's need to be forgiven (described in 1:8–2:2), it is apparent that such Gnostic strains were wreaking havoc on the peculiar view of ethics in this community.

John likewise uses grammar carefully. "We know that *we have come to know* him" disguises a perfect tense verb, which in Greek means not simply that knowledge is a one-time enlightenment, but rather a past experience with ongoing present consequences.[2] Knowledge for John is experiential, not speculative and abstract. It reveals itself in present activity, namely, the continuing reflex to obey God.[3] Therefore, people who make some claim that they know God must have evidence in their daily lives that they are conforming their decision-making to his will.

John's habit is to make a statement, offer a negative example, then reinforce his point by repeating the first statement in more depth. This is the pattern here, for verse 4 now describes the person who

---

2 This is the function of Greek perfect tense verbs in this construct

3 The present tense of "*obey* his commands" demands this interpretation of obedience as an ongoing daily activity.

feigns intimacy with God and rejects obedience (the same descrip-tion is given in 2:11). John's words are severe: This person is a liar. In 1:8 we learned that the denial of sin is evidence that truth is not in a person. Now we learn that the denial of obedience means the same thing: Truth is absent. We must keep in mind the central place of "truth" in Johannine vocabulary. Truth describes Jesus (John 14:6), the Holy Spirit (14:17), and the word (17:17). Truth is the principle of spir-itual integrity that should accompany all worship that is empowered by God's Spirit (4:24). Therefore, John is here *not* simply saying that someone who fails to obey has missed the point; instead, such people are seriously disconnected from God.

On the other hand (1 John 2:5), the profile of true Christians is quite the opposite: They *keep* God's *word*. John offers two important points. (1) Throughout these verses he employs the Greek word *tereo* ("to keep") in order to describe obedience. Brown argues convincingly that this verb means more than observance.[4] Its use in the LXX and elsewhere implies duration and perseverance: to observe diligently, to guard care-fully, to suddenly realize a truth—and to protect it.[5] In other words, "to keep God's word" goes far beyond mere conformity to law. It expresses a zealous desire to adhere to God's will. On the other hand, in verses 3–4 John used "commands" to describe God's will, and now in verse 5 it is changed to "word." John is well known for his variation, so that no difference of meaning exists here.

(2) Mature Christians make complete (*or* perfect) the love of God. This thought provides an exegetical puzzle. In English and in Greek "the love of God" can mean different things. Is this God's love for us, as the NIV translates it (a subjective genitive, see 4:9)? Or is it our love for God (an objective genitive, see 2:15 and 5:3)? Or does it mean love that is like God's love (a genitive of quality)? All three interpre-tations have been used for this verse, and some even think that John is intentionally ambiguous or is not making a sharp distinction.

I am inclined to see this as an objective genitive ("our love *for God* reaches perfection"). After all, throughout these verses John is outlin-ing how we might express fidelity and obedience *to God*. He is look-

---

4. R Brown, *The Epistles of John*, 252.
5. Cf the use of the verb to describe Jesus' watchful care over his disciples in John 17:12

ing for the signs of response that show our desire to act in such a way that we unveil our devotion to the Lord. Of course we understand from a wider theological perspective that such obedient love does not arise unless God's own love first inspires it. But this is not John's present purpose. By "perfection" John has in mind the maturation of the steadfast believer. Perfect obedience springs from perfect love. When we have discovered God's inexhaustible love for us, we love him utterly, *and this is expressed tangibly in obedience to his will.* This dialectic between love and obedience is a constant theme in the Fourth Gospel. In the Upper Room, Jesus says, "If you love me, you will obey what I command" (John 14:15). Later he adds, "If anyone loves me, he will obey my teaching. . . . He who does not love me will not obey my teaching. These words you hear are not my own; they belong to the Father who sent me" (14:23a–24; cf. 15:10).

This, of course, adds yet another practical problem: *To what extent is perfection possible for the believer?* Christians in the Wesleyan-Holiness tradition have always taken a keen interest in verse 5 because of its stress on perfection. Our application of it below should do likewise.

Obedience and the Life of Jesus (2:6–8)

THE SECOND TEST of authenticity, of genuine spiritual vigor and life, has to do with living as Jesus lived (2:6–8). If we claim to live in him, we must also walk as he did. The verb used at the beginning of this affirmation, however, is a specialized Johannine term, *meno*, which occurs in John's Gospel forty times and in his letters twenty-seven times. "To live in him" goes beyond merely imitating Christ in lifestyle or "living as Jesus lived." This verb generally describes the indwelling of the Christian in God (1 John 3:24; 4:13ff.) or in Jesus (John 6:56; 15:4ff.; 1 John 2:27–28; 3:6). It may even depict God indwelling us (1 John 3:24; 4:12–13, 15–16). Therefore, many translators prefer "abide" or "remain" as a way of conveying the sense of permanence and duration, of interior participation and connection with God. In this sense, the word parallels what we heard in verse 4. To know God truly is to abide in him deeply. And in each case, the outgrowth of such knowing and indwelling is obedience.

John holds up the earthly life of Jesus as a model to be imitated. This is the first time he has done this, and it is an important development, given the controversy in his church.[6] *As earthly conduct is an essential part of faith, so too the earthly life of Jesus is an essential model for our lives.* This, of course, indicates some consensus about the earthly life of Jesus and suggests that these Christians had at their disposal an account of Jesus' life. The numerous parallels with the Fourth Gospel no doubt tell us that (as we outlined in the introduction) this Gospel was well known in this community. And now John is making an appeal to it directly.

Verse 7 contains a fresh, impassioned tone. John slips into the first person ("*I am* not writing") and addresses his audience as "beloved."[7] The Greek term *agapetoi* (based on *agape*, "love") is used sixty-one times in the New Testament and seems to have been a common early Christian term of endearment (Rom. 12:19; 2 Cor. 7:1), which John uses frequently (1 John 3:2, 21; 4:1, 7; cf. "my dear children" in 2:1). It almost seems as if for the moment John is leaving the arguments and slogans of the controversy behind and is writing to his flock from his heart about the true character of a discipleship that pursues the center of God's will, namely, that we love one another.

But how is the command to love not new (v. 7a)? On the one hand, it has been around since the Old Testament (see Lev. 19:18; Matt. 19:19), and thus even Jesus appealed to it directly (Mark 12:28–34).[8] But in another sense, this church had the Fourth Gospel and knew well Jesus' words in John 13:34, "A new command I give you: Love one another. As I have loved you, so you must love one another" (cf. 15:12; 1 John 3:23). Therefore, John's exhortation is anchored in an authority not even his opponents can challenge. It is "from the beginning"— which refers, as it does in 1:1; 2:13; and 3:8, to the events surrounding Jesus' life and ministry.

And yet there is still something new in this (v. 8). The ancient command has taken on a new form since the coming of Christ. Initially, Christ himself exemplified this love by demonstrating his self-giving love for us. He fulfilled the law of love in a way never before seen. But more, Jesus has enabled this love to be realized in the present age

---

6. John does this also in 1 John 3:16, when he uses the sacrificial life of Jesus as a model for sacrificial service for others.

7. The NIV translates this word as "dear friends," but this misses the power of John's endearing language.

8. This command to love characterized an exhortation throughout Christian communities. See Rom. 12:14; 13:8–10; Eph. 5:2; James 2:8; 1 Peter 2:17).

among his followers. Hence, the truth of love is evidenced "in him" and "[in] you." In other words, a new era has dawned, a new age has come, a new empowering light is shining, all of which give the church new possibilities for love and a new imperative (see v. 8b). The *newness* John describes is an eschatological reality now at work among Christians.

So once again John is providing a test for spiritual reality. In the first test, obedience was the natural outgrowth of an intimate life with God. Now we learn that the second test of life is a love that bears the quality of Christ's love.

Obedience and Love (2:9–11)

THE FIRST TEST (2:3–5) contained a warning about falsehood; the third test (2:9–11) does the same. The dreadful prospect remains that some may claim to have the intimacy with God that John has described all along—but it is a delusion. Being "in the light" repeats the eschatological analogy of 2:8. Since the coming of Christ the world has changed, a new potential for spiritual conduct has been realized. A new light is shining. And yet some will claim to be a part of this new reality while all along still living outside of it.

The tests in this exhortation are cumulative: To know God and to abide in him mean to obey, and to obey is to exhibit Christlike love. But the ultimate test of such obedient love is whether we are able to love the unlovely. Thus John's severity is unrelenting: To hate a brother or sister in the church means one is "in the darkness" and has been blinded (vv. 9, 11); to love them means that one is living "'in the light'" (v. 10).[9] Love becomes a genuine value only when it is tested, only when we must reach beyond ourselves and love someone we do not wish to love. This is the caliber of love John has in mind.

It is easiest for us to think that John is referring to his opponents here, to people who exhibited less than godly character in John's church. They have made aggressive doctrinal denials and denied the value of practical behavior as a hallmark of true spirituality. And it is appropriate for John to exhort them. But in this congregational struggle I am convinced that John is also speaking to his own followers.

---

9. Of course, John would affirm that loving people outside the church is required as well. Jesus loved his enemies However, John's interest is specialized in the present verses. He is addressing an inner-church struggle and the attitudes that have evolved within it.

They do not have license *to hate* even though they are in the right. Hate is not an occasional outburst of anger; it is an attitude that has become a habit.[10]

There is a curious phrase attached to verse 10 that lends some support to this interpretation. The NIV renders it, "Whoever loves his brother lives in the light, and *there is nothing in him to make him stumble.*" However, the Greek literally says, *"stumbling [skandalon] is not in him/it."* The original is ambiguous on two counts: (1) The pronoun can refer to the believer ("him") or to the light ("it")—the grammar works perfectly either way;[11] (2) the stumbling may refer to the believer's falling down (thus the NIV and many commentators), or it may mean that there is nothing in the believer that will cause *others* to fall down. A *skandalon* is a trap or an object that makes one trip. Metaphorically, it is something that causes one's demise or downfall.

Smalley argues convincingly that in most New Testament uses, the *skandalon* word group refers to something that causes *others* to trip (Rom. 14:13; 1 Peter 2:8; Rev. 2:14).[12] The verbal form of *skandalon* carries this meaning in the Fourth Gospel (John 6:61; 16:1). If this is the correct interpretation of verse 10, John may have in mind *Christian misbehavior* that may drive more people out of the church. Therefore, a better translation might be, "There is nothing in him to cause anyone to stumble." Naturally, such a warning would apply to the believer as well, but John has chiefly in mind indignant, persistent attitudes of anger that might widen the fissure already splitting the church.

THE COMMAND TO love and obey is universally understood, and thus it is not difficult to carry forward themes found here to our context. Moreover, John's setting is not unlike many today, in which difficult relationships within the church have paralyzed the church's mission. Christians who claim to have an intimate walk with God, who say that they are "in the light," and who yet pro-

---

10 "Hating" is a present participle in Greek, suggesting an ongoing activity

11. Greek scribes often preferred seeing the reference to light and moved the pronoun in the sentence so that it would be nearer its antecedent The sense is that if you are in the light, it is harder to stumble because your sight is excellent

12. S. Smalley, *1, 2, 3 John,* 62.

mote their own spiritual prowess, sometimes find themselves in bitter conflict with others making the same spiritual claim.

Distilling the timeless features of the passage demands that I understand the particular setting of John's letter as well as the message brought there. But to build a bridge to our century I need to discern what themes can have universal value when I find myself in an analogous setting or perhaps even an entirely different setting. It is clear that John has a unique church landscape on his mind: There are those outside the fellowship who exhibit error and hostility, there are those inside the fellowship who continue to be faithful to John's teachings, and there are no doubt those in the middle—Christians who give an ear to both sides. I am speculating on this third group because while evidence for it is slim, experience tells us that they are there. Perhaps this group is trying to play a reconciling role. Or perhaps they have not decided where to align themselves. John's tendency is to use broad brush strokes, to paint things black and white. And yet church life is generally more nuanced than this. In other words, I have to be cautious, lest I introduce the same polarity into my church that John seems to be describing for his.

There are other reasons to be careful. John's absolute, dualistic view of things leads him along other risky paths. Those who fail his tests are "liars," "the truth" is not in them, they live "in the darkness," and they are "blinded." To what extent does the absence of godly behavior jeopardize one's claim to be Christ's follower? John's demand that we test ourselves opens up a constellation of questions about assurance. These criticisms of errant would-be Christians were heard in chapter 1, but in that case we were clearly dealing with people who had left the fold. Their theological errors were obvious. Now something different is at hand. John's strong language is being applied to believers *within the church.*

All of this springs from a unique view of the church that John is promoting. John expects the church to exhibit the real presence of Christ so powerfully that he can even use eschatological language to announce its character (2:11). He can even describe the maturity of Christians as reaching *perfection* (2:5). This is a view of the church that is unlike anything I see today. John's church was a bridgehead in its culture. It was an underground movement that had to stand together in strength or else it would die. Perhaps it was the jeopardy of his situation that gave his ecclesiology such urgency. And following from this, perhaps it is the absence of our perception of threat that makes our ecclesiology so lax.

If the eschatological language of John is foreign to our context, the same is true with the passage's central themes, love and obedience. As I have suggested, they can be understood today, but it is another question whether our society genuinely wants to hear such absolute commands. We have built a world based on free choices, not obedience. We have viewed love as attraction, which, when the feeling passes, may be directed elsewhere. We rarely hear calls for obedience and love *as work*. In each case such calls may cost me my freedom. They may limit my spontaneity. They may put boundaries around what I can and cannot do. Recently in a premarriage counseling session at a Naval air station chapel, a young couple affirmed their love for each other but refused to work on hard compromises. The young lieutenant in front of me was even unwilling to stop seeing a former girlfriend despite his engagement and the objections of his fiancée! He remarked, "I didn't think marriage was just more rules, chaplain. Sure, I'll love my wife, but I don't want love taking away my freedom."

This attitude that flees from obedience and sees love as a passing affection is prevalent today. And to bring John's message to an audience that has accepted it will take some serious bridge-building. I was fortunate. The young man in my office was in the Navy. He was an Annapolis graduate and an ace helicopter pilot. "Look," I said, "there are rules for the flightline, right? What you can wear, where you can walk, when you can't smoke. You obey them because you know that if you don't, you can get killed—and you can kill others. It's obedience to the rules that makes flying possible, that makes you complete your mission. Life is a flightline. Marriage is your mission. Our counseling is your preflight briefing. Freedom comes from disciplined obedience." For the first time in our hour together I thought I had caught this pilot's attention. But in his heart he was not eager to hear what John would say about obeying and loving. But we both realized that in order for helicopters or life to work, there has to be fidelity to guidelines that will not flex.

A WELL-KNOWN PASTOR from Florida once said that there was nothing wrong with his congregation that a couple of funerals would not fix.[13] Of course, after we smile, it dawns on us—soberly—that this is exactly what we occasionally want. Every pastor can think of people who seem to have too much time on their hands and too much of the church on their minds. They are obsessed with the church and make it their business to straighten out everything from table linens to the pastoral staff. I have met many people like this and have often wondered what they were doing at the church or what personal needs were being met by being there. Did they enjoy the tension they created? Did they have any perspective about the harshly destructive behaviors they brought? One constant characterizes their presence: Rarely did they exhibit a deeply pious, Christlike demeanor. Instead, they were inflexible, angry, manipulative, and coercive. And they would never guess that their behavior had this effect.

This passage levies severe tests on all who would claim to be followers of Christ. To what extent, it asks, is our faith simply a matter of pious slogans ("I know him, live in him, and am in the light" were the Johannine slogans)? To what extent do I seriously reflect the demeanor of Jesus Christ? Am I known as obedient and loving or simply as religious? As the text lays these challenges at my feet, it also opens up a variety of fresh ideas.

(1) *Do we unwittingly neglect the call to obedience?* Many of us recoil at the mere word "obedience." I often meet students who have grown up in conservative churches and families where obedience and righteousness were pounded home so often that today they have been pushed aside as vehicles of death and suffocation. *Obey?* such students ask. *God loves me. Let me simply enjoy him and live.* For some of us, promoting obedience is difficult particularly when we ground our salvation in the rich goodness and charity of God. Nevertheless, John could not be clearer.

Sometimes I wonder if our concern to support the Reformation teaching about grace has sabotaged any hope for this call to obedience. We frame the theology of the New Testament as a series of juxtapositions: the synagogue versus the church, Jesus versus Moses, Paul versus the Jerusalem legalists, grace versus law. In doing so, we forget

---

13 Stephen Brown, speaking at Wheaton College Chapel, September 8, 1993.

that Paul's first concern was *works of Jewish ritual that were thought to earn some benefit from God.* Paul can at once say that the Christian life should display *good works* and yet that we are not saved *by works.* Paul endorsed no compromise to the believer's pursuit of righteousness. The same is true of Jesus. In his Sermon on the Mount he said that our righteousness must exceed that of the Pharisees (Matt. 5:20). He was openly critical of Pharisaic behavior but still told his followers to take note of what they had to say (23:3). This is a difficult paradox: Personal righteousness and obedience are an essential component of our faith and yet do not form the basis of our salvation. It is no wonder that theologians continually debate the synthesis of these themes and ask if the "gospel according to Jesus" has long been neglected.[14]

(2) *Can the call to obey be abused?* Admittedly, there are other theological settings, other arenas of Christian life, where obedience arises to become the center of things. Conformity and obedience become watchwords as everything from our social life to our financial decisions are legislated. What happens when a pastor or a church demands *inappropriate* obedience? I recall meeting a refugee from such a congregation, who was told once that she would simply have to leave the church if she could not conform to the pastor's teachings about quitting her job and staying home with her elementary school-age children.[15]

Simply put, what—or whom—should we obey? Naturally, our impulse is to say that we obey the Lord. But how is his will manifest? John refers again and again to what was "since the beginning" in order to say that the teachings of the Jesus of history, found today in our Scriptures, should be the basis of our obedience. This is the perfect place for us to begin. But it does not solve the problem of the abuse of authority. Many Christian leaders go further and say that their interpretation of these Scriptures or their application of them in the church is authoritative. And here absolute conformity is sometimes demanded. Frequently it is a teaching, such as a view of charismatic gifts or women's ordination. It could even be a lifestyle issue, such as the use of alcohol. On occasion these "authoritative" teachings may become bizarre. I have heard a pastor preach that all of the women in his congregation

---

14 This is the title of John MacArthur's book on the subject, in which he challenges church teachings that neglect obedience as they affirm grace. See page 108.

15. For further examples of this pattern of control, see R. Enroth, *Churches That Abuse* (Grand Rapids: Zondervan, 1992).

must *never* wear trousers but always wear skirts—and any who disagree must leave. A congregation I know of in California required its members to give their property deeds to the pastoral staff. Another church gives specific biblical instructions on how to breastfeed infants.

This is abusing the call to obedience. As Christian leaders we need to employ restraint when we call our people to obey. We may need to be minimalists, grounding ourselves constantly in the Scriptures. Human leadership can be fallen leadership. Therefore, our reflex must always be to point men and women to the ultimate authority in God's Word.

(3) *And if we disobey?* At once this raises a vital theological question, which must be handled with care. John is nothing short of absolute in his description of those who disobey: They are liars (2:5) and walk in the darkness (2:9). Can the absence of obedience disqualify someone as a Christian? I think of Jesus' sobering words in Matthew 7:21–23, which conclude the Sermon on the Mount.

> Not everyone who says to me, "Lord, Lord," will enter the kingdom of heaven, but only he who does the will of my Father who is in heaven. Many will say to me on that day, "Lord, Lord, did we not prophesy in your name, and in your name drive out demons and perform many miracles?" Then I will tell them plainly, "I never knew you. Away from me, you evildoers!"

This passage is followed by our Lord's parable about building our houses on rock. Hearing Jesus' words and *doing* them compares with a person whose house has an unmovable foundation.

Taking a passage such as this at face value comes with significant risk. Above all it demands that the measure of saving faith can be seen in some tangible outworking of grace and goodness in a person's life. The timeless theological problem is here, however: How do we preach such a theme without destroying Christian assurance or making obedience a criterion for salvation?

In recent years this debate has been launched again by John MacArthur of Grace Community Church in California. In his book *The Gospel According to Jesus*, MacArthur argues that our emphasis on grace has emptied the gospel of its sharper edge; many who say "Lord, Lord" simply will not enter the kingdom of heaven. The following paragraph represents the book's tone and outlook:

The gospel in vogue today holds forth a false hope to sinners. It promises them they can have eternal life yet continue to live in rebellion against God. Indeed, it encourages people to claim Jesus as Savior yet defer until later the commitment to obey Him as Lord. It promises salvation from hell but not necessarily freedom from iniquity. It offers false security to people who revel in the sins of the flesh and spurn the way of holiness. By separating faith from faithfulness, it leaves the impression that intellectual assent is as valid as wholehearted obedience to the truth. Thus the good news of Christ has given way to the bad news of an insidious easy-believism that makes no moral demands on the lives of sinners. It is not the same message Jesus proclaimed.[16]

This volume has opened afresh an age-old debate and inspired yet more authors who have taken exception with MacArthur. There is a delicate balance here that each of us must find for ourselves. On the one hand, we dare not compromise the pivotal doctrine of grace. And yet there must be a call to discipleship that shows how such grace has transformed the disciple. It must be a call that makes room for important, difficult passages, such as James 2:14–26. It must be a call that sobers, that makes us check our Christian resolve—all without sacrificing the loving character of God.

(4) *The absolute command to love.* Not enough can be said for the importance of love in 1 John. However, the pastoral problem is that we speak of it so often that we have become anesthetized, dulled from hearing afresh its demand on us. *Of course we're loving. We're Christians, aren't we?* Three thoughts come quickly to mind. (a) Does this mean that Christians cannot have disagreements? That Christians cannot be angry? That emotions of dissent must be repressed? We would likely disagree, and yet this command is often used to inhibit fair and passionate disagreement in church life. It is much like the biblical injunction not to judge (Matt. 7:1), which is then turned into a denial of critical discernment. I believe John is describing a sustained attitude that repudiates another. It is a disposition of heart that condemns and criticizes out of habit and has not been shaped by the selfless love of God.

---

16. J. MacArthur, *The Gospel According to Jesus What Does Jesus Mean When He Says, "Follow Me?"* (Grand Rapids: Zondervan, 1988), 16.

(b) This command is also a call to reconciliation. The test of obedience to the command to love surfaces when we come to terms with those whom we have difficulty loving. And the first step in this direction is reconciliation. When I was in seminary, I participated in a two-year internship at a church in California. I was supervised by a staff member who, frankly, seemed never to appreciate what I did. It was a difficult relationship. And as a fledgling intern-minister, it became one of the most painful and anger-filled formative experiences of my life. Fifteen years later we met again and were reconciled. And we laughed—healing laughter—when we discovered that both of us then were profoundly unhappy and caught up in strenuously difficult ministries that had ruined our chances to see each other clearly. The command to love is a command to work at relationships that have gone wrong.

(c) While John is eager to see love promoted, that does not mean that we are to be naive about those who would hurt us. John distinguishes carefully in these letters between those who are "deceivers," who belong "to the world," and Christians who belong to the family of God. In 2 John 10 he explicitly states that such people are not to be welcomed into our lives.

This teaching requires thoughtful discernment since, in the interests of evangelism, we are called to go into the world. At the same time, we must be warned that the world holds dangers. There are *intellectual* dangers, which lure us into patterns of thinking that rob us of the simplicity and immediacy of Jesus. There are *moral* dangers, lifestyles and attitudes that deal with everything from corrupt obsessions with money to destructive views of sexuality. There are *religious* dangers, passing gurus who can out-evangelize most evangelists. I even wonder if there are *theological* dangers, a sort of fossilized orthodoxy that does not promote Jesus but rather promotes doctrine, deceiving its adherents that they actually possess the true gift. Dangers are everywhere. And even though we should be generously open and loving, we must also be shrewdly discerning and wise.

1 John 2:12–17

🌿

I WRITE TO YOU, dear children,
because your sins have been forgiven on account
of his name.
13 I write to you, fathers,
because you have known him who is from the
beginning.
I write to you, young men,
because you have overcome the evil one.
I write to you, dear children,
because you have known the Father.
14 I write to you, fathers,
because you have known him who is from the
beginning.
I write to you, young men,
because you are strong,
and the word of God lives in you,
and you have overcome the evil one.

15 Do not love the world or anything in the world. If
anyone loves the world, the love of the Father is not in
him. 16 For everything in the world—the cravings of sinful man, the lust of his eyes and the boasting of what he
has and does—comes not from the Father but from the
world. 17 The world and its desires pass away, but the
man who does the will of God lives forever.

Original Meaning

IF WE HAVE been following John's argument
thus far, the present text, particularly verses
12–14, seems to fuel the observation of many
interpreters that portions of the letter lack
logical coherence. However, these verses are a parenthesis, a pause,
designed to reassure John's readers about their own relationship to
God and, as Stott says, to rob counterfeit Christians of their false assurance.[1] Therefore, we will find that a connection with the foregoing
verses and those that follow is tenuous at best.

---

1. Stott, *The Epistles of John*, 95

While the exhortation given in verses 15–17 seems straightforward, the parenthesis of verses 12–14 presents some exegetical difficulties. Initially, it is clear that there is a symmetry here: three groups ("children," "fathers," "young men") are addressed twice, and the second time repeats those words over again. Is this duplicate material? Are we to seek nuances of difference?

Moreover, just what is the meaning of these titles? Do we understand these literally, as age-groups? Are they symbolic of maturity (young converts, mature leaders, etc.)? Is this a literary device that actually refers to all members equally? Some have argued persuasively that perhaps John has two groups in mind. His first reference to "children" echoes his habit of how he refers to Christians throughout his letters (cf. 2:1). Then the following two titles ("fathers," "young men") describe old and young alike.

A third question surfaces regarding the verb John employs. "I write" is in the present tense three times in verses 12–13 but changes to the past (aorist) tense in verse 14.[2] The past tense, of course, might refer to another writing (the Gospel or another letter) or to a portion of the present letter already penned. This latter option, sometimes called an epistolary aorist, permits a writer to refer to his present work as if completed and is likely the best way to view the present construction.

I prefer to view the first title as an address for all John's followers. This makes the best sense of the order of the names (otherwise we would expect "fathers" to come first). Furthermore, "children" is commonly used in the Johannine literature for whole communities, while there is no evidence that "fathers" or "young men" are ever used in this way.[3] We have, then, a symmetry here that is helpfully outlined:

I write to you:

children (*teknia*)	because	sins/forgiven
fathers (*pateres*)	because	you have known him/ beginning
young men (*neaniskoi*) because		overcome/evil one

---

2 The NIV translation obscures this difference making all six verbs present tense. The NRSV distinguishes them with "I am writing to you" and "I write to you."

3. See Brown, *The Epistles of John*, 298–300

I have written to you:

children (*paidia*)	because	you have known the Father
fathers (*pateres*)	because	you have known him/ beginning
young men (*neaniskoi*) because		you are strong, word/God, overcome/evil one

This symmetry is virtually perfect, except that the term for "children" changes (*teknia/paidia*) and the clauses that follow are rearranged in the second set. For the sake of clarity, I will cluster the names.

Words for John's Children (2:12, 13c)

IT WAS COMMONPLACE among early Christians to address their followers with family terms. John does this frequently (see on 2:1).[4] Here the first term, *teknia*, likely is a general title denoting a parent/child relationship. The second term, *paidia*, is probably synonymous, although some think that it implies the subordination of the child. No doubt the two words merged since Jesus in the Fourth Gospel uses each for his disciples (13:33; 21:5).

Two themes reassure John's followers of their place in God's household, each of which has been heard before in the controversy and debate of previous verses. (1) Their sins "have been forgiven" (perfect tense) on account of Jesus' name (see 2:1–2). There is nothing insecure about this; it is a completed fact because Christ has died and satisfied the requirements of salvation. (2) They "have known the Father" (perfect tense again). This is the natural result of their redemption and renewal (see 2:3–8). Freed from sin, they have been given a new consciousness of God's intimate fatherhood over them. This, of course, is precisely what gives the title of "child" its poignancy. Christians are children of God because they know the fatherhood of God as no other can. Thus the unique Christian response to God is *"Abba!* Father!" (Rom. 8:15), a privilege shared by no one else.

Words for Elders (2:13a, 14a)

IT IS UNPARALLELED to find in the New Testament Christians referred to as "fathers," since it generally serves as a metaphor for ancestors

---

4. See also 2:28; 3:7, 18; 4:4, 5:21.

who have died (2 Peter 3:4). In Acts 22:1 we may have an instance of senior or elder Christians being given this title, but this is rare. Its general meaning here likely refers to those who are mature in the faith (if we disregard the use of the word "elder" for a church office). Above all, we must not think that John has in mind the *men* of this congregation exclusively. Paul's Jewish custom is to address adults widely with such titles as "brothers," all along implying that he has the entire Christian church in mind, women included.

Like the children in 2:14, fathers too "have known" God. Everyone, mature and immature alike, shares this same privilege. But there is a difference, for fathers have known "him who is *from the beginning*." This may refer to God exclusively—or it may refer to Jesus, whose preexistence is important to John.[5] We have seen thus far that "from the beginning" is an important phrase in this church. It has been used in reference to the message that was passed on about Jesus (2:24; 3:11) or even about Jesus himself (1:1). Even the command to love is "since the beginning" (2:7). This suggests that those who are mature in the faith, whose spiritual maturity and experience reach back many years, have a knowledge of God that is anchored securely in the things of the past. It is their seasoned wisdom that makes for steadfast faith in the present circumstances.

Words for Younger Christians (2:13b, 14b)

IF THE ELDERS of the community provide a steadfast anchor of faith, it is the youth—men and women alike—who are here engaging the battle of living that faith in the struggles of the world. The young are often strong, and it sometimes follows that young believers exhibit spiritual strength too. Their knowledge of God brings a zeal not found among those more mature.

Thus John affirms them by saying that they are strong and that God's word abides within them. As Stott suggests, there is no small hint here that the word of God is likely the very vehicle that brings strength.[6] But that strength is there for a purpose: It has overcome the "evil one." In 3:8, 12 we learn that the spiritual life can be a war of spiritual forces, a conflict with the devil. Paul too affirms this by saying

5. So Marshall, *The Epistles of John*, 139.
6 Stott, *The Epistles of John*, 98

that our struggle is not with humankind but with "authorities" and "powers" (Eph. 6:12–18). Even the Fourth Gospel depicts this landscape of divine forces led by Christ at war with the powers of darkness.

John does not, however, urge the young to defeat these forces. Rather, he says that they "have overcome" them already (another perfect tense). Again and again the Christian life is being celebrated as an accomplished fact. When did this victory take place? Satan was found in defeat when at the Incarnation his kingdom came under siege (cf. Col. 2:15). As 1 John 5:18–20 says, even though the world is under the control of Satan, those who have been born again, who "know God," whose sins have been forgiven, are protected by Jesus Christ, who is Satan's victor through his cross and resurrection.

The Love of the World (2:15–17)

JOHN NOW TURNS to the principal exhortation of this section. Smalley suggests a symmetry connects this unit with the foregoing.[7]

15	Love of the world	Love of the Father
16	comes from the world	comes from the Father
17	the world passes away	the one who obeys God remains forever

It is a warning. Two choices stand before everyone—even in the church: Either we love the Father or we love the world. Affirmations for John's loyal followers (vv. 12–14) now become warnings that they do not fall away into spiritual duplicity—parading spiritual things while the heart is possessed by the world.

It is crucial to maintain a firm understanding of vocabulary in this section. Key words such as "world," "love," and "life" must be read with their original meaning in mind. When John uses the word "world" (Gk. *kosmos*), he can mean either the created material universe, which is good (2:2; 3:17; cf. John 1:10), or the world of sin that stands in aggressive opposition to God (1 John 4:3–5; 5:19). This latter idea operates here, for *kosmos* represents the unredeemed world, a world under the control of Satan (5:19; John 12:31; 14:30); it lives in darkness (John 1:5; 12:46) and lies under God's judgment (9:39). This is again John's dualism at work, but here we see it as an ethical dualism

---

7. S. Smalley, *1, 2, 3, John*, 80

rather than a cosmological dualism.[8] To John, the material world is good and will find renewal someday. Yet there are those within it who follow evil impulses and reject God; they deserve criticism.

There is a further difficulty when John says that we should *not love* this world. This is different from the command to love in 2:10, where the object of love is a fellow believer. Nevertheless, there is a tension with John 3:16, where we learn that God *loves* the world. Even though the world is a place of disbelief, God's love for it does not cease (1 John 2:2; 4:14). He actually set out to save and repair the world he had made. Should we not then love the world too?

John has in mind that Christians are to avoid an infatuation with worldly godlessness, with the realm of darkness that brings base pleasures. Such affection is incompatible with the true love of the Father (v. 15b). In verses 16–17 John lists the three characteristics of such affections; these verses shape the meaning of verse 15.

(1) *The desire of the flesh* (NIV, "the cravings of sinful man"). The Greek word *sarx* (lit., "flesh") possesses various nuances. Some commentators take it to mean sensual or sexual desires, and certainly this may be suggested. On the other hand, the LXX never uses *sarx* with reference to sensuality but often uses it to refer to humanity in general, particularly as it stands in contrast to God. In other words, John has in mind any desire, any sinful interest, that draws us away from God or at least makes continuing fellowship with him impossible.

(2) *The desire of the eyes* (NIV, "the lust of his eyes"). The same noun as is used in the first phrase, *epithymia* ("desire"), is repeated here. This develops further the arena of "sinful desires" against which John is warning us. This word may, of course, refer to a sinful interest in what can be seen. On the other hand, the eye is often a metaphor for sinful passion that corrupts (cf. Matt. 5:28). Examples include Eve's looking at the forbidden tree, which was "pleasing to the eye" (Gen. 3:6), or David's lustful looking at Bathsheba as she bathed (2 Sam. 11:2).[9]

(3) *Boasting in one's lifestyle* (NIV, "boasting of what he has and does"). The third description now moves from two forms of inappropriate interest and passion to an unholy pride in what one has. The "boaster" (Gk. *alazon*) is someone who pretentiously "promises more than he can perform" and, in antiquity, "often describes orators, philosophers,

---

8. Ibid , 83
9 Stott, *The Epistles of John,* 100.

doctors, cooks and officials."[10] It is used in Romans 1:30 and 2 Timothy 3:2, two of Paul's vice catalogues. The object of this boasting is life.[11] The Greek term here is unusual. *Bios* (as distinguished from *zoe*) describes the basic stuff of living—the materials of living—and appears in 1 John 3:17 in an unusual phrase that makes the meaning explicit: "the life of the world," which the NIV rightly translates "material possessions." Thus, John has in mind an attitude of pretentious arrogance or subtle elitism that comes from one's view of wealth, rank, or stature in society. It is an overconfidence that makes us lose any notion that we are dependent on God.[12]

These three characteristics are frequently compared with the temptations of Eve in the Garden of Eden or of Jesus in the desert (wrong interest, wrong passion, and pride), but the parallels seem weak. John is rather sketching a sweeping portrait of what it means to be seduced by worldliness and the allure of sin.

In 2:16b–17 two reasons are given why these interests are wrongheaded. (1) They do not spring from the Father and therefore will ultimately destroy a relationship with him. (2) As an eschatological reason, "the present age is doomed."[13] Christ has brought a completely new value system to history. And practically speaking, those who are utterly invested in the world and its passions will see it vanish. Only those whose passions rest in the Father will continue forever.

THIS IS JOHN'S third exhortation in a series that began in 1:8. He is continuing a dualistic outlook by building within his congregation a sense that there are two fronts, two dimensions, about which his followers need to be concerned. There is initially "the world" outside the church, an environment intrinsically opposed to God though loved by him. Christians should be aware of the temptations and threats of this world and equip themselves so that they do not fall prey to them. Then there is a group within the church itself who hold an "unworldly" array of convictions. People within the

---

10. G. Delling, "ἀλαζών, ἀλαζονεία," *TDNT*, 1:226–27.
11. The construction should be viewed as an objective genitive.
12. Brown, *The Epistles of John*, 212
13 Stott, *The Epistles of John*, 101

Christian community need to develop the strength of their fellowship and be alert to those who might compromise the faith and diminish the quality of life together.

Each exhortation increases the sense of "boundary" between the spheres of the world and the church. Subtle theological distortions give way to genuine perversions of doctrine. A world that seems indifferent to God is now disclosed as being utterly inimical to him. People that seemed to be sitting on the border—worldly Christians, we might say—are identified as threatening. Teachers of error suddenly become instruments of the devil.

Through these exhortations John is building an ecclesiology that is nothing short of separatist. A separatist worldview is one that draws a sharp line between us and the non-Christian world. It calls us apart radically, demanding that we sever most links with a hostile environment. John reassures those within the fellowship and severely condemns life outside of it. In the fourth exhortation (2:18–27), those within the fellowship who have succumbed to the world's allure are given the harshest rebuke. John paints a portrait of a community under siege, a community infiltrated by saboteurs with hostile opposition at every turn. Is separatism good? Is it wrong? Its moral value is hinged directly to the character of the environment surrounding the church. If the church is threatened by a hostile, aggressive society, separatism might be a valid strategy for survival.

Such an outlook might look like this:

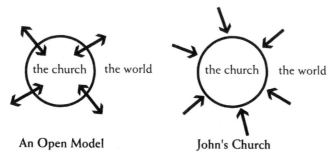

An Open Model   John's Church

How do I bridge this worldview with my own? How do I convince my Christian community that severe boundaries might be appropriate? In fact, I suspect that many in the church are convinced that the mere notion of *boundary* is inappropriate. They live with a cosmology that innocently sees the world as benign. Many evangelicals do not see the world as hostile. They do not see that its values, its politics, its educational systems, and even its social life are opposed to the church. As I write, ABC national news has carried the remarkable Dallas story of the Christian conversion of Norma McCorvey, otherwise known as Jane Roe, the original plaintiff for abortion rights in the landmark 1973 case Roe versus Wade. Once an abortion leader, she has been baptized, confessed to the fraud of the 1973 Supreme Court case, and now speaks of early abortions as sin.[14] Norma McCorvey is now prolife—as a Christian—and the ABC interviewer's hostility on TV was tangible. The nation was told that this woman was now emotionally troubled and that this was no conversion but a political ploy of the Christian "right." We must not be fooled. The world is seriously hostile to the growth of the kingdom. Yet we do not want to be separatist; we sometimes want to be inclusive lest any accuse us of being self-righteous, even cultlike.

Therefore John's ecclesiology—his doctrine of the church—requires that we forge a new worldview. Unless this view of the world changes, John's warnings about the dangers inherent in the world—its offensiveness, its aggressiveness, its rejection of the truth—will seem irrelevant. When I take an ecclesiology such as this into the twentieth century, it forces me to ask difficult questions about how we live in our communities. How do I view the threat of the world? What warnings do I give to equip my people without making them fearful? What strategies do I use to forge a strong community that is not vulnerable to the spiritual dangers and threats of the world? This discussion may begin with these verses but must continue for many sections to come. Some might urge that this question of managing the boundary between church and world is John's consuming interest throughout this letter.

MANY OF US fail to discuss the boundary between the church and the world. As a result, we fail to think of strategies to equip our people to manage a life lived in both spheres. Five fields of inquiry open up some of John's principal con-

---

14. In the original case, McCorvey argued for an abortion on the basis that she had been raped. This was not true.

cerns. Three strategies and two warnings are given to equip and strengthen the church.

(1) *Does assurance reduce vulnerability?* In verses 12–13 John writes to his "children" that their sins have been forgiven and that they have known the Father. As a pastor John is discerning something important. The first threat to faith, the fissure in an otherwise rock-solid Christian life, comes when I doubt the validity or the certainty of my convictions. When someone comes along and suggests that *more complete knowledge* of God or *genuine certainty* of salvation is available elsewhere, I am forced to rethink the basis of my faith. If I am assured of my convictions and confident in the truth I embrace, such questions cannot make me vulnerable.

I am often intrigued by stories of men and women who are swept up into a new religious movement. It may be the authoritative teachings of some new evangelist or perhaps a new church promoting a new experience or teaching. On closer inspection I find there is something lacking, some absence of confidence in this person, doubting that what he or she had received in Christ was exhaustive and complete. John writes in these verses not simply to make his followers feel better, but to help them know more completely that their Christian experience is true, authoritative, and complete. If the strength of our Christian resolve is firm, external religious pollutants have only limited influence.

What does this imply for the conduct of ministry and preaching? Preaching should not simply explain, it should equip. Instruction should not simply reiterate the tenets of faith, but do so with reference to those who might undo faith. Assurance limits vulnerability. The degree to which we are sure of ourselves before God will determine the degree of our vulnerability.

(2) *Senior believers are anchors of the faith.* Recently in one of my classes we were discussing how Jesus worked miracles and cast out demons in the Gospels. In order to launch a discussion of the contemporary relevance of these passages, I showed an unusually powerful video of Catholic priests and laypersons conducting an exorcism. It described their spiritual preparation and the remarkably difficult task of such ministry. After the film, I asked my students (whose average age was about twenty) to comment on it. One of the first respondents stunned me: "These people look so old that I can't imagine how they can do

something like this." The bulk of the team was made up of men and women in their fifties and sixties who had vast experience in this work.

The response stunned me because it unveiled a complete disregard for the contribution of senior members of the Christian community, people whose experiences and maturity gave them a savvy about the Christian life that could be found nowhere else. In other less dramatic ways, the church similarly disregards the resources of its senior members. John's reference to "fathers" is not an appeal to give respect to those who are simply older (though such is appropriate). Age does not give a person intrinsic spiritual authority in the church. But John is indicating that senior believers—who often are older but who may not be elderly—provide an unparalleled service: Their faith is anchored "from the beginning."

I noted earlier that "from the beginning" is an important phrase in this letter. It suggests that those whose faith reaches far back, who understand the genesis of Christian belief, who recognize the importance of Jesus' life and work, and who know the Scriptures after long study—that these women and men are anchors of stability and wisdom. When such strength is set aside in favor of the exuberant zeal of youth, the church becomes vulnerable to those who would redirect it from its historic and biblical moorings.

(3) *Young believers can be exemplars of the faith.* John does not fail to include the contributions of those who are young in the faith. These are believers—sometimes school children, sometimes adults—who have not lost the freshness and vitality of their "first love" for Christ (cf. Rev. 2:4). They are transparent, vocal, and passionate. They are another form of strength for the church.

This is perhaps why I enjoy teaching at an undergraduate college. College students exhibit a thorough-going zeal and abandon for God that can be found in few other places. And this strengthens me and challenges me. John writes that such believers are "strong," are rooted in God's Word, and are succeeding in battle with "the evil one." This brings to mind soldiers—Marines maybe!—who know how to handle the front lines and are eager to be there. One only has to visit Inter-Varsity's national mission's conference called *Urbana* to see what I mean. The passion of these men and women for the Scriptures is undiminished. They are eager to make new discoveries as they study. They listen for God's voice, and when they hear it, they are likely to leave their nets and follow Jesus. They are exemplars of faith.

But life in a congregation does not always see things this way. Those who hold leadership, who broker influence and power, often look at the impulsiveness and recklessness of this sort of faith and distrust it. They do not oppose it; they simply ignore it, and since they often control the decision-making bodies of the church, they can marginalize it. John knows that youth bring virtues that have been lost with the passing of years. When these virtues are absent, the church is vulnerable.

(4) *The theological problem of the world.* John's ecclesiology is difficult for many of us. We are not to love the world or *anything* in it. Of course, we can redefine this by saying John really has in mind those things that are abhorrent to the godly life: sinful cravings, lust, and pride (v. 16). But this does not sweep away the problem. John believes that the world outside of Christ is a treacherous place that can do irreparable harm to believers.

If we take this view seriously, we will have to change the tone of our preaching. We must be candid about the threat of the world. We must be forthright that a *boundary* does exist between our lives in Christ and the life promoted in the world. Unfortunately, for many of us such preaching is difficult, if not embarrassing, because our lives are so utterly enmeshed with the world. And because we fail to warn believers in our churches about the character of the world, they become vulnerable to its influences. Paul had no difficulty with this sort of candor. He drew strict boundaries between the world and the church. The Ephesians were told to arm themselves for this battle (Eph. 6:10–18). The Corinthians were told to discern worldly wisdom from godly wisdom (1 Cor. 1:20–31) and to exhibit a conduct that is unlike the world's (2 Cor. 10:3). John encourages this sort of speech. He speaks of "overcoming" the world because of its inherent hostility to us (1 John 5:4–12).

It is not difficult for most of us to generate examples of how the world has lost its moral compass. Any perusal of print, television, or film media will render examples in abundance. Just sample HBO or the USA network for a month. But it is the more subtle incursion of hostile values that concerns me. For example, when Disney movies are no longer safe fare for children, something has changed. I recently watched *Rin Tin Tin K9 Cop* on the Family Channel with my youngest daughter and was astounded at the violence. The opening scene showed a captured Rin Tin Tin tied to the trigger of a huge shotgun (if he moved, his head would disappear), while the criminal poured gasoline around the dog and lit it. Fortunately the police came and filled the crook with bullets. All this in less than five minutes! Is this family fare today? Two hours later a slight move to another channel will produce even more amazing adult fare. Must I be tolerant?

No doubt examples from the media are only symptomatic of a deeper, more tragic catastrophe that is at work in our society. In 1975 Jacques Ellul published an influential book called *The New Demons*, in which he outlined the forces at work in the secular world.[15] We have witnessed the erosion of a Christian consensus undergirding society, and this has been joined with a "sacred" devotion to science and materialism, which now give us our cosmology. Yet while this is going on, new modern myths—new pagan religious forms—are erupting everywhere.

More recently Carl Henry announced the same judgment on the severity of the world's fall in *Twilight of a Great Civilization*.[16] He offers a penetrating critique of the moral and intellectual downfall of our society and calls on the church not only to erect boundaries, lines of demarcation separating church and world, but also to take the offensive, to attack the neo-paganism on our doorstep. The world is now a theological problem. When will we draw a "line in the sand"?

(5) *To what extent have worldly values invaded the church?* The allure of the world is strong. To cite a minor example, the allure of wealth, and of power in particular, has invaded our ranks. John is explicit in verse 16 that worldly desires and a boasting in our lifestyle should find no home among Christians. The world, he remarks, is going to disappear (cf. 1 Cor. 7:31), and therefore we should invest in places where "moth and rust" cannot enter (Matt. 6:19–20). Jesus tells a disturbing story about a man who fills barn after barn—mutual fund after mutual fund—and then one evening the Lord says, "This very night your life will be demanded from you" (Luke 12:16–21; cf. Matt. 16:26–27).

And yet how often do we defer leadership in the church to those who have been successful by worldly standards? Possessing wealth, having a successful business, wielding influence in the world—these things do not in themselves mean that one should have spiritual author-

---

15 J. Ellul, *The New Demons* (New York: Seabury, 1975).

16 C. Henry, *Twilight of a Great Civilization: The Drift Toward Neo-Paganism* (Westchester, Ill.: Crossway, 1988).

ity in the church. I recall on two separate occasions watching the leadership of a major Christian organization and a large, successful church defer completely to Christian laypersons in power because they had enjoyed secular success. "Why is he in charge?" I asked someone. "Because so many people work for him here—or would like to," came the answer. John is clear: When secular, worldly power forms the basis for Christian leadership, new demons have entered the church, and once more the church is vulnerable.

But the problem of the world's influence over the church's life runs far deeper than cosmetic examples of secular success running church boards. David Wells has written a brilliant study that not only outlines the ongoing intellectual, religious, and cultural corruption of the world, but how these post-Christian values are shaping the church's witness and thought. He shows that Western culture is being upended and the church is awash with change. Modernity has rearranged the reality of God in such a manner that he no longer makes a real difference in the church of today. Wells calls this a "silent revolution" that is barely noticed by its victims. As a result, the church is producing a "weightless God," who is of no consequence to those who believe. Listen to his comments in this regard:

> It is one of the defining marks of Our Time that God is now weightless. I do not mean by this that he is ethereal but rather that he has become unimportant. He rests upon the world as inconsequentially as not to be noticeable. He has lost his saliency for human life. Those who assure the pollsters of their belief in God's existence may nonetheless consider him less interesting than television, his commands less authoritative than their appetites for affluence and influence, his judgments no more awe-inspiring than the evening news, and his truth less compelling than the advertisers' sweet fog of flattery and lies.[17]

According to Wells, the church is in trouble (but barely knows it) because it has failed to discern the corrupting influences of the world, erect formidable boundaries, and make potent and compelling claims for the truth.

---

17 D Wells, *God in the Wasteland The Reality of Truth in a World of Fading Dreams* (Grand Rapids Eerdmans, 1994), 88

1 John 2:18–27

DEAR CHILDREN, THIS is the last hour; and as you have heard that the antichrist is coming, even now many antichrists have come. This is how we know it is the last hour. ¹⁹They went out from us, but they did not really belong to us. For if they had belonged to us, they would have remained with us; but their going showed that none of them belonged to us.

²⁰But you have an anointing from the Holy One, and all of you know the truth. ²¹I do not write to you because you do not know the truth, but because you do know it and because no lie comes from the truth. ²²Who is the liar? It is the man who denies that Jesus is the Christ. Such a man is the antichrist—he denies the Father and the Son. ²³No one who denies the Son has the Father; whoever acknowledges the Son has the Father also.

²⁴See that what you have heard from the beginning remains in you. If it does, you also will remain in the Son and in the Father. ²⁵And this is what he promised us— even eternal life.

²⁶I am writing these things to you about those who are trying to lead you astray. ²⁷As for you, the anointing you received from him remains in you, and you do not need anyone to teach you. But as his anointing teaches you about all things and as that anointing is real, not counterfeit—just as it has taught you, remain in him.

Original Meaning

WHEN WE MOVE to the fourth exhortation, John turns up the heat considerably. Suddenly we are told about the imminent crisis looming over his congregation. We read about "antichrists," "the last hour," and those who are leading many astray. And here for the first time we have an explicit description of those in his church who brought these divisions, former disciples who left the fold and yet continued to create havoc in the church. In this section John does two things: He equips and warns. He looks for safeguards that will help protect his people from the corrupting, hostile intentions of his opponents, and he is forthright in his warnings about them. In previous exhortations John uncovered the opponents' threats along moral or ethical lines: They were worldly and engaged in sin that they defended. Now John looks to doctrinal error (as he did abstractly in 1:1–4) and explicitly lists its ingredients.

The Problem: Dissolution and Controversy (2:18–19)

THE URGENCY AND passion of John comes through not simply in his form of address ("dear children," Gk. *paidia;* cf. 2:13) but in his announcement that it is now "the last hour." Two things signal to John the arrival of this hour. (1) The appearance of "antichrist," technically, anyone who opposes Christ, represents a focused hostility toward the gospel.[1] (2) The dissolution of his own congregation (seen in the departure of some Christians) indicates that the antichrist has now laid siege to John's church.

The first of these signals presents a difficult problem. In what sense is it "the last hour"? How can John be right since, to put it frankly, quite a few "hours" have passed since this letter was written and the end has still not come? Some scholars have been critical, arguing that for New Testament writers like John the phrase "the last hour" implied the period of time just before the end and therefore, logically, John was wrong. This view suggests that the early Christians believed in the imminent arrival of Christ in power (his second coming) and that his delay brought a major crisis on the church. Peter, for instance, acknowledges that people were scoffing at the church because Christ's announced second coming had not happened (see 2 Peter 3:3–7).[2]

---

1. The term *antichrist* appears only in the Johannine letters (1 John 2:18, 22, 4:3; 2 John 7). This may refer to a single person or more likely it refers to a disposition of hostility to the things of Christ and a denial of his sonship. As such 'the spirit of antichrist' could describe many opponents of the church.

2. Some interpreters have sought to soften the problem, noting that John does not write "*the* last hour" but rather leaves the phrase without a definite article. This suggests that John had in mind an era of time (it is "*a* last hour"), not a specific period when Christ returns.

However, another view is more helpful. John may be speaking theologically rather than chronologically. The early Christians understood that the first coming of Christ brought a change of eons, an unparalleled period when the knowledge of God, the presence of his Holy Spirit, and the defeat of Satan were at work. They were fond of speaking about this era eschatologically, for it encompassed elements of the "world to come." Christians were experiencing the last days or the last times, as if to say, all that was left for history to culminate was for Jesus to return a second time; that coming would complete what this era had begun (see Acts 2:17; 1 Cor. 10:11; Heb. 1:2; 1 Peter 1:20; cf. Joel 2:28; Mic. 4:1).

In this framework, the last times formed a last hour in which the struggle with evil and the unveiling of God's power would intensify (1 Tim. 4:1; Jude 18), though the exact knowledge of when the eschatological era was being culminated remained unknown. Jesus was clear that speculation about the end of the world was inappropriate (see Mark 13:32, Acts 1:7). Yet he still gave an outline of those things that would characterize this era (Mark 13:28–37). There would be a cascade of falsehood and evil putting the church on the extreme defense. False christs and false prophets would be one feature (Matt. 24:24; Mark 13:22; cf. Rev. 13; 19:20). Paul even tells the Thessalonians to watch for "the man of lawlessness," who is the antichrist, a powerful broker of evil forces (2 Thess. 2:1–12). Consequently, John is reminding his readers that the concentration of evil they are now experiencing fits perfectly the formula announced by Jesus and his apostles for the end of time.

The most helpful image to explain this view of history comes from J. H. Newman, a nineteenth-century pastor.[3] History has changed its direction, says Newman. It runs "not towards the end, but along it, and on the brink of it; and is at all times near that great event, which, did it run towards it, it would at once run into. Christ then is ever at our doors." Since the coming of Jesus, history has a new urgency, a sense that its end is at hand and the powers of the future are impinging upon it. Marshall cites Newman and illustrates his views thus:[4]

---

3. Cited in Marshall, *The Epistles of John*, 149ff., who in turn gives credit to F. F. Bruce's 1970 commentary for the full reference. See J. H. Newman, "Waiting for Christ," in *Parochial and Plain Sermons* (London: n p., 1896), 241

4 Ibid., 149–50

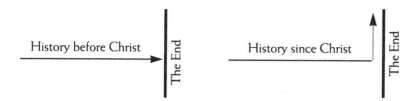

Thus, at any moment history could lapse over the line and bring about the end. And history's proximity to the line (The End) will be signaled by the devastating events described here and elsewhere in the New Testament.

How long will this time take? Sometimes the "last hour" refers to a short period (John 4:23); sometimes its length is longer (16:2). Peter warns that God's measuring of time is not like ours, for to the Lord a thousand years is like a day (2 Peter 3:8–10). God is above time. But when the end does come—and here the New Testament writers are in one accord—it will surprise everyone, including Christians. It will be seen by unbelievers as an unexpected catastrophe (Matt. 24:36–44; 25:1–13, 14–30; Mark 13:32–36; 1 Thess. 5:2; 2 Peter 3:10).

But what has prompted John's interest in the end times? John sees in the personal catastrophe of his congregation echoes of the eschatological evil that waits on the world's horizon. The work of antichrist has been successful in his own church. Verse 19 gives us our first explicit description of the secessionists. These are men and women who once lived as a part of John's community but have now departed. And no doubt, since he mentioned antichrists in the previous verse, John views these people and their teachers/leaders as bearing the spirit of antichrist. They stand opposed to correct teaching and deny essential tenets of the faith (2:22; 4:3–6). In fact, they have broken a cardinal rule of the Johannine community by failing to love or failing to remain in community when disagreements were intense.

Their departure is evidence, says John, that they were never a part of the church in the first place. Their falsehood has been unveiled. This judgment presents us with a number of serious theological problems that we should discuss in our application. Were these people ever Christians? Does this mean that the church is made up of believers and unbelievers today? And if they were and are not now Christians, what does this imply for our understanding of the perseverance of the saints?

The Protection: Anointing (2:20-21)

JOHN WORKS TO equip his faithful followers regarding the deceitful teachings of these secessionists. There is a play on words here in Greek. If the secessionists represent the antichrist (*antichristos*), now we learn that John's Christians bear an anointing (*chrisma*) that can aid and protect them. *Antichristos* and *chrisma* originate from the same Greek verb, *chrio*, "to anoint."

But what is this anointing? The Greek word simply means "what is rubbed on," whether it is ointment or paint or medicine. In the New Testament (and Judaism) it took on a specialized use, referring to the gift of the Holy Spirit that would hallmark the reign of a king (2 Sam. 2:7), the authority of a prophet (Isa. 61:1), and the Messiah (11:1). "Christ" thus means "Anointed One," since by definition the Messiah is filled with God's Spirit in an unparalleled way.

Thus when John speaks of the Christian's anointing, he likely has in mind their endowment with the Holy Spirit, a gift that is able to give all knowledge.[5] Some interpreters see this instead as a body of teaching that empowers the believer against heresy.[6] I disagree. John's Gospel again and again refers to believers as recipients of the Spirit (14:17, 26; 15:26; 16:13). John's community defined its membership with reference to the Spirit. In 1 John 4:13 certain knowledge of life with God is discerned *pneumatically*. Men and women in this congregation received the Holy Spirit and through this mystical experience gained a new knowledge of life.

If this was the character of teaching in John's church, then it is also likely that the secessionists justified their teachings with the same pneumatic, or spiritual, authority. John 16:13 says clearly that the Spirit would have more to say than Jesus had spoken. It is not difficult to speculate that the secessionists took up this promise as fuel for their own inspiration; their words completed a theological picture that Christian tradition did not know.

---

5 The NIV adds the word "truth" in verse 20, "and all of you know [the truth]." The Greek text simply says, "and you have an anointing from the holy one and you know everything (*panta*)." If we follow some manuscripts and spell *panta* as *pantes*, it becomes the subject of the verb, "and all (*pantes*) of you know." It seems best to take the first option, giving the verb an object.

6 W. Grundmann, "χρίω, κτλ," *TDNT*, 9.579–80, I H Marshall and C. H Dodd are similarly inclined

Curiously, John does not confront the secessionists with his own apostolic authority as Paul did the Judaizers in Galatia. He realizes that in such a context, this sort of authority is useless. Instead, he must give tools from within the pneumatic setting that will strengthen his followers' faith. No longer must they be victimized by others claiming a unique, prophetic endowment. John therefore tells his followers that they too have the Spirit; *they have an endowment of equal power* and must discern the truth spiritually—through the vehicle of the Spirit within them. John does not deny the power of the Spirit (as many pastors might). Instead, he wants his people to test the spirits (4:1–6).

In the Johannine literature the Spirit is called "the Spirit of truth" for good reason (John 4:17; 15:26; 16:13; 1 John 4:6). Here in verse 21 John writes that one by-product of having the Spirit of God is knowing the truth. That is, no teaching from the Spirit will ever diverge from what has been revealed to us in Jesus Christ. In John 14:26 the Spirit will recall what Jesus said in history. In 16:13 the Spirit will not speak on his own but "will speak only what he hears." Therefore, the work of the Spirit must always submit to the revelation we have in Jesus Christ. If anyone comes along with a claim to have the Spirit and contradicts what we know of Jesus in history, that is, as recorded in the Gospels, his or her anointing is fraudulent. This is one meaning of John's repeated phrase to hold on to "what you have heard from the beginning" (v. 24). These "beginning things" are the events and words in Jesus' life, especially as recorded in the Fourth Gospel. For the Johannine community, they form the bedrock of the church.

The Heresy: Incarnational Christology (2:22–23)

JUST AS THE opponents of John have been explicitly identified, so now the false teaching they have been promoting is outlined for us. At first reading it sounds as if these people are denying the messiahship of Jesus. But this is unlikely since they were once members of John's church and understood the gospel story. The crux is where we put our emphasis in the statement in verse 22. They are not disputing Christ's messianic credentials; rather, they disputed that Jesus—the man of Nazareth—qualified as this messianic figure. The liar is the one who denies that "*Jesus* is the Christ."

This denial is clearer if we look ahead in this letter. John's opponents struggled with the notion of incarnational Christology, namely, the notion that God could become human—fully flesh—when he sent his Son as the Christ. "This is how you can recognize the Spirit of God," John writes in 4:2–3: "Every spirit that acknowledges that Jesus Christ has come in the flesh is from God, but every spirit that does not acknowledge Jesus is not from God. This is the spirit of the antichrist, which you have heard is coming and even now is already in the world." Second John 7 is similarly explicit: "Many deceivers, who do not acknowledge Jesus Christ as coming in the flesh, have gone out into the world. Any such person is the deceiver and the antichrist."

We learned earlier the propensity among Hellenistic Christians to entertain some forms of dualism in which the realms of God and humanity were kept strictly apart. The Christian religious system was agreeable everywhere with the exception of this one point. Greeks argued that God's divinity could not be compromised with the things of this earth (see above on 1:1–4). Spirit and flesh were utterly separate, and those who truly had the Spirit, who were initiated into secret wisdom and knowledge, realized the utter enmity between these two spheres. John's response is unequivocal. People who teach like this are "liars" (v. 22) and have nothing to do anymore with either the Son or the Father (vv. 23–24). In a word, they are no longer Christians.

It is interesting to reflect on why John finds this one theological point so important and why any compromise is unacceptable. In a word, to deny incarnational Christology is to deny important theological interests in revelation and soteriology. (1) Incarnation—that is, historic enfleshment in time and space—means that God has genuinely penetrated our world and made himself known. Truth is not a matter of experience but a matter of history. Our vision of God is anchored in *what has happened objectively*, not in our perception of who he may be. Incarnation makes revelation possible because God has signaled once again his love for this world and his desire to show himself to it. The Fourth Gospel urges again and again that Jesus is the *human display* of the Father (John 1:18; 14:1–14). This is an important point that still needs to be underscored, for we live in a world that denies the objectivity of truth and the possibility of revelation.

(2) Incarnational theology is essential to our understanding of salvation. It is the true union of God and flesh, the complete fusion of divinity and humanity, that makes Christ's sacrificial death potent. He represented our humanity on the cross by truly bearing our humanity

to Golgotha. And he now represents our humanity before the Father by truly bearing our transformed humanity before him in the resurrection/ascension. John rightly saw that the loss of this one doctrine was critical for the intellectual survival of the church. Without it, the center would be removed from the Christian faith.

Objective and Subjective Safeguards (2:24–27)

JOHN'S ANTIDOTE TO this problem is interesting. He suggests two weapons that should always be available and ready in the Christian's arsenal. Objectively, John believes that right belief is rooted in our recitation of the historic facts about our faith. Subjectively, we need to hone our skills of spiritual discernment so that those who come bearing some spiritually compelling doctrine can be weighed by the Spirit of God within us.

In 2:24–25 John seeks to anchor orthodoxy in "what you have heard from the beginning." This is a phrase we have already heard several times (1:1; 2:7, 13, 14) and will hear again (3:8, 11; 2 John 5, 6). The earliest objective teachings, the things grounded in Jesus' historical ministry, serve as anchors when theological storms sweep across the church's deck. This is the assured avenue for knowing the truth about the Father and the Son and the eternal life that comes from them. No doubt John has in mind the Fourth Gospel, which bore a firm witness to Jesus' historical ministry. Its pages were quickly becoming the standard by which theology would be judged. As we mentioned in the introduction, some scholars think that in this period not only did the Fourth Gospel discover a new value, but an early edition of it may have enjoyed a fresh editing by the Evangelist. Critical passages such as John 1:1–18 may have been penned at this time, including especially 1:14, with its crystal-clear affirmation of Jesus' incarnation.

But John goes further. More safeguards are needed for his people. When false teachers with charismatic authority are leading people astray (v. 26), men and women need to be equipped to confront them spiritually as well as intellectually. That is, subjective safeguards are needed too. Therefore, in verses 27–28 John echoes what he said in verse 20 and once again affirms the qualitative importance of the average Christian's anointing in the Spirit. No impostors can come along and say that their anointing is superior or that they have more of Jesus than someone else. On the contrary, the gift of the Spirit is the same for all.

We should be careful, however, not to think of this objective and subjective preparation as entirely separate. Intellectual readiness is not distinct from spiritual readiness. To John, the Spirit's work encompasses both: It is the Spirit who enlivens our thinking and gives discernment to our reflection; it is the same Spirit who likewise awakens our spiritual faculties, giving us gifts of wisdom, discernment, and knowledge.

The aim of all this is preparation (v. 27). John writes that "you do not need anyone to teach you," though not as a denial of the teaching office in the church! He is not setting aside the authority of pastors trying to instruct their congregations. Rather, *John is invalidating the authority of the false teachers.* If they were validating their new theological insights through the authority of the Spirit, as I suspect they were doing, and if John's congregation likewise shares in this Spirit *equally,* this self-promoting authority diminishes.

John goes on to make a final suggestion. There are true and false anointings, true and false spiritual experiences. An anointing that leads to error, that misrepresents Christ—an anointing that detracts from "what was from the beginning"—may be no anointing at all. It may in fact be a falsehood. Thus John will not permit anyone to say that the Spirit inspires rival theological points of view. Only one inspiration comes from the Spirit of God—the anointing that affirms the church's historic beliefs in Jesus Christ. Again, as in verse 24, inspiration must forever be judged at the bar of historical revelation. Any that cannot pass must be deemed untrue.

 ALTHOUGH THE CHURCH today is not frequently assailed by the sort of theological heresy outlined here, nevertheless there are substantial parallels between John's experience with schism and his attempt to equip his congregation. The denial of Jesus' humanity has come up in certain quarters of the church, and no doubt it should not be overlooked.

But the Johannine context described in these verses introduces a larger topic, a topic germane to church life today: What do we do when schism puts us in its grip? What do we do when members of the congregation feel that they are being led under the direction of the Holy Spirit into new areas of belief and experience? And worse still, what do we do when pastoral authority is rejected *because (it is claimed) such authority is not in touch with the power of God to speak today?*

John's response is crucial for my understanding. First, John has an eschatological outlook that puts such erroneous teachings and church ruptures in their proper context. They are characteristic of the last days, characteristic of the tenor of the time when Christ will return and the end will break upon us all. He is not so much announcing "the end" as he is describing the present as bearing features that betray those of the end.

This is an important distinction. John is not apocalyptic, saying that the end is coming tomorrow; he is writing and living within an eschatological schema that says there are features present in his day that go along with the end times, and when these features begin to accumulate in history, two things are true: The end *may* break upon us and we must therefore be ready.

While certain themes may be difficult to bridge to our era, I am convinced that men and women today live with an eschatology. That is, the cumulative crises of recent decades have shaped a worldview that knows a terminus. This is perhaps one of the distinguishing marks of the so-called "Generation X," people born after 1960. They bear little confidence that the world can improve, and they often live out a pessimistic eschatology.

The popular recent book *Thirteenth Generation: Abort, Retry, Ignore, Fail,* by Neil Howe and Bill Strauss, describes in breathtaking detail the pessimistic outlook of these young people. Listen to one college graduate:

> I think we are all in a sense doomed. [I'm talking about] downward social mobility. We hear a lot about the great social mobility in America—with the focus on the comparative ease of moving upwards. What's less discussed is how easy it is to go down. And I think that's the direction we're all heading in. And I think the downward fall is going to be very fast. . . ."[7]

---

7 N. Howe and B Strauss, *Thirteenth Generation Abort, Retry, Ignore, Fail* (New York: Vintage, 1993), 99

It is here that Christians can interpret that despair. John's community despaired as well—just consider the odds against them in their pagan world. But John gives hope through his Christian explanation of things: Disintegration is an expected result in history and God is watching history unfold. This is an important "bridge point" that will connect powerfully today. Jill Nelson, a high school student in Washington, D.C., believes, "The way society presents it, I'll either be strung out on drugs, a manager at McDonalds or a lawyer."[8] Christian ministry to Jill has high potential when it addresses her desperate view of history.

Second, John also has a strategy for equipping his people so that they will not fall prey again. He understands that they must be armed to confront the many prophets and inspired leaders who come along. This too connects vitally in our day because the same problems exist. Religious movements continue to flourish, and all promise to deliver compelling answers and experiences. Remarkably, young people who are sharply critical of the church and "religion" are easily swayed by these new prophets. Furthermore, within healthy, growing congregations voices of authority—voices claiming to be empowered by the Spirit—challenge the course of life as usual. John says there must be a strategy. Christians must be equipped to discern new voices that claim to be from God.

Finally, John is unashamed to use an assertive, aggressive tone to fight for the well-being of his flock. Here we have the universal pastoral dilemma that turns on two cherished values in the church: our commitment to unity and our commitment to the truth. Every church in every age has wrestled with this theme, and John's wrestling is a struggle from which we can benefit. But the problem also has practical and personal dimensions. Does this mean that friendships should dissolve for the sake of the truth? Does this mean that the church should chastise—or even expel—some who deny what is true? Each of these dimensions within the passage beg for attention in our modern churches today.

---

8 Ibid , 108.

DEALING WITH CONFLICT paralyzes most of us. It is painful because if we are honest and confront people with their misbehavior, relationships may be ruined and in some cases whole communities fractured. In a church context, the paralysis is the same. There are occasionally those who step forward with alluring influence and erroneous teaching, *and they gain a following.* Our impulse is to correct them gently and heal what divisions may have occurred so that the community will remain intact. The unity of the body of Christ is often foremost on our minds.

These verses are interesting because John has experienced precisely this sort of conflict. His church has been ruptured by members who have departed—members who have split the congregation—because they saw things differently. But although the situation is painful, John is not paralyzed by it. He interprets it and tells the remaining members of his congregation how to address it.

(1) *Building an eschatological climate.* Throughout history the church has often suffered the assaults of heresy and persecution and tried to interpret them eschatologically. That is, when the Christian life begins to bear the weight of these troubles, when signs of tribulation increase, life is approximating the climate that characterizes the end of time, and therefore the church takes hope and is warned. We can graph the church's life as an irregular line that moves between eras of comfort and eras of persecution. This cycle has repeated itself for centuries, and in some cases Christians have misunderstood their histories, urging an apocalyptic message that the end is at hand.

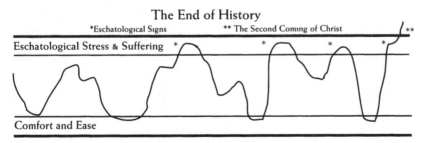

The End of History

John would have us build a climate in the church that heightens eschatological awareness so that when troubles overwhelm us, instead of predicting confidently the arrival of the end, we will say that we are in a period that hallmarks features of the end and that in this instance may actually carry us over the threshold that ends human history. The above chart illustrates the cycles of life the church has known. Times of ease are followed by times of struggle. When struggle occurs, such experiences begin to sound like the sufferings listed in, for example, Mark 13. This does not necessarily mean that the end is here, but that the end will be characterized by suffering such as this. And one day such suffering will be greeted by the return of the Lord.

All of this serves one purpose: to equip Christians so that they are not discouraged when severe difficulties and turmoil erupt. *Eschatological readiness, in other words, has a pastoral function.* It interprets struggle and dispels the despair that accompanies it. It teaches us to watch for changes in history, to watch for "antichrists," and to be alert for times when history betrays elements of the end.

Of course, one problem that accompanies this outlook is the irresponsible predictions of the end offered by each generation's apocalyptic prophets. In 1991, during the height of the Gulf War, I happened to visit a Christian family bookstore and scanned the "prophecy shelf." And there it was: Saddam Hussein of Iraq was boldly being introduced as the Antichrist. Curiously, I also found an older book still in print, saying the same thing about Mikhail Gorbachev, the leader of the former Soviet Union. Writers like Dr. John Walvoord (former president of Dallas Seminary) were making confident predictions:

> The rise of military action in the Middle East is an important prophetic development. While wars in Korea, Viet Nam, and Europe were not necessarily prophetically significant, all end-time prophecy pictures the Middle East as the center of political, financial, and military power at the end time."[9]

The New Testament communities were not unaware of the problem of unrestrained apocalyptic voices. In Mark 13:5 Jesus describes those who exploit apocalyptic passions, and in 2 Peter 3:3–7 Peter describes cynics who jeered at Christian predictions of the end.

---

9 J Walvoord, *Armageddon, Oil and the Middle East Crisis* (Grand Rapids· Zondervan, 1991), 48. The extent of this fantastic interest is hard to imagine. I have been interviewed by Christian TV and radio programs whose sole interest is to determine if the current array of politics in the Middle East, particularly the Palestinian Peace Accords, fulfills prophecy and is a sign of the end

Nevertheless, the New Testament does not warn us about eschatological zeal as much as it does about the prospect of losing an eschatological vision. Be ready, Jesus and Peter urge, for the coming of the end will be like a thief in the night (Matt. 24:43–44; 2 Peter 3:8–10). The challenge of Christian leadership is discerning how to promote an eschatological worldview without inspiring doomsday apocalypticism.

(2) *The problem of errant believers.* John never tells us explicitly the history or the character of the people who have left the church. Were they faithful Christians once but had now moved into the darkness? Were they lapsed Christians? Or were they never really a part of the community in the first place? First John 2:19b seems to deny their membership: "Their going showed that none of them belonged to us." By *belonging* does John mean that they were never a genuine part of his community? Or more severe still, does he mean that they were never Christians in the first place?

This opens a veritable host of theological questions. Is it possible for believers to step into wrong doctrine and thereby jeopardize their entire standing before God? Does this error make impotent God's grace in their lives? If such errors are possible, where is this doctrinal threshold, this line that may be crossed? How do I avoid inflicting fellow Christians with fear and anxiety, or how do I avoid the temptation of using this threat as inappropriate power over my people? While there may be a number of critical theological or spiritual issues that, if denied, place our lives in jeopardy, John's letter places significant emphasis on one issue: the doctrine of Jesus Christ. Whenever the exclusive place of Jesus Christ is jettisoned, when his lordship is lost, serious consequences follow.

It is interesting to me that these people left the church *voluntarily.* Is this John's pastoral strategy? Compare this with Paul's expulsion of a notorious sinner in 1 Corinthians 5:1–5! John stood firm and would not compromise on the essentials of belief and experience and permitted the secessionists to discover their own discomfort alone. And after a while, they departed.

But of course, we cannot be naive. It is not simply that these people were wrongheaded in their beliefs. They were in error and were aggressively teaching others to join their ranks and to abandon the traditional teaching of the leadership. In that sort of pastoral setting, the stakes are high. I cannot imagine that John was simply passive, gently coaxing everyone to find a middle ground theologically. He no doubt moved to the offense (his tone in this letter makes it everywhere evident) and kept up the pressure, urging conformity with what had been taught from the beginning.

(3) *Struggling with authority in a charismatic setting.* Today while mainline denominations are experiencing breathtaking declines, charismatic/Pentecostal churches are witnessing strong growth. In fact, the explosion of Christian life in Africa, Asia, and Latin America is chiefly charismatic in nature. A friend who is a pastoral leader in West Africa put it to me succinctly once: "Our churches seek power—your American churches seek reasonable faith. We are pursuing the more biblical model!" In Evanston, on the north side of Chicago, and in Wheaton near our college, the Vineyard Fellowship, a charismatic denomination, is growing at rates other Protestant churches can only envy. Another rapidly growing church is the Episcopal Church—now with dance, banners, healing services, charismatic worship, and record growth.

What does a pastor do when a faithful believer, newly filled by the Holy Spirit, challenges pastoral authority on the basis of that Spirit? I once attended the Society of Pentecostal Studies, a national fellowship of charismatic and Pentecostal scholars, and remember hearing pastors confide how authority issues in their congregations were some of their most difficult problems. If the Spirit plays a prominent role in congregational life and if speech gifts and teaching gifts are commonplace, pastoral authority has difficulty appealing to intellect or office.

John realizes this and does not attack his opponents on the basis of such institutional or academic authority. He makes two appeals. First, he assures his followers that *every* Christian bears the Spirit and therefore, by implication, the average believer does not need to be led about as if uninitiated: 2:20, "you have an anointing . . . and all of you know!" 2:27, "the anointing you received from him remains in you, and you do not need any one to teach you!"

When Christians are not given a theological system that incorporates pneumatology, they are vulnerable to spiritual sabotage. I recall when I was in college going to my pastor and asking about baptism in the Holy Spirit. Someone had told me that without it, I was an incomplete Christian. I have two painful memories. At first my pastor appeared stumped and speechless. Then he reached for an old thick concordance to see where the Bible talked about such things. He barely knew where to look. My confidence in him evaporated in minutes. My charismatic friend had even said, "Perhaps even this pastor does not have the Spirit." As I look back, I do not think that this was the case. The Spirit fills our lives and works among us in ways we cannot begin to measure. Nevertheless, this pastor had not learned—and therefore could not teach his people—about the things of the Spirit (or spiritual warfare). He could not interpret the growing charismatic context. As a result his people were ill-equipped to address authoritative charismatic leaders. At the age of twenty I knew that in my heart I was leaving this pastor's fold.

Therefore, it is crucial that we equip our laity with a complete understanding of Christian discipleship as intimately linked to the Holy Spirit. That is, when we talk about receiving Jesus Christ, we need to express this in terms that incorporate the Holy Spirit. The Spirit is not separated from Jesus; the Spirit is Jesus himself returned to us in power. He is Jesus-in-Spirit. John makes this clear in the Farewell Discourse of his Gospel (John 14–16). The coming Spirit is portrayed as the returning Jesus; the promised Spirit-experience is also a Jesus-experience.[10] We need to cultivate a *Christocentric pneumatology* that at once joins our view of Christ as Lord and our experience of Spirit as his powerful presence. Once Christians cultivate the powerful presence of Christ-in-Spirit, once they view their discipleship through their anointing, they will rarely be frustrated by such teachings.

John's second appeal is found in verse 24. In this charismatic setting, he reaches for a teaching authority but cannot appeal to his own role or position. He does not say, "Look, I'm an apostle and I know what Jesus said." His opponents would simply say that Jesus is in them as well. Consequently, John appeals to the Scriptures as the plumb line against which all teaching must be measured. A pastor with such a strategy is thus not pointing to himself/herself as having theological jurisdiction. Rather, the Scriptures, what was taught "from the beginning," bear all authority. The Bible thus brokers theological disputes. In John's situation, he no doubt appealed to the Fourth Gospel and little else (since the New Testament as we have it was unavailable). But we have the full armor of God and must appeal to the full breadth of our Scriptures.

---

10. See G Burge, *The Anointed Community. The Holy Spirit in the Johannine Tradition* (Grand Rapids Eerdmans, 1987), 137–43

Few books explain this unity of Christ as Spirit as effectively as Thomas Smail's *Reflected Glory: The Spirit in Christ and Christians*.[11] Following academic study in Glasgow and Basel (under Karl Barth), Smail began his ministry as a parish pastor in his native Scotland. But then he had a profound, overwhelming experience in the Holy Spirit in the 1960s, which brought him into leadership in the charismatic renewal in the United Kingdom. This book is Smail's attempt to give a theological explanation to the lost role of the Spirit in the church. To my mind this often overlooked book should be on every pastor's shelf.

Smail explains the centrality of the Spirit for every dimension of our faith—from our understanding of the Gospels to the sacraments. But his chief concern is to argue that Christian experience is an experience of Jesus-in-Spirit. Christian life is not merely a cognitive embrace of Christ; it is an engagement, an encounter with Christ in the Spirit. Are these two blessings—Christ and the Spirit—or one? Smail remarks:

> [If we ask,] "How many blessings are there?" the NT answer is "essentially one." God has given us his one gift of himself in his Son, and everything else is contained in him. "Blessed be the God and Father of our Lord Jesus Christ, who has blessed us *in Christ with every spiritual blessing* in the heavenly places" (Eph 1:3). However many and varied our spiritual experiences, they all have their unity and significance in the fact that they all proceed from him, reflect him, and glorify him. He is the center and unity of all that comes to us from God, and anything that does not derive ultimately from that center, whatever its experiential quality, is without Christian value or content.[12]

Therefore, experiencing the Spirit must be an experience of Jesus, and experiencing Jesus must be an experience of the Spirit. Smail warns that the charismatic/Pentecostal error is to make the Spirit's blessing separate from Jesus. On the other hand, noncharismatics explain the Christian experience of Christ without reference to the Spirit. In his view both approaches are wrong.

---

11. T. Smail, *Reflected Glory The Spirit in Christ and Christians* (Grand Rapids: Eerdmans, 1975).

12. Ibid., 45.

(4) *Is division the ultimate pastoral catastrophe?* When a congregation suffers a severe division in its fellowship and splits, pastors experience anxiety, shame, and loss. Certainly, they wonder, more could have been done. Perhaps they should have been more gentle or worked harder at compromise. They feel blame if their church loses numbers. No matter what the explanation for the schism, most people on the outside will infer that there has been some pastoral deficiency, some failing in leadership, insofar as unity could not be maintained.

John's letter impresses me with the number of times he speaks about the love of the community. First John 2:10–11 is a clarion call to fidelity and unity in the body of Christ. Unity, therefore, is seriously valued by John.

However, one awkward thought comes through these verses: *There comes a time when leadership must sacrifice unity for the sake of the truth.* Sometimes right belief is more important than cohesion and oneness. Unity is not the ultimate virtue in the Christian faith. John here is a coconspirator in the splitting of his church because he has stood firm in the truth. Certainly he mourned for these people, but he did not regret his decision (2:18–19).

This, of course, leads us to a question of pastoral leadership that we cannot answer. At what point is it appropriate to sacrifice unity? At what point is the communion of believers secondary to the truth? What truths bear such importance? As I write, evangelicals such as myself serving in mainline denominations struggle with just these questions. Unity that does not regard the truth we know in Jesus Christ may be a unity not worth cherishing.

1 John 2:28–3:10

A ND NOW, DEAR children, continue in him, so that when he appears we may be confident and unashamed before him at his coming. ²⁹If you know that he is righteous, you know that everyone who does what is right has been born of him.

³·¹How great is the love the Father has lavished on us, that we should be called children of God! And that is what we are! The reason the world does not know us is that it did not know him. ²Dear friends, now we are children of God, and what we will be has not yet been made known. But we know that when he appears, we shall be like him, for we shall see him as he is. ³Everyone who has this hope in him purifies himself, just as he is pure.

⁴Everyone who sins breaks the law; in fact, sin is lawlessness. ⁵But you know that he appeared so that he might take away our sins. And in him is no sin. ⁶No one who lives in him keeps on sinning. No one who continues to sin has either seen him or known him.

⁷Dear children, do not let anyone lead you astray. He who does what is right is righteous, just as he is righteous. ⁸He who does what is sinful is of the devil, because the devil has been sinning from the beginning. The reason the Son of God appeared was to destroy the devil's work. ⁹No one who is born of God will continue to sin, because God's seed remains in him; he cannot go on sinning, because he has been born of God. ¹⁰This is how we know who the children of God are and who the children of the devil are: Anyone who does not do what is right is not a child of God; nor is anyone who does not love his brother.

IN MOST OF John's exhortations we have witnessed his twin agenda: (1) to expose those who distort the truth through their false teaching and living, and (2) to reassure those who are staying the course in faithfulness to his teachings about Christ. After an explicit denunciation of his opponents in the previous exhortation, John now turns to build up his followers, strengthening their confidence before God. True, he cannot set aside the threats of his opponents (3:7) and even adopts severe language for those in their ranks (they are "of the devil," 3:8, 10). Nevertheless, the thrust of his message is to strengthen through exhortation, in order to decrease his followers' vulnerability by shoring up their assurance.

This is an important observation when we interpret many of these verses. For instance, in 3:4–10 John talks about the children of God not sinning. He is not trying to instill fear or threaten his followers with losing their salvation. In 3:2 he says clearly that they *are* children of God right now. Rather, he wants to encourage them to stay on a course *in which they are already confirmed*.

Brown notes an interesting symmetry in the section.[1] After an introductory word about continuing in Christ in verses 28–29a, two antithetical affirmations are launched:

- Everyone who acts justly (2:29b)
- Everyone who acts sinfully (3:4a)

These section heads are then followed by discussions (3:1–3 and 3:4b–6) that outline in greater detail what John has in mind. Then in 3:7–10, John contrasts behavior of just and sinful activity in order to distinguish the children of God and the children of the devil.

Moreover, the passage contains nine stylistic peculiarities that stand out.[2] Nine times the subject of a sentence is "everyone who," followed by a Greek participle (Gk. *pas ho* . . .). Also, if 3:1–3 is set aside for the moment (see below), the result is four antithetical pairs with the same structure and opposite themes.

---

1. Brown, *The Epistles of John*, 379ff.
2. Ibid., 418ff. On p. 419 Brown also shows how these verses can be arranged into an inverted parallelism or chiasmus.

29b	*everyone who* acts righteously	has been born of God
(3a	[*everyone who has this hope based on him*]	*makes himself pure*)
4a	*everyone who* acts sinfully	is really doing sin
6a	*everyone who* abides in him	does not commit sin
6b	*everyone who* commits sin	has never seen him
7b	*everyone who* acts righteously	is truly just
8a	*everyone who* acts sinfully	belongs to the devil
9a	*everyone who* has been born of God	does not act sinfully
10b	*everyone who* acts unrighteously	does not belong to God

What, then, do we make of 3:1–3? If John's strong affirmations are in 2:29b and 3:4, then 3:1–3 is a exclamation, a parenthesis in which the apostle pauses to reflect more deeply on what it means to be born of God. Even his choice of words is telling: "How great is the love the Father has lavished on us, that we should be called children of God!"

The Confidence of God's Children (2:28–29)

THE FIRST WORDS of verse 28 ("And now, dear children"[3]; cf. 2:12, 18) introduce a new section that builds on the earlier exhortation (2:27, "remain in him") and expands the thought in a new direction. John now uses the hope of Christ's coming as a fresh impetus for faithfulness.[4]

Two phrases are used to describe the second coming of Christ. (1) The first is "when he appears," a reference to Christ's "appearing." This expression occurs elsewhere for Christ's first coming in the Incarnation (1:2; cf. 3:5, 8). The verb actually means "to reveal"; in a sense John is thinking of the coming of Christ as a time when our Lord will be unveiled visibly before the entire world. (2) The other expression is the Greek term *parousia*, which was originally used for the arrival of

---

3 These words (Gk *kai nun, teknia*) serve as a common signal beginning a new section (John 17:5; 1 John 2 1, 12) Because John's flow of thought is not obvious, commentators often prefer to break the paragraph at 2:29 or 3:1. This division is supported by Marshall, Brooke, Schnackenburg, Stott, Bultmann, M. Meye Thompson, and Bruce.

4. Some critics have sought to question the authenticity of this passage because it is one of the few places where John indulges in futurist eschatology. John 5:25–30, however, supports the same eschatological outlook

a ruler or celebrity, accompanied by great interest and celebration.[5] Christ, John affirms, is going to arrive, and his appearing will at once dramatically set right the present circumstances and identify those who have been allied with him.

Christ's appearance will produce two reactions. Some people will experience confidence, while others will experience shame. Literally, the latter group will "shrink from him," while the former will enjoy confidence and assurance, even poise. The Greek term here is a favorite in the New Testament to describe the candor and ease with which Christians may approach God in prayer (Heb. 4:16; 1 John 3:21; 5:14). In 1 John 4:17 this will even be our disposition on the day of judgment. There is one important footnote, however. John's warning about shame is not meant to threaten Christians, who are born of God. He is here addressing those who stand in opposition to Jesus, for whom his climactic coming will be a catastrophe of the first order.[6]

Further confidence can be found in verse 29. When we exhibit God's righteous character, we show that we are born of him, just as a child might show the features of his or her parents. Knowing God and his righteous character fully leads to its imitation. But it does not work the other way around. Doing righteousness is not a precondition for being born of him, nor is it the means to divine birth. As Stott says, "A person's righteousness is thus the evidence of his new birth, not the cause or condition of it."[7]

The Identity and Purity of God's Children (3:1–3)

MENTION OF REBIRTH in 2:29 inspires John to reflect in praise on the splendor of God's love for us. The NIV fails to translate the first exclamation: "*Behold!* How great is the love the Father has lavished on us!" John expresses his wonder at this, using an unusual word to express the utterly foreign nature of this love. The Greek term *potapen* means "of what country" and thus implies that God's love is so unusual, so unearthly, so unique to our experience, that we barely expect its result: "We are called children [Gk. *tekna*] of God " (cf. Matt. 5:9). This

---

5 *Parousia* occurs only here in the Johannine literature, but it is a common term used by Paul (1 Cor. 15 23; 1 Thess 2:19, 3:13, 4 15; 2 Thess 2:1; etc.)

6. Thompson, *1–3 John*, 85

7 Stott, *The Epistles of John*, 118.

transaction is not imaginary, and John buttresses it with a final phrase to cement it firmly ("And that is what we are!"). Marshall points out that this is an act of "legitimation," in which a father names his child and thereby makes a permanent claim to identity and ownership.[8] Hence it is not in the child's hands! Rather, this identity is entirely in the Father's hands, so that the child's security is assured.

Further confidence in our place with God is found in our relation with the world (3:1b). The intimate knowledge shared between the believer and the Father is now contrasted with the absence of such knowledge found in the world. The NIV makes a free translation of 3:1b, changing its meaning slightly. The verse begins with the Greek *dia touto* ("on account of this"), which the NIV has referring forward: *"The reason the world does not know us is that* it did not know him." This means that the world's ignorance of us is theological: It has never known God and thus cannot recognize his children.

On the other hand, some say that the phrase should refer back to what was in the previous sentence in 3:1a.[9] A literal translation might read: "Therefore, we are called children of God—and so we are! For this reason the world does not know us."[10] We might paraphrase 3:1 thus: "God has given incredible love to us! He has even made us to be his children! And this is the reason the world does not know us, for the world has not known the Father either." This second reading is striking because it suggests that the children of God, *because of their relation with the Father,* have become an enigma to the world. Of course, it is true that the world has not known the Father as well, and this contributes to its ignorance of and hostility toward God's people.

Again and again John repeats that *now* we are God's children. It is an established fact that God's love controls. In 3:2 John reflects on how this fact will have consequences in the future. If now we have a glimpse of what it means to have the presence of the Father within us, when Christ comes there will be yet more overwhelming experiences for us. He will appear, we will appear just like him, and then we will

---

8 Marshall, *The Epistles of John,* 170–71.

9. Ibid., 171; Bultmann, *Johannine Epistles,* 48; Westcott, *The Epistles of John The Greek Text with Notes and Addenda,* 3d ed (1892, repr. Grand Rapids: Eerdmans, 1966), 96.

10. Brown gathers impressive evidence in defense of the NIV reading, *The Epistles of John,* 392.

see him exactly as he is.[11] In that day there will be an immediate and unmistakable unity between us and the Father. This is reminiscent of Paul's thought in 1 Corinthians 2:9: "No eye has seen, no ear has heard, no mind has conceived what God has prepared for those who love him." Inherent in this idea is Paul's notion that we will share in the glory of Christ (Rom. 8:17–19; Phil. 3:21; Col. 3:4).

Verse 3 contains the apostle's summary of his reasons for confidence in the Christian life. Fully knowing the Father's love, witnessing God's righteousness at work in us, experiencing the alienation of the world, and sharing a fresh confidence and joy at the prospect of Jesus' return—these things build renewed joy and assurance among Christians who may be struggling. This was certainly the setting for John's church with the schism that challenged his leadership and was poised to rend the church in two.

However, John's pastoral purpose here is not simply to reassure his readers' wavering faith. Ultimately his purpose is ethical. If we set our minds on the confident basis of God's promise, we will feel differently, and this will renew the character of our living. "Everyone who has this hope in him [Christ] purifies himself, just as he is pure" (v. 3). "Purity" (*hagnos*) occurs only here and refers to the absence of any stain. But John does not have ceremonial or ritual purity in mind. A mind singularly focused on meeting Jesus will discover a renewed power to pursue righteousness so that "when he appears," our righteousness will resonate with him. This recalls the words of Jesus in Matthew 5:8, "Blessed are the pure in heart, for they will see God."

God's Children and the Children of the Devil (3:4–10)

THE PREVIOUS DISCUSSION about righteousness and purity leads John to reflect on the tension between sin and perfection in the Christian life. As Stott illustrates, themes repeat themselves systematically:[12]

	1 John 3:4–7	1 John 3:8–10
Introduction	whoever does sin	whoever does sin
Theme	sin and lawlessness	sin and the devil

---

11. On the notion of seeing Christ or God in heaven, see Matthew 5:8; John 17:24; 1 Corinthians 13:12; 2 Corinthians 5:7; Hebrews 12 14.

12. Stott, *The Epistles of John*, 121.

The purpose of Christ's appearing	Christ appeared to take away sin	God's Son appeared to destroy the devil's work
Logical conclusion	no one who remains in him keeps on sinning	no one born of God keeps on sinning

The New Testament contains a number of general descriptions of sin, its character, and its compulsions (Rom. 1:18–3:20; James 4:17; 1 John 5:17; etc.). But few passages are as clear as 1 John 3:4–10. John's firm condemnation of sin suggests that he has in mind the secessionists, who have made some claim about sinlessness (see on 1:8–10). Paul confronted the same problem in Romans 6, where some believers had apparently viewed sinfulness as an opportunity to exercise the grace of God more fully. John is not only affirming the universality of sin once more, but is describing its inner character. *Sinners break the law.*

John's use in verse 4 of the term *lawlessness* (Gk. *anomia*, from *nomos,* "law") can be viewed in two ways. He may possibly be referring to the moral quality of sin as a breach of some divine command. Indeed, this is true. To commit sin is to offend a rule or word given by God. Many read the verse in this light and believe that John is describing the essence of sin. John's heretics were viewing immorality with indifference, and he writes to confront them.[13] In this sense lawlessness and sinfulness are virtually synonymous and interchangeable (and thus appear that way in the LXX).

But other interpreters have gone a different direction.[14] It seems unusual for John to interject a legal image here, since no hint of such a framework has yet appeared. Moreover, this is John's only use of *anomia,* so we cannot compare his use of the word elsewhere. Perhaps, therefore, it carries another meaning. In 2 Thessalonians 2:3, 7, the word describes "one who is lawless," one who stands in direct opposition to Christ at his second coming (hence the "man of lawlessness" in some translations). Therefore, John may mean that those who sin *participate in a lawlessness,* otherwise known as a rebellion, that is characteristic of the devil. This interpretation is helpful because in his previous section (see 2:18) John has described the antichrist and unveils the outbreak of evil that will accompany the end of the world.

---

13. Ibid., 122.
14. Technically, the term *law* does not appear in verse 4.

This interpretation finds added support if we follow the symmetry of the passage and look at 3:8. Here John makes the alignment crystal clear: Those who sin participate in the devil's work because they share the inherent character of the devil (v. 8a). Therefore, the decision to sin or not to sin is really a decision to reflect the character of Christ or Satan. John is describing what it means to be a true child of God—or of the devil (v. 10).

But, John adds, Jesus came to destroy all sin (3:5b, 8b). This means initially that his substitutionary sacrifice "carried away" our sins (cf. John 1:29) and the punishment that accompanies them. But John has more in mind. Jesus himself is pure—there is no sin in him—and if that is the case, his work also includes opposition to any sinfulness. In other words, Jesus' works include *both* removing the guilt of sin and defeating its presence altogether. Jesus is concerned with both justification *and* sanctification.

In order to make the point unmistakable, John goes on to say that no one who is truly in an intimate relation with Christ "keeps on sinning" (3:6). The same thought is repeated in 3:9 and 10 with different nuances (see also 5:18). Those who are born of God—those who have received the "seed" of God[15] and who are children of God—keep themselves free from sin. In fact, 3:9 makes the statement boldly: Such people "cannot go on sinning" because they have "been born of God."

John's characteristically bold statements in these verses have led to numerous struggles for the average Christian. *Does this mean that perfect holiness is God's expectation for me?* Initially, we can dismiss the notion that John believes Christians can be sinless. In 1:8–2:1 (cf. 5:16–17) he has said just the opposite, and we must allow that he is not contradicting himself one chapter later. Some have suggested that John is addressing different issues in 2:1 and 3:9. In the earlier section he is confronting proto-Gnostics, who have denied ethics in their embrace of a higher spirituality. The apostle rejects this. But in the present verses John presents an ideal, a vision of Christian character that is godly and above reproach. He would hardly say, "Be as much like Christ as you can." Rather, he would urge us to take on Christ's perfect character (even though it is an ideal beyond our reach).

---

15. John's use of the word "seed" could refer to the life God gives or even his word. It is likely that it may refer to the Holy Spirit, which, as John has insisted, is the exclusive endowment of the believer (cf. 1 John 2:20, 27).

A helpful solution is used by the NIV, concentrating on the tenses of the verbs. In Greek a present tense (in certain forms) indicates continuous, repeated activity.[16] Four key occurrences demand attention. (1) In 3:6a and 5:18 John says (lit.) that Christians "do not sin." The Greek verb "to sin" appears in the present indicative, and the sense is that we should not have the ongoing, self-endorsing habit of sin. (2) In 3:6b the construction uses a present participle (lit., "the one who sins," or better, "the one who continues to sin") to express the same notion. Once again, a participle with a present tense implies ongoing activity. (3) In 3:9a, a different verb is used ("to do sin"), and sin appears as a noun. Again, it appears as a present tense. (4) Finally, in 3:9b John describes Christians as "not able to sin." Both the verb ("to be able") and its infinitive ("to sin") appear in the present tense. It is useful to outline these verses carefully since they can be difficult in most English translations. Using this interpretation, John may well be emphasizing that ongoing, habitual sin should find no place in the believer's life.

But a number of interpreters have outlined problems with this view.[17] Chiefly, it seems that John may not be diligently following the grammatical function of present and aorist tenses this carefully. Among these scholars most see these texts controlled by the theological situation of the Johannine crisis. John is confronting people who seem to say that Christians are *free to sin* (since ethics is irrelevant anyway by their accounting). In 3:7 their influence is mentioned and a warning is sounded. Therefore the real subject is the permissibility of sin[18] or a sort of perfectionism that has no regard for morality.

Even if John does affirm that Christians will indeed sin, still, he is making a strong case for the holiness of the believer. In fact, those commentators in the Wesleyan or Holiness tradition (e.g., Marshall) point out that even within Judaism there was the expectation that in the era of the Messiah, surprising holiness would be commonplace (Ezek. 36:27).[19] Thus the New Testament writers (who viewed them-

---

16 Another tense, the aorist (a type of past tense), indicates individual or singular action in certain forms. In 2·1 John uses the aorist ("But if anybody *does sin*") to say "If someone commits *a sin*, Christ is our advocate "

17 See Smalley, *1, 2, 3, John*, 159ff

18 There are a number of solutions to this problem of sinlessness in 1 John, and the subject has received extensive scholarly attention I have given only the barest outline For an extensive survey, see Brown, *The Epistles of John*, 412–17

19. Marshall, *The Epistles of John*, 181–82

selves living in that era) fully expect near sinlessness to accompany the Christian life.

This is a subject that will take some discernment in our application below. Its pastoral implications are immense, and we will have to ask how closely this teaching squares with the practical experience of the Christian life.

WHILE MANY OF the sections we have studied in 1 John are shaped entirely by the apostle's conflict with the secessionists, the present section has a remarkable universal applicability. This is not to deny that the Johannine doctrinal struggle still influenced the passage. First John 3:7 provides an explicit warning against the author's opponents. Nevertheless, the congregational division, the crisis of leadership, and the corruption of orthodox Christology are not limited to John's first-century context. Therefore, as I read the passage and distill its meaning for today, my task seems to be easier. John is giving an exhortation that evokes themes that can be sounded in any age and context.

When John describes the essential meaning of living like God's children, two emphases are placed in the forefront: assurance and righteousness. Perhaps these two can even be subsumed under a wider category: *transformation*. In the midst of the conflicts in his church, John desires that his followers exhibit a thorough-going change in how they view themselves and their relationship with God. His people need a renewed vision for who they are and what God desires them to become. It is through the renewal of that vision that a transformation will occur—and that transformation will bear measurable fruit: They will discover greater *assurance* in their identity as God's children and will begin to exhibit the *righteous* character of Jesus Christ.

However, these exhortations are not aimed at simply making the Christians in John's church feel better. *His intentions are not purely therapeutic.* That is, his goal is not simply to help them have a victorious Christian life. We must always keep in mind that the Johannine context here is adversarial and that John's aim is therefore to strengthen his followers and protect them and so to make them less susceptible to the challenges and corruptions of his detractors. Consequently, when John speaks about perfection among Christians, he may well have in mind the secessionists, who seemed to deny ethics. But he no doubt has others in mind as well—his own followers, whose righteousness in comparison with their opponents should be stellar.

At the same time, there is much in this passage that offers sound pastoral therapy for Christians who, while not experiencing the threats of any opponents, still feel the same insecurities that one under threat may feel. In other words, even though the Johannine adversaries may be absent in a modern context, the symptoms that are native to such conflict (insecurity, vulnerability, etc.) are still with us today. And John's words about assurance and righteousness can thus play an essential role.

Therefore, it seems that my interpretative task, which calls for me to bridge these themes to my own day, is fully possible. Believers are looking for reassurance about their place before God and for some way to understand God's unyielding call for righteousness that does not create legalism. Unfortunately, my experience suggests that while we must balance these issues, we have not done well. Men and women of faith hear the call to holiness but cannot comprehend the nature of their security before the Lord. John's themes can be immediately bridged, but we need new, creative ways to express these truths today that powerfully reach our own people.

EVERY PASTOR AND Christian leader wants to strengthen the spiritual stamina of his or her flock. This is particularly the case when, as in John's church, opponents are at the door or in the pews. The natural question is, *What strategy works best to reinforce Christian discipleship?*

This passage opens up as many questions as it resolves. Yet it leads us into areas of reflection that are extremely pertinent even if we do not have all of the answers. John is a pastor with a pastor's heart. Therefore he knows, through the guidance of the Holy Spirit, what issues need to be addressed.

(1) *Assurance and rebirth.* Throughout this passage (and much of the letter) John repeats again and again that divine rebirth is a necessary feature of Christian discipleship (see 2:29; 5:1–2). This is the source

of our power to live a life not plagued by sin. It also gives us confidence that our identity is completely found in Christ and that even when he comes again, we will be filled with self-assurance.

When I was growing up as a child in a Lutheran church, such thoughts about divine birth were truly perplexing. We were baptized, we were confirmed, and we were regularly taught that discipleship included such practical matters as Bible reading, prayer, the Lord's Supper, and personal piety and obedience. For good measure Luther's *Shorter Catechism* was even given a place in our personal devotional lives! John's remarks about rebirth, however, implied to me that there was an experiential dimension to Christianity that I was missing. When John writes to tell his followers that it is their rebirth that gives them assurance, what happens when they cannot anchor their spirituality in some powerful ecstatic experience that validates the presence of God in their lives?

In order to answer this question, we must first look at what happens when a pastoral theology makes *experience* the centerpiece of Christian discipleship. Students at my college, for example, often ask one another to tell their "conversion story." This seems to reinforce the notion that a valid Christian life must have a dramatic beginning or at least a dramatic component. In evangelical/fundamentalist circles this may be a profound conversion experience. Among charismatics, it may be an ecstatic experience such as speaking in tongues or a healing.

Of course I am not denying that Christians must be born again—John 3 makes that perfectly clear!—nor am I saying that a powerful, transforming experience with the Holy Spirit should not be an important part of the Christian faith. I simply wonder if experiential theologies, that is, preaching that reinforces the centrality of experience, make faith tenuous. If *what I feel* in my Christian walk is where my assurance is anchored, then my confidence is frail indeed, for I cannot continue to manufacture those experiences nor can I reinvent them. And as time passes on and the earlier experiences become more and more dim, I find that they have less and less power to reassure me.

I am instructed by John's teaching that *feeling* the power of rebirth is not the foremost measure of being reborn. For John it lies elsewhere. My moral impulse to do right, to obey God's Word, to live an ethical life, is the first by-product of divine rebirth (2:29; 3:9). Admittedly, such ethical maturity lives in conjunction with a thoroughly informed orthodoxy (John would have it no other way). But it is Christian behavior, behavior that the world does not recognize and that the world finds incomprehensible, that shows us that something divine has happened within us, that we have been reborn.

It is interesting to note that throughout the Johannine literature the world not only fails to recognize Jesus but also cannot comprehend the behavior of his followers (John 15:18–27). This is further testimony to the foreignness of the experience of the Spirit. But what are the things the world finds impossible? John gives us little help, but we may speculate that it has something to do with our undivided devotion, loyalty, and obedience to the person of Jesus, *even when that devotion denies our self-interest.* This is the gist of John's message. Christian love for God and one's neighbor is a sacrificing love that is animated by supernatural power; it takes its model from what God has shown us in Jesus Christ—sacrificial love—and then extends that same quality of love within the world (John 16:12–17; 1 John 3:1).

(2) *Assurance and adoption.* In 3:1–3 John gives a second way we can know about our security with God. John remarks that we are to be known as children of God, and this ascription comes from his love that he initiates in our behalf. This leads John to an exclamation of praise.

A few years ago our family had the privilege of adopting into our home a little four-year-old girl named Grace. I have often reflected on how this experience is so much like our experience with God as he makes us his own. It was not Grace's merits that made the adoption happen, nor was it someone forcing us to do it. We decided independently that this was something we wanted to do. And one day, on February 20, 1992, all of us went to the Illinois court building in downtown Chicago, where a judge with solemn black-robed dignity and the smack of a gavel forever changed one little girl's name.

When John thinks about our status as "God's children," he has in mind this sort of absolute, unyielding decision initiated by God on our behalf. That is what leads John to exclaim, "How great is the love the Father has lavished on us that we should be called children of God!" It is an unmerited love, an unmerited adoption, a divine choice whereby we utterly become the Lord's possession. When this conceptual framework is firmly a part of our consciousness, when we discover that our security with God is out of our hands and firmly in his, assurance comes naturally. Confidence in our Christian identity comes simply through finding that God holds us secure. If we do not feel like a child of God or if others say that we do not exhibit certain criteria confirming our status as God's children, it makes no difference. *A divine gavel has fallen.*

I am frankly astonished at the number of times I have explained to classes of Christian college students about the unmerited love God has for us—how we are his children and he will never "unadopt" us—and how in the course of my explanation students from strong evangelical churches literally will cry. Their tears have nothing to do with the character of my presentation; instead, they point to the *insecurity* they have learned at their home churches. "If I don't feel like God's child, maybe I'm not." "If I can't always act like God's child, perhaps I never was." My office has witnessed such statements from the children of our evangelical households every semester for years.

(3) *Assurance and eschatology.* John writes in 3:3 that everyone who holds to his or her eschatological hope is purified. That is, if we have an expectation of the imminent return of Jesus and realize that we will be identified with him and unveiled as his children, it will have a galvanizing impact on our lives. Our faith will be strengthened and our resolve to live a godly life will increase.

But I wonder if this is really what happens. Apocalyptic preaching that reinforces the Second Coming and our meeting the Lord Jesus must be handled with extreme care. I believe many average Christians are filled with anxiety and fear at the thought of the Second Coming, and they wonder if *for them* it will be a day of joy. Using passages such as 1 Corinthians 3:10–15 and Jesus' parable of the talents in Matthew 25:14–30, many Christians teach that the day of Jesus' return will be a day of reckoning for everyone. When he comes back, he will want to know what we have been doing with the heritage he left behind.

John's purposes run along different lines. In 3:2 he says, "*Now* we are children of God," and *since* we bear Christ's image, when he appears, we will be like him. The return of Jesus will disclose the truth about God's relationship with us, not evaluate whether that relationship is satisfactory. Peter refers to this event as one of celebration and joy for believers (1 Peter 4:13), and Paul thinks of it as a time of divine reward (2 Tim. 4:8) and genuine encouragement (1 Thess. 4:18).

(4) *Righteousness and rebirth.* In the commentary section above I made clear John's intention when he speaks of the sinlessness of believers.

Those who are children of God, who bear Christ's character and are born of him, are not plagued with ongoing habits of sin. One evidence of God's presence in their lives is their sanctification. Yet while John urges us toward holiness, he is candid that perfection is not completely possible since he honestly says elsewhere that sinfulness is characteristic of every human (1:8; 2:1–2). There is thus a tension here, which is accompanied by a number of profound pastoral problems. On the one hand, we candidly admit to our fallenness and announce God's generous forgiveness. On the other hand, we exhort one another to pursue holiness, to become Christlike as we grow in Christian maturity.

Christian traditions differ on how they handle this delicate question. Some traditions, particularly in the Holiness churches, stress the demands of righteousness strenuously. In the Reformed tradition the emphasis on God's grace and love has made many of us uncomfortable with bold calls to holiness. For those of us in this latter community, the uncompromising words of John must be sounded again. "No one who lives in him keeps on sinning" (3:6). Sadly, there are many in our churches for whom habitual sin is nothing of real consequence. Even among Christian leadership, not everyone is comfortable speaking forthrightly about purity and righteous living.

(5) *Righteousness and assurance.* The difficult theological problem that attends to the subject of perfection is whether or not someone who continually sins, who consciously breaks God's law, puts himself or herself in spiritual jeopardy. That is, can habitual sin so violate our status as children of God that we lose any privileges that come through such a relationship? Another way to frame this question is to ask whether continuous sin reflects that we have already violated our status as God's children, or perhaps never known it in the first place.

This brings us full circle as we return to the subject of assurance. John's intention is to exhort his followers to superior Christian discipleship in a way that will strengthen their faith. Therefore, his appeals to holiness emphasize not the impossibility of sin but the connection to Christ. "*No one who is born of God* will continue to sin" (3:9). The assumption throughout is that John's audience *is* born of God, that they enjoy a redeemed place with the Father. *In light of that privilege, sin should have no place.* Holiness becomes an imperative fueled not by fear of jeopardy but by a heartfelt response to the security that God's love gives us. Cosmetic changes appear in our lives in response to threat. Permanent change comes to us when we are safe and assured in God's love; this safety must be anchored in the objective work of Christ on the cross.

However, at the risk of taking away the assurance that I have so carefully protected in the preceding paragraph, I cannot help but feel troubled by verses such as 3:6, 8, and 10. John seems to sound a warning here, a final and terrible warning, that lives characterized by sin, lives willfully disobedient and unrighteous, cannot be lives that are born of God (3:9), that know him and abide in him (3:6). Such persons possess the dreaded prospect of eternity without God. They are "the children of the devil" (3:10). Setting our pastoral concerns about assurance aside, does this warning have a valid place in the teaching and preaching of the church? It is like those passages in Hebrews that every Calvinist prefers to avoid, particularly Hebrews 6:1–8 (also chaps. 3 and 4), where the writer *warns* Christians not to fall into disbelief *as did the Israelites who fell in the desert and failed to enter the Promised Land.*

However I communicate this, I must weigh carefully the measure of exhortation and the measure of grace I serve up. I must be honest about both. But in the end, my aim is to strengthen, not to tear down; to fortify belief and resolve, not to weaken them through severe exhortation.

1 John 3:11-24

THIS IS THE message you heard from the beginning: We should love one another. ¹²Do not be like Cain, who belonged to the evil one and murdered his brother. And why did he murder him? Because his own actions were evil and his brother's were righteous. ¹³Do not be surprised, my brothers, if the world hates you. ¹⁴We know that we have passed from death to life, because we love our brothers. Anyone who does not love remains in death. ¹⁵Anyone who hates his brother is a murderer, and you know that no murderer has eternal life in him.

¹⁶This is how we know what love is: Jesus Christ laid down his life for us. And we ought to lay down our lives for our brothers. ¹⁷If anyone has material possessions and sees his brother in need but has no pity on him, how can the love of God be in him? ¹⁸Dear children, let us not love with words or tongue but with actions and in truth. ¹⁹This then is how we know that we belong to the truth, and how we set our hearts at rest in his presence ²⁰whenever our hearts condemn us. For God is greater than our hearts, and he knows everything.

²¹Dear friends, if our hearts do not condemn us, we have confidence before God ²²and receive from him anything we ask, because we obey his commands and do what pleases him. ²³And this is his command: to believe in the name of his Son, Jesus Christ, and to love one another as he commanded us. ²⁴Those who obey his commands live in him, and he in them. And this is how we know that he lives in us: We know it by the Spirit he gave us.

Original Meaning

I HAVE ALREADY suggested in the introduction (see pp. 41–44) that a natural break in the letter occurs at 3:11. This is a convenient division for a number of reasons: (1) It gives near balance to the letter's two halves (1:5–3:10 and 3:11–5:12). (2) If the Gospel of John was any model for the structure of the letter, its emphasis on the light and truth of God in the first half of John is followed by an emphasis on love in the community, a subject found in the second half. (3) First John 3:11 contains the phrase, "This is the message you heard from the beginning," a near copy of 1:5, "This is the message we have heard from him." In each verse the word "message" is the Greek word *angelia*, which occurs only at 1:5 and 3:11. Furthermore, the noun *angelia* can be translated "gospel," so that John defines "the gospel" as light and love, the twin themes of his letter.

This is not to say that there is a harsh break between the two sections. The emphasis in 3:11 is linked to 3:10 (loving one's brother or sister).[1] And in each section John intertwines the subjects of love and light as key concerns in his church. Indeed the two sections are linked in many ways, much as the two halves of the Gospel of John are linked. For instance, in the Fourth Gospel, the "Jews'" are Jesus' opponents, but after chapter 12, his interest turns to the quality of his followers' lives together with him (chaps. 13–17). Yet Jesus continues to speak of his opponents, though they noticeably slip into the background.[2] The same phenomenon happens in 1 John. The first half defines carefully the difference between those who live in the darkness and those who embrace the true light given in Jesus Christ; they are children of God, while the secessionists are children of the devil. Now in the letter's second half, John focuses on the quality of his followers' lives together. As Brown puts it, "The secessionists are still much in mind, but now one hears less directly of their boasts and claims. The secession has torn the life of the Johannine community, and the author is taking pains to rebuild that life. He does this by giving full stress to the gospel of loving one another."[3]

---

1. First John 3:11 likewise begins with *hoti*, meaning "for" or "because," making the subject of this verse grammatically dependent on 3:10.
2. See Brown, *The Epistles of John*, 468.
3. Ibid.

A clear subdivision runs from 3:11–24. First John 4:1 not only introduces one of the most clearly defined units in the letter but changes John's topic abruptly. Furthermore, 3:11 buttresses the command to love as coming from the beginning, and 3:23 reminds us that this exhortation comes from Jesus. These two verses are even constructed in the same grammatical form.[4]

The structure of the unit is simple: John follows his initial exhortation to love with a negative example (Cain) and in this finds a warning for those in the church who exhibit aggressive hostility (3:12–15). After this, he cites the positive example of Jesus, who loved even as far as death (3:15–18); in this John finds an appeal to love with full action, not mere words. John concludes with words of assurance that indicate how we can be certain we are pleasing God in how we live (3:19–24).

The Tragic Example of Cain (3:11–15)

GENESIS 4:1–16 HAS always been a potent story to show the destructive impulses that accompany envy. This is an archetypal story in the Old Testament (John's only Old Testament allusion in this letter), which was well known in the Christian community (see Matt. 23:35; Luke 11:51; Heb. 11:4; 12:24; Jude 11) and widely discussed in Judaism. Since Satan has always been the destroyer of life (John 8:44), it makes sense that in some fashion Cain was working under his inspiration, even though this is not mentioned in Genesis. Brown lists in detail the remarkable fascination of Judaism and the early Christians with the Cain story.[5] Philo (a Jewish contemporary of Paul), for example, wrote four works on Cain![6] In Christian literature (Heb. 12:24; Pseudo-Clementine Homilies) the Cain and Abel story is generously used, particularly as a foreshadowing of the martyrdom of Christians. Abel's sacrifice was pleasing to God; Cain's was not. In the Christian church, the envy and revenge harbored by Cain were compared to the feelings of the opponents of Christians, whose sacrificial lives were pleasing to the Lord.

---

4. Each exhortation employs a Greek *hina* clause
5. Brown, *The Epistles of John*, 442–44.
6. In some medieval Jewish writings, Cain is the offspring of the union of Eve and Satan, though this is not a first-century tradition.

In verse 13 John makes this comparison. The passions that fueled Cain's jealousy and hatred are now fueling those opposed to Christians. And this includes not simply non-Christians outside the church but also Christians—brothers and sisters—who reside within the fellowship.

John furthers his thoughts in verses 14–15 to reinforce the antithesis he has created between those who love and those who hate, between those who possess life and those who are already living in death. Those who exhibit love for Christ's family demonstrate that *already* they are enjoying the eternal life promised them. This is not to say (and it cannot be stressed enough) that one way to gain such life is to love others earnestly. That is not John's point. He is simply underscoring that *because* such love is already going on, we have a tangible sign of Christ's salvific work in progress.

Verse 15 echoes the severe exhortation found in Jesus' Sermon on the Mount that our inner motives and attitudes weigh as seriously as our actions in God's moral economy.

> You have heard that it was said to the people long ago, "Do not murder, and anyone who murders will be subject to judgment." But I tell you that anyone who is angry with his brother will be subject to judgment. Again, anyone who says to his brother, "Raca," is answerable to the Sanhedrin. But anyone who says, "You fool!" will be in danger of the fire of hell. (Matt. 5:21–22)

In other words, anyone who hates is willing to deny life to his or her opponent and in one sense already has committed murder (cf. 1 John 2:9–11; 4:20). But the reverse is also true: Those who exhibit love, who forgive freely and value their neighbor, bring life, healing, and goodness to others. These are nothing less than divine qualities.

The Superior Example of Jesus Christ (3:16–18)

IF CAIN PROVIDES a negative example, Jesus offers an utterly different model of what it means to live in community. He gives life.[7] Since

---

7. The Greek text does not refer specifically to Jesus in verse 16, rather, it uses the emphatic pronoun *ekeinos* ("that person") But throughout 1 John, this is how the author refers to Christ (cf. 2·6, 3 3, 5, 7; 4:17). Thus the NIV rightly interprets and expands the verse

God's essence is love (4:8–12), Jesus, who bears the presence of God in our midst, offers these divine gifts of love and life to us.

John uses the example of Jesus for two reasons. (1) Christ is a *model* for us to emulate. Thus in verse 16b we learn that we ought to exhibit the same quality of love and life to our communities. In verse 17 this notion takes an interesting turn: If we possess the "life [*bios*] of the world"—that is, if we possess "material possessions" (NIV) or "the world's goods" (NRSV)—and refuse to share, shutting down our feelings[8] for those in need, we are not giving life (*zoe*) to those who are suffering. Worldly *bios* can interfere with godly *zoe*. Christ as God's Son possessed more than we can ever imagine; yet he did not keep what he had selfishly but gave of himself voluntarily for others. Paul uses the self-giving of Jesus in a similar way in Philippians 2:5–11. Christ's model of self-sacrifice *ought* to inspire us to levels of giving.[9]

(2) But John has a second, equally important interest in the death of Jesus. In verse 16a we learn that Jesus' death is also a *revelation* of God's effort on our behalf: "Christ laid down his life for us." The verb used (Gk. *tithemi*) here is of special interest to John and generally describes "setting aside" something, such as a garment. In John 13:4, for example, Jesus "sets aside" his garment when he washes his disciples' feet. In John 10 Jesus describes himself as the good shepherd who "sets aside" his life for his sheep (10:11, 15, 17). In 13:37–38 and 15:13 he does the same for his followers. This peculiar Johannine construction suggests "divesting oneself of something" that is precious and personally valued.[10]

First John 3:16 might be called John's version of Mark 10:45, that "the Son of Man did not come to be served, but to serve, and to give his life as a ransom for many."[11] A number of scholars even see this verse as a Johannine variation of Isaiah 53:10.[12] Jesus' service for us is not simply in revealing to us self-sacrificial love. His death is not merely an

---

8 The Greek text actually refers to closing our "bowels" (KJV) or intestines (*splanchna*), meaning the seat of emotions—much like we use the word "heart" today.

9 I stress "ought" here because John's Greek sentence employs this strong verb (*opheilo*) in verse 16.

10. Westcott, as cited by Stott, *The Epistles of John*, 143.

11. Smalley, *1, 2, 3 John*, 193

12 Ibid Smalley cites C. Maurer, "τίθημι," TDNT, 8: 155–56; J. Jeremias, "παῖς θεοῦ," TDNT, 5:708–10, idem, "ποιμήν, κτλ," TDNT, 6.496.

ethical model; it is a genuine offering, a genuine giving of his life. This is further supported by the appearance of the Greek *hyper* ("on behalf of"), which is a common sacrificial term that occurs only here in 1 John.

Verse 18 serves as a sort of summary—and a plea (cf. "Dear children"). Love that fails to take the form of action on behalf of others is nothing more than religious rhetoric. No doubt the context of the Johannine schism fueled this concern. Religious weapons were being wielded with devastating consequences. John is eager for his community to exhibit *visible* signs of love—love that acts on the order of Christ's saving activity.

Shoring Up Christian Confidence (3:19–24)

SOME COMMENTATORS HAVE viewed verses 19–24 as a major digression in the letter's thought.[13] John's topic shifts abruptly from a discussion of practical examples of love to Christian assurance. Both verses 19 and 24 employ the phrase "this is how we know," suggesting that assurance is John's new concern. No doubt Smalley is right when he says that the full phrase in verse 19a actually governs the entire section, "This then is how we know *that we belong to the truth.*"[14] John's community is a community under siege, and his followers need reassurance that they are indeed on the side of the angels, that they possess the truth.

John's words of assurance are linked to the foregoing exhortation about love. "In this" (NIV, "This then") should be taken as pointing backwards to verses 11–18, so that when the crisis of self-examination comes, the first evidence of our security with God is our obedience to the command to love.[15] The NIV makes the verb tense present ("we know") when it is actually future. In other words, John is equipping his church, planning for a future episode when self-doubt and self-incrimination might paralyze them.

If we repunctuate verses 19–20, we can better clarify John's thought, particularly if we make the first clause clearly point to what comes

---

13 If the manuscript evidence tells us anything, it indicates that scribal questions were in abundance concerning these verses (particularly vv 19–20) Textual variations abound Commentators have struggled to organize John's meaning

14. Smalley, *1, 2, 3 John*, 199–200 The reference to "truth" serves as a literary link with the foregoing

15 This interpretation of "in this" is the one taken by most commentators, although in many cases the Greek expression *en touto* points to what follows rather than to what precedes

before.[16] Initially, therefore, John is making two points, which we can paraphrase in this manner:

19a: "In *this* [the love and obedience we exhibit, vv. 11–18] we will know that we are of the truth."

19b–20: "We will reassure our hearts in his presence whenever[17] our hearts condemn us, because (1) God is greater than our hearts, and (2) God knows all things."

This paraphrase gives a clear strategy about what to think when moments of profound insecurity overtake us. Our assurance is anchored in God and God alone, never in our own ability to generate feelings of confidence. John is urging that God is the final arbiter of our personal spiritual well-being. We do not look into our hearts to see if we feel secure and then use this as evidence of our security in the truth. If our conscience condemns, God overrides its verdict. This is possible for two reasons: God is mightier than our hearts, and he knows far more about us than we can ever imagine.

The setting of our insecurity "before God" that was suggested in verse 19 is explained in verses 21–22. When all self-condemnation is gone, when God's opinion of us is foremost in our minds, we enjoy a newfound boldness in our relationship with him, which is discovered principally in prayer.

The astonishing statement in verses 21–22 echoes other similar forms of confidence found in passages such as John 14:13–14; 16:23–24: *Whatever we ask will be given to us!* John says much the same in 1 John 5:14–15, but there modifies the statement with a condition: If we ask anything *according to God's will*, we will obtain what we ask. It is common in the Scriptures to find conditions attached to such promises: We must pray in Jesus' name (John 14:13) or abide/remain in Jesus and keep his commands (John 15:7). Here John says that we must do "what pleases him"; this presupposes a quality of intimacy that is in touch with God's very heart. Thompson comments, "Prayer according to God's

---

16. Marshall, *The Epistles of John*, 198. Such repunctuation for the sake of clarity, interestingly, is exactly what so many of the ancient scribes were doing when they edited the text.

17. This translation requires that the second *hoti* in the sentence be read not as "because" or "that" but as a relative pronoun connected with the following *ean*. The third *hoti* clause introduces a causal clause.

will (5:14) is prayer that understands what is pleasing to God (3:20) and makes its petitions accordingly."[18] Therefore prayer such as this springs from a fruitful and intimate relationship with God that has already matured.

If it is true that our relationship with God can be viewed through the lens of our obedience (v. 22), it now makes sense to review exactly what this means (vv. 23–24). Some have taken this letter wrongly as supporting a minimalist view of the Christian faith, that if we love one another we are Christians. The command of God to obey has two foci, and they enjoy a "fundamental unity."[19] We are to believe in God's Son, Jesus Christ, and to love one another. Verse 24 makes explicit that the success of such love only comes when we are living in intimacy with the Son, an intimacy that takes place when the Son is genuinely living in us and we in him. But the formula goes even further. This indwelling, this intimacy, is made possible by the Spirit he gives to us (cf. John 14:23–27).

Therefore, John's description of the Christian life is at once theological *and* ethical. God has sent his Son, through whom we receive life, and in turn God has poured the life of his Son into us through his Holy Spirit.[20] The virtues of the Christian life cannot be lived apart from a relationship with God, a relationship defined and sustained by Jesus Christ.

Bridging Contexts

LURKING BEHIND THESE verses are hints of the struggle within John's church now viewed from a different vantage point. It is potent to think about the behavior of Cain as a murderer and reflect on the Johannine division that fills out the background of this letter. John's interest in the Cain story is in how the brothers destroyed each other because of *anger fueled by religion*. John himself was facing a religious struggle, a struggle for spiritual power even if it meant inflicting religious casualties. "People who get in the way," some no doubt thought, "must be eliminated." Cain met his challenge with brutality—the word *sphazo* (3:12) actually means

---

18 Meye Thompson, *1–3 John*, 109.
19 Marshall, *The Epistles of John*, 201.
20 The inherent Trinitarian framework in Johannine theology is evident here

"butchered" and occurs frequently in a sacrificial context in the LXX (see Gen. 22:10). Thus, it implies a religious butchering—a slaying wed to piety, murder laced with prayer.

In such a setting, how is this type of conflict viewed from the inside? What pastoral priorities come to the forefront when the wonder of religion is dashed because religion itself is being used as a weapon? This pastoral question has been illustrated for me in an interesting way among the pastors of the churches in Palestine, where Christians are experiencing severe violence, justified with religion by the Israelis: "God has called us to purge this land and take it. Our Scriptures justify our behavior." In such a context, what is a Palestinian pastor to do? How does one shepherd severely abused people? How do we keep people from abandoning religious faith when faith is corrupted and twisted in violent ways?

This is where I must try to distill the pastoral setting and carry it with me to my own Christian context. John's strategy becomes my own. I find it interesting how John strives to maintain two things. (1) He begins with the cohesion and purity of his congregation. He urges them to avoid fragmentation, not letting the spirit of fighting pollute their fragile lives together. Yet this is the very thing so many of us experience today. The Johannine context of inner conflict is not unfamiliar to us. I have witnessed laity in revolt over the trivia of church life—such as the time of the worship service. I have mediated between pastors who work together publicly and yet behind the scenes indulge in a lethal war. John's church was fragmented; our churches are fragmented. Religious righteousness has been as much a weapon for us as it was in John's day. Therefore, these verses need to be—must be—bridged to our own generation.

(2) John is also concerned that we care for those who are wounded on the sidelines. The fragmentation of corporate bodies ends up fragmenting individual lives—men and women who suffer grave doubt or debilitating disillusionment because of conflict. Here again, the timelessness of John's message cannot be more clear.

Woven through these verses is John's insistence that Christians exhibit a purity and innocence like that of Jesus Christ. The very qualities that they have criticized the world for not having *must* appear within the Christian church. If the world is hypocritical and hostile, the church should have integrity and peace. Therefore, we must work to shore up weakened souls, to strengthen flagging spirits that are under siege and being fragmented.

Like no other, this passage forces us to reflect on the character of fragmented communities. How are they destroyed? How are they healed? Can people like Abel still be murdered in Christian community? Even though John refers to this struggle as the hatred of *"the world,"* we must keep in mind that these secessionists have come from within his own church (2:19–27). This is a congregational—or denominational—struggle.

Essentially John is asking one basic question: If someone claims to be changed inwardly, to what extent is this change a reality *outwardly?* Does it affect our relationships with our peers, with the needy, with those we call "our opponents"? And when this fragmentation explodes, what is the collateral damage? What is the cost in human hearts and weakened faith?

 I AM INCREASINGLY convinced that every Christian community struggles with fragmentation. Sometimes it is overt, with hostility out in the open. At other times it involves covert and subtle maneuverings for power that gently destroy others in the community. John would have us ask if the spirit of Cain is still alive and well in our churches.

(1) *Is this exhortation about insiders or outsiders?* John fails to clarify one thing. When he says that we must love our brothers, is he still referring to the secessionists? Or is he referring to his faithful congregants? In other words, is he speaking about cohesion in the church or about how the church should love its enemies?

One could argue that since these errant believers had left the fold, they were no longer to be labeled "brothers"; hence, we are here being called to love those within Christ's church. In this case the exhortation would sound like this:

> Our opponents have demonstrated that they are people of hate; therefore, they cannot have Christ's life in them. But our ranks should witness no such thing. Our community is a community of love, and we treat one another accordingly.

All nineteen uses of the *adelphos* word group ("brother/sister") in these letters leaves some ambiguity about how narrowly we should define the term.[21] Certainly the secessionists had *once* been "brothers," yet now they have become "enemies." At the least John is saying that his exhortation is aimed at inner-church conflict, but I am convinced that he has more in mind. The access these people seem to have to the congregation suggests that many still view them as part of the fold, as still being members of the church. But John is drawing no line, as if to say that some on one side deserve only enmity and those on "our side" deserve only love.

Furthermore, if love is to be characteristic of his community, such love must encompass *anyone* who contacts that community—enemies included. In 3:9 Christ models the love we are to show, and he loved not only his followers to the end (John 13:1) but also his enemies (Matt. 5:44; Luke 6:27, 35). Yet curiously, Jesus' command to love our enemies appears nowhere in the Johannine literature. Was this an area of struggle for the church? Can we sometimes find personal or theological reasons to withdraw fellowship from others?

(2) *Is conflict justified?* Most of us are able to justify some sort of hostility when we perceive that our opponents are either incompetent or in the wrong. Perhaps they are in error theologically. Perhaps as leaders they are out of their depth. Perhaps they have lost our respect and (in our view) are impeding the advance of the church. It is in such contexts that we witness breathtaking examples of Cain in ourselves and in others. In Christian contexts I have heard theological professors utter aloud words designed to destroy. In church committees I have seen power brokers maneuver themselves over the lives and feelings of others without any hesitation.

Of course, John's implication is that since these opponents fought us first, since they departed from the community, it proves that they do not have life in them (3:15). John then turns the thought on its head. *Their misbehavior, however, cannot ever become a justification for our misbehavior.* Fire must not be fought with fire. "We know that we have passed from death to life, because we love our brothers" (v. 14).

But this opens up a whole range of troubling questions. Certainly we are to stand firm and refuse concessions to those teaching spiritual

---

21 *Adelphos* ("brother") occurs eighteen times in the letters, *adelphe* ("sister") occurs once (2 John 13)

error. Certainly we cannot hand over the church to false shepherds. Church history—from Nicea to the Reformation—is replete with examples of men and women who exhibited conflict in defense of truth. But how do we discern the difference between justifiable conflict and inappropriate hostility? There is an interesting example of this conflict in the pages of the magazine *Christianity Today*.[22] In one issue John Woodbridge wrote an article entitled "Culture War Casualities. How Warfare Rhetoric Is Hurting the Work of the Church." Among the offenders, Woodbridge named James Dobson. Two months later Dobson responded ("Why I Use Fighting Words"), and *Christianity Today* even invited Woodbridge to supply a rejoinder ("Why Words Matter"). The point for our purposes has little to do with the Christian concern for Western culture. What makes the exchange interesting is how these two men were trying to negotiate their conflict. Dobson tried to defend his words as justifiable; Woodbridge wondered if such language was appropriate and helpful.

(3) *High fashion hatred.* John the pastor understands that hatred and division are not always overt. For most of us there are sophisticated ways to avoid the command to love.

But John draws an unexpected parallel between hating and murder in verse 15: "Anyone who hates his brother is a murderer." This means that attitudes qualify. This brings to mind Jesus' teaching in the Sermon on the Mount in Matthew 5:21 (see above), where Jesus draws a straight line between murder and hatred. In what sense, I wonder, do we display attitudes that bring death to those around us? How often does polite civility disguise undisclosed feelings of antipathy and aversion? Usually such feelings can never be disguised completely, and in the end they destroy.

Moreover, John draws another unexpected parallel between love and generosity in verse 17, but this time it is about apathy toward those in need. One measure of love is the degree to which people blessed with material wealth distribute that wealth within the community. This is a surprising and unsettling thought! Church mottoes often describe congregations as "friendly" or as "a place where Christ's love is genuine." Imagine a church where Christ's love was *generous—not metaphorically, but financially!* Admittedly, there are countless practical problems with this sort of thinking, and many (particularly the

---

22 *Christianity Today*, March 6 and June 19, 1995.

wealthy) will be quick to point them out. But John could not be clearer. James makes the same argument. A church is no loving community if the rich are simply friendly to the poor and send them on their way after the coffee hour (James 2:14–17). This also means that the financial well-being of church members—their suffering and struggles as well as their successes—should become the interest of pastoral care.

I have always been intrigued to see how poor churches in urban areas frequently have ministries that deal directly with financial need. Some offer short-term loans. Others have full-scale mortgage programs. I know one church that even has housing and employment programs for street people.[23] Curiously these are the churches with little cash flow, and yet they recognize that practical financial need is essential to ministry and harness surprising sums to meet these needs. On the other hand, affluent churches, *where more resources are available,* rarely enter this arena.

(4) *Sources of spiritual malaise.* This entire section suggests that the church is to become a life-giving community. It should be a place where men, women, and children are healed, not hurt; where the rich take genuine responsibility for the poor; where lives flourish both spiritually and materially. Conflict, struggle, rejection, community fragmentation—all can lead to despair and doubt. When a community loses its solidarity, when its shared vision and life evaporates, personal faith begins to wane. Here in Chicago I have learned of two large churches whose congregations lost influential pastors due to struggle, and in each case over 25 percent of their people disappeared from the membership roles. As one former member said to me, "If Christian leaders can behave like this, I'm not sure if Christianity is true in the first place."

First John 3:19–24 is John's answer for pastoral care. As we have seen, his foremost concern is to remind believers that God is greater than all of these things and that therefore, when self-incriminating doubt swamps us, we need to understand his sovereignty and strength. He lists at least three strategies that should be a part of every Christian's arsenal.[24] If these are pursued, we should enjoy a confident and

---

23. See Wayne L. Gordon with Randall Frame, *Real Hope in Chicago* (Gand Rapids: Zondervan, 1995).

24 Smalley, *The Epistles of John,* 199, and most commentators list six points that John makes to reassure the believer. I have distilled the three most significant; the others can be subsumed under these three

vibrant spiritual relationship with God despite the struggle and fragmentation around us.

First, we should have *faith* in Jesus Christ (v. 23). This means that the confidence of our faith is not anchored in the church, in other believers, or in our pastor. The words of Jesus, found in the Scriptures, should be more audible to us than the words of those fragmenting the world around us.

Second, we should be *obedient* and do what pleases Jesus (vv. 22–23). In particular, this means we do concrete acts of love for others, acts that are unexpected and fueled by the love we witness in Christ himself (v. 16). Such deeds, John assures us, will become signs for our hearts that indeed we belong to Christ. Thus we become known in our community not as protagonists, not as theological watchdogs, but as unabashed lovers of the unlovely.[25]

Third, we should be *filled* by the Holy Spirit (v. 24). This means that our Christian walk is not only a matter of doctrinal orthodoxy or ethical purity, but is also mystical and spiritual. In verse 24 John says that Jesus Christ will live in us and that the vehicle for this indwelling is the Holy Spirit. Assurance does not spring simply from vigorous works of obedience or orthodoxy, but from the interior life. We know that Christ lives in us *by the Spirit he gave us* (cf. 4:13). It should therefore be commonplace for us to find evidences of the Spirit that signal Christ's presence. Regarding John's community, I am convinced that it was comfortable with what we today would call "charismatic evidences" (gifts of prophesy, healing, etc.). The Spirit is not an insignificant array of feelings, but ushers a concrete presence and reality into our lives.

---

25. On the subject of confident prayer in 3 22, see comments on 1 John 5.13–15.

1 John 4:1–6

D
EAR FRIENDS, DO not believe every spirit, but
test the spirits to see whether they are from
God, because many false prophets have gone
out into the world. ²This is how you can recognize the
Spirit of God: Every spirit that acknowledges that Jesus
Christ has come in the flesh is from God, ³but every
spirit that does not acknowledge Jesus is not from God.
This is the spirit of the antichrist, which you have heard
is coming and even now is already in the world.

⁴You, dear children, are from God and have overcome
them, because the one who is in you is greater than the
one who is in the world. ⁵They are from the world and
therefore speak from the viewpoint of the world, and the
world listens to them. ⁶We are from God, and whoever
knows God listens to us; but whoever is not from God
does not listen to us. This is how we recognize the
Spirit of truth and the spirit of falsehood.

**Original
Meaning**

JOHN'S DISCUSSION OF our assurance in 3:24
by referring to the Holy Spirit brings to mind
the larger subject of spiritual discernment.[1]
God has given us his Spirit, and as we have
seen, this anointing was emphasized in John's community (2:20, 27;
3:24; 4:1–3, 13). Yet particularly in communities that stress spiritual
empowering, it is necessary to weigh the claims of those who say they
are spiritually enlightened. Or, as John insists, we need to "test the
spirits." Paul makes the same claim to the Corinthians, who likewise
lived in a pneumatic community and needed to weigh the authority of
prophetic voices (1 Cor. 12:1–3; 14:29).

One essential idea is presupposed throughout this passage: Two
spirits are active in this world, "the Spirit of truth" and "the spirit of false-

---

1. It seems clear that 4:1–6 is a self-contained unit. Note its frequent use of *pneuma* (7
times) and the abrupt change of subject in 4:7

hood" (4:6). That is, there is the Spirit who comes from God, who glorifies and elevates his Son, Jesus Christ (John 16:14), and there is the spirit of antichrist (1 John 4:3), which is welcomed by the world (4:5) and sabotages the truth about Jesus (4:2). In these verses John provides two tests so that Christians will be able to discern the difference.

Dangerous Prophet-Teachers (4:1)

WE HAVE SEEN suggestions throughout this letter that the schism that had John's community in its grip was being fueled by false teachers (e.g., 2:22–23). Now we learn that they are pneumatics, teachers claiming that their words are inspired by the Spirit of God. In verse 1, John calls them "prophets" because technically a prophet is the mouthpiece of some spirit.[2] And as John acknowledges, among those who call themselves prophets, there are many frauds (cf. Matt. 7:15; Mark 13:22; Acts 20:28–30; 2 Peter 2:1).

It is important to pause and gain some appreciation for this problem in the early church. House churches were isolated in cities throughout the Roman empire. In the early years there were few formal creeds (such as the later Creed of Nicea) to give doctrinal guidance, nor were the Scriptures available as we have them today. No one owned a "New Testament," and at best the early Christians only had random collections of letters from the apostles and collections of stories about Jesus. Therefore oral communication was essential. Churches relied on emissaries from their leaders, who relayed information from other communities and taught. Paul sent out Timothy and Silas in this capacity, and John sent out elders as his spokespersons (3 John 5).

But problems came when prophets or teachers arrived claiming an authority that was not rightfully theirs. Paul had to address the problem of unauthorized teachers in Galatia and Thessalonica. Because some churches received false letters (see 2 Thess. 2:2), he even decided to sign his correspondence with recognizable markings (Gal. 6:11; Col. 4:18; 2 Thess. 3:17). This phenomenon meant that churches could fall prey to unscrupulous itinerant prophets and teachers, and John's churches were no exception (cf. 2 John 7). Consequently,

---

2. Stott, *The Epistles of John,* 153.

Christians had to be ready to assess the message they heard and the spirit that inspired it.

John's First Test: What They Say About Jesus (4:2–3)

THIS IS THE only time the Greek word for "testing" (*dokimazo*) occurs in the Johannine literature, although it occurs often in the New Testament (twenty-two times). It appears in Paul's letters when he challenges his churches to assess the validity of irregular teachings (see 1 Thess. 5:21; 1 Tim. 3:10). Testing the spirits may refer to a spiritual apprehension, such as Paul's understanding of the discernment of spirits (1 Cor. 12:10). In this case, John would have in mind charismatic leaders in the congregation who spiritually intuited the authenticity of these prophets' lives. Just as Jesus could "see" the spiritual bonds of a person before a deliverance—that is, spirit seeing spirit—so the Spirit of God would equip Johannine believers to recognize God's Spirit in others. On the other hand, John's thought may be nothing more mysterious than weighing objectively what was being said by these prophets. Perhaps this engaged different gifts in the Johannine church—elders, teachers, and leaders with wisdom and knowledge, who could weigh what was said and compare it with what had been taught previously.

But what should one test for? The Spirit of God always glorifies the Son of God (John 15:26; 16:13–15; 1 Cor. 12:1–3). Thus the first test centers entirely on one's view of Jesus Christ: "Every spirit that acknowledges Jesus Christ has come in the flesh is of God."[3] We saw earlier in 2:18–22 (as well as 1:1–4) how incarnational Christology was at the heart of this community's struggles. Behind these words John is urging three things about our belief: (1) that the man Jesus of Nazareth is indeed the divine Word of God; (2) that Jesus Christ was

---

3. There is considerable debate concerning how we should understand this verse See Smalley, *1, 2, 3 John*, 222–23, Brown, *The Epistles of John*, 492–93. Some view this verse as evidence of a dispute with Cerinthus's claim that Christ descended on Jesus at his baptism and thus translate it, "Whoever confesses Jesus as the Christ come in the flesh." Others keep "Jesus" and "Christ" together [so the NIV], making the doctrine of the incarnation central and taking "Jesus Christ" as the preexistent Lord who becomes flesh. Here the stress is on the creedal fact of incarnation Still others (e.g, Smalley, Brown) view the entire phrase as confessional and descriptive, "Whoever confesses Jesus Christ incarnate," emphasizing his personhood and its mode of existence

and is fully divine as well as fully human;[4] and (3) that Jesus is the sole source of eternal life since he alone reveals the Father to us and atones for our sins.

John sees this confession as central to Christian discipleship. If Jesus, the man from Nazareth, were not our divine Lord, his sacrifice on the cross would have limited importance. If he were not divine, we would have little confidence that the Father had been revealed to us. The nature of discipleship would likewise be placed in question. Our human lives, our ethics, are important because God has deemed our humanity important through the incarnation of his Son.

But note further that this affirmation is not simply a matter of holding a creed. In 4:3 the confession is abbreviated: "confessing Jesus" is John's real interest.[5] He looks for believers to embrace with their words and their hearts the truth of the Incarnation. Smalley comments that this is the "heart of the apostolic gospel," which requires "a right estimate of [Christ's] identity (an eternal and an historical humanity) together with a personal acknowledgment of his Lordship."[6] In the New Testament even the demons recognized the fact of the Incarnation (Mark 1:24; 3:11; Acts 19:15), but they did not embrace this truth by confessing Jesus' lordship. Behind the creed is a person, and it is to this person, Jesus Christ, that John demands our allegiance.

To fail to hold to Christ's incarnation is to reflect the pernicious "spirit of the antichrist" that lives in the world. Is this simply a spirit of error? Of erroneous human judgments? Or is this spirit demonic? John's dualism no doubt personified evil, and he viewed those who stood against Jesus Christ as working in league with the devil (2:13; 3:8, 10, 12; 5:18–19). In all five uses of "antichrist" in the Johannine letters, this denial of Jesus Christ is the antichrist's principal interest (2:18–22; 4:3; 2 John 7).

Marshall points out that the Greek text does not mention "the spirit" when the NIV translates "*the spirit* of the antichrist" (although it should be supplied grammatically). In this manner John avoids any implicit

---

4 The perfect tense of the verb "*has come* in the flesh" betrays John's emphasis on the continued significance of this incarnation right up to the present; see Smalley, *The Epistles of John*, 222–23

5. Some ancient manuscripts expand the verse by adding "Jesus *who came in the flesh*," in order to harmonize it with verse 2

6 Smalley, *The Epistles of John*, 224.

comparison between the Spirit of God and this so-called spirit.[7] It is a point well taken. John speedily assures his readers in verse 4 that the Holy Spirit in them is more powerful than this spirit in the world. John's spiritual dualism claims that the Spirit of God is unrivaled and that those who reside in the Holy Spirit have no reason to fear.

It is interesting to compare 4:1–3 with 2:18–22. In the first section, having a right relation with the Father leads to a correct view of the Son. In the second, having a right relation with the Spirit leads to a similarly correct view of the Son. In each case the Son is central in all true contacts with God. Jesus Christ is the only point of communication between heaven and earth.

John's Second Test: What the World Thinks About Them (4:4–6)

JOHN'S SECOND TEST has to do with audiences. Who celebrates this teaching? Where does it find a ready following? John frequently refers to "the world" (twenty-four times in the letters), and in some cases he sees it simply as a place of benign unbelief. God loves this world and sent his Son to save it (2:2, 15, 17; 4:9, 14; 5:4–5; see discussion on 2:15–17). But John also sees "the world" as a place of genuine hostility to God, a place where the forces of evil and falsehood are marshaled (3:1, 13; 4:1). In fact, in 5:19 he says that the world is under the power of the evil one.

It comes as no surprise, therefore, that if false prophecies (such as those of the schismatics) originate with an ungodly spirit, these utterances will find a ready reception in the world (v. 5). On the other hand, it is the response of the church, the community of true believers, that can test the veracity of a word from the Lord (v. 6). God's people know his voice—like sheep with a shepherd (John 10:4ff.)—and their corporate judgment should be trusted. There is also a harmony, a correspondence, between the Holy Spirit in the believer and the Holy Spirit in the prophet. When God's Spirit inspires a prophet, his people will discern God's truth.[8]

---

7. Marshall, *The Epistles of John*, 208, n.12

8. Paul employs this same strategy in 1 Corinthians 14:29, where the words of prophets must be tested by the discernment of the church

Here, then, are John's two tests. This is how we can discern "the Spirit of truth and the spirit of falsehood" (v. 6). Christians must judge the Christological correctness of anyone's teachings. If the incarnate Christ has been theologically removed, if Christology is not at the center of what someone says, we are right to be suspicious. In addition, if the community we have always trusted, if the church as the historic custodian of truth, refuses this prophesy, we should be warned. Moreover, if it finds a ready reception in the world, we should flee because it may be a message that has originated with the evil spirit that dominates that world.

Bridging Contexts

JOHN'S COMMAND THAT we "test the spirits" is apt for our generation since there are so many competing claims to religious truth today. Cults, sects, and new religious movements abound. There are even countless house churches led by untrained teachers whose theological acumen and spiritual maturity are dubious. In a city of forty thousand near me, one study conducted by Wheaton College's graduate school found dozens of these religious communities recruiting members all around the city's major congregations, and the pastors were virtually unaware of what was happening.

But there is a difficult twist here as well. Our society prizes religious tolerance and pluralism to such a degree that many of us have begun to believe that such "testing" betrays a narrowness of vision that is overly critical, even judgmental. In 1994 a number of mainline churches sponsored a conference called "Reimaging God," in which pagan worship forms were embraced and traditional orthodox teachings were openly attacked. To "test the spirits" today will take considerable discernment and not a little courage. Nevertheless, John's command is clear: Such testing is the responsibility of every generation.

Bridging this text to the contemporary scene obligates me to ask how this testing should take place. John's two tests, incarnational Christology and the response of the world, were designed for a particular historical context. In some cases those tests may be useful for us, but it is an open question whether they serve as a universal arbiter in questions of orthodoxy. For instance, some doctrinal errors would pass John's test. Mormons, for instance, agree that Jesus was human and divine, *but his divinity was not unique to him*. Harold Camping, the prophet who announced on his thirty-nine radio stations that Christ would return to earth in September 1994, likewise passes the test, even though his abuses to reasonable interpretative methods are well known.[9] As John Walvoord, former president of Dallas Seminary, remarked, Camping is "practicing a method of interpretation that no one else recognizes." New questions therefore have to be written in each generation to address theological challenges as they come along.

Because John's tests are limited to one historical setting, they also tend to be limited in scope. Other essential beliefs about Jesus that go beyond his incarnation, such as his miraculous powers, his resurrection, and his second coming, might be included in other circumstances. John mentions none of these because they were not issues sharply defining fidelity to the apostolic witness in his circumstances.

Each generation, then, must forge its beliefs, anchored to the doctrines laid out in the Scriptures with an eye on the contemporary challenges the church must confront. A quick look at the past illustrates how this has been done already. The historic Christian creeds (Nicea, Chalcedon) did precisely this: They formulated statements of faith on matters essential to their time and place. Each age has every imagined heresy, and it is the responsibility of every generation's leadership to rise up and confront gross departures from the truth. In our century, the Barmen Declaration (1934) was written by German Christians to reject the Nazi claim that God was at work in the nationalistic aspirations of the Third Reich and that the government could therefore make a divine claim for obedience. Other more recent generations have felt called to clarify questions of biblical authority, sexuality, and social justice. One ought not give timeless guidance here for no one can predict what "the spirits" will say to each generation. We must simply be ready, as the Johannine Christians were, to confront wrong thinking and willful unbelief.

But perhaps this is where I worry most. Among the students I teach I find that most of them are eager to tell how they feel about a particular question, but few of them are capable of giving a coherent,

---

9. See "End-Times Prediction Draws Strong Following," *Christianity Today* (June 1994), 46–47.

objective, carefully reasoned argument for or against it. The same is true among adults in the church, where adult education programs, rather than equipping men and women to "test the spirits" of their day, help them cope with feelings they have in the crises of their lives. Both are important, but one is sorely neglected.

The Johannine call here is to build a Christian maturity that can use theological radar to spot intruders who want to upend the church's beliefs. This is high-tech radar that can tell the difference between pleasure aircraft and lethal bombers, between minor issues and colossal errors that deserve a fierce struggle.

THE SPIRITUAL LANDSCAPE is no less confusing today than it was for John two thousand years ago. Challenges to the gospel and the flourishing of new religious movements seem commonplace. And in some cases the church has endorsed their growth. A Presbyterian Church (U.S.A.) presbytery in Missouri recently sent $41,000 from its church-wide benevolence offering to a local Muslim school "to aid the poor and oppressed." Yet does not such charity advance the theological mission of a faith that denies Christ and directly competes with the church? One Presbyterian pastor, Alan Krummenacher, defended the grant as "a bridge for understanding and cooperation."[10] Such examples as this abound. Otherwise splendid overtures of Christian generosity become confused with the ultimate mission of the church.

Therefore the discernment John encourages must become a vigorous part of every congregation's ministry. Nevertheless, there are difficulties and challenges to its application. We must know where to apply it and how narrowly.

(1) *The church is called to be the custodian of the truth.* When John says that we must "test the spirits," he is addressing the corporate body of Christ. Throughout 4:1–6 his verbs are plural ("together all of you test the spirits"), implying that this spiritual discernment is an obligation of the gathered body and its leadership. Therefore, it is not simply permissible but is incumbent on the church to weigh what is being

---

10. See "Educator Quits Over Grant to Muslims," *Christianity Today* (June 1994), 65

taught within its ranks. National bodies and local congregations must evaluate everything from curricula to Sunday school teachers.

In some instances this has made many uncomfortable, especially when it leads to a struggle at the denominational level or even within a local parish. As one person put it, "The church should be loving and accepting, not critical." This is correct. Our custodianship should not make us so harshly critical that we disqualify every different point of view in a congregation. On the other hand, we cannot be negligent either. We cannot accept all things in the interest of accepting all people.

But as soon as I say this, another question haunts me: *How do I cultivate a discerning spirit without becoming cynical?* This is a practical question implicit in John's command for discernment. Unfortunately, John's letter does not address it. There is a sickness that lurks behind this worthy command: It can make me unteachable. Soon I am weighing the words of everyone—including my pastor—and I alone become my own arbiter of truth. No doubt John's interest in the importance of the gathered community—the church—is a signal reminder to us. The *church* is the custodian of the truth, and my impulse to critique, to analyze, or to judge must be worked out in the community of the church's leadership. My voice, which by itself sounds righteous and orthodox, may sound different when heard by other thoughtful leaders. This calls for a humility and courage that is willing to submit to the corporate voice while still retaining its passion and vision.

(2) *The centrality of Christology.* John affirms a delicate balance throughout his writings between the humanity and the divinity of Christ. He will compromise on neither. I wonder if this same concern is alive in our church today. I frequently force my students to think carefully about the coherence of Christian theology by neglecting one of Christ's two dimensions. If he were not fully human, what would this mean for our confidence in his revelation of the Father? How would it affect his work on the cross or his return to the Father? If he were not fully divine, what would this mean for these same categories?

I remember with great fondness and appreciation a seminary professor at Fuller Seminary speaking passionately to us about the delicate balance of Athanasian Christology.[11] Such a balance between human-

---

11. Dr Ray Anderson, professor of theology.

ity and divinity—its symmetry—is *the distinctive feature* of Christian thought. Today my students barely know that it is Athanasius they are hearing. John wants us to cultivate such an instinct. He wants us to feel it intuitively when Christological symmetry is broken by accident or heresy.

(3) *How do we unmask false teachers?* John warns us that false prophets/teachers may lay siege to the church, but he gives us little direction about how to do this or what to do with these teachers when they are uncovered. He has at least two concerns: (a) False teachers should not have access to the church as a platform for their teachings, and (b) people should not be deceived by what they hear in the church. This means at least that the church should be a spiritual refuge where experimental teachings or controversial points of view are checked. Practically speaking, when I send my daughters to Sunday school, I deserve the assurance that the teacher in the class is not there simply because she is the only one who volunteered. The church must guarantee that those who teach are theologically and spiritually qualified to do so.

The danger of unmasking false teachers is that the community of Christ may become unduly intolerant of diverse points of view. Individuals may see themselves as commissioned to flush out those whose outlooks differ. This is not what John has in mind. He desires that the leadership of the church prohibit any from leading who might undermine the heart and soul of the Christian faith.

(4) *Where or who are these spirits today?* Throughout this passage John tells us to test the spirits. If John's outlook is dualistic (see above), I have to be ready to test for genuine spiritual forces in my community. To be candid, I have to admit to the possibility of demonic influence among those who want to sabotage the church. John does not tell us about spiritual warfare as Paul does, but as I noted in the introduction, there is ample evidence to suggest that he led a "charismatic" or pneumatic community. The spiritual warfare described in Ephesians 6 was no doubt familiar to him. John thus wants us equipped for spiritual battle. *Does this mean discerning spirits? And does it also mean deliverance and exorcism?*

Many of us recoil from the thought that such fantastic ministries should be a part of the church's work. But they must be. Today Christians who have grown up in the wake of the charismatic renewal are comfortable and look for a pastoral ministry that "encounters" spiritual forces. Twenty-five years ago young people would have scoffed at the idea of the demonic, but no more. I recently spent a day with a friend who is the chaplain aboard one of the Navy's newest guided missile cruisers. He told me of the many faith groups in the ship's crew of four hundred. There were Jews, Catholics, high church Protestants, Mormons—everything, including Satan worshipers. This ship is a cross section of the world and its willingness to flirt openly with the demonic.

I met a young Presbyterian pastor and his wife during a conference in Michigan where I was speaking. In our conversation they spoke late into the evening about his first pastorate in Florida. Early one morning on his first week he entered the darkened church only to see demonic spirit-apparitions that had been witnessed by many others. This spirit-encounter required a ministry to deliver this church from its bondage.[12] This is, of course, a highly unusual situation. But other destructive spirits need to be named and confronted in our churches—spirits bringing illnesses, sin, and destruction to Christ's body. It is not eccentric to hold such a view. Any Christian cosmology that posits a personal God and angels should also have room for a personal devil and his cohorts. I shared these stories with a Hispanic pastor from south Texas, who smiled and said, "Our communities have known about these realities all along."

Others have pursued a more basic application. Perhaps this "spirit" is something wider, something more universal. These may be the forces that shape me and my community for better or for ill. Some are certainly demonic; some are simply the spirit of the age in which I live. These latter spirits require discernment lest I become victimized by voices that have more to do with the world and its passions than with Jesus Christ. I referred earlier to Jacques Ellul's book *The New Demons*,[13] where he describes tendencies of thought and behavior that are inflict-

---

12 The church had been built on the site of an old house used for decades for Satanic rituals. And before that the site had been an ancient Indian cemetery Are these things important? As an example of how far this discussion and its pastoral dimensions have gone, a whole branch of literature on this sort of phenomenon, called "territorial spirits," has evolved. See Peter Wagner, ed., *Territorial Spirits Insights on Strategic-Level Spiritual Warfare from Nineteen Christian Leaders* (Chichester, Eng Sovereign World, 1991)

13. Jacques Ellul, *The New Demons* (New York Seabury, 1975)

ing our age with dreadful spiritual diseases. Many others are sounding the same alarm. The great irony is that Christians, who have a theology that should equip them to sift the impulses of the world, do it least, whereas unbelievers, who have no such theology, are leading the way in describing the moral bankruptcy and general wretchedness of our day.

In 1993 David Wells's award-winning book, *No Place for Truth*, set out to diagnose what has been happening to the modernity of the West—and it makes grim reading.[14] The "new demons" he describes have created a decaying intellectual environment that has no use for truth, no interest in a transcendent God, and indeed no way to conceptualize any notion of revelation. That God would become human in Christ is not simply rejected (as had been done in liberalism), but now is *incomprehensible*. What has evolved is a new pagan mind. Lesslie Newbigin makes the same point in his *Foolishness to the Greeks*.[15] This author describes how the basic conceptual categories that lie behind Christian thought cannot be presupposed any longer.

Are destructive spirits at work in the world? In the church? There can be no doubt that they are. The church must be equipped to combat all forms of evil, along with its gritty ugliness in encounter ministry, its wily sophistication in the intellectual currents of the day.

---

14 D. Wells, *No Place for Truth· Or Whatever Happened to Evangelical Theology?* (Grand Rapids Eerdmans, 1993).

15. L Newbigin, *Foolishness to the Greeks· The Gospel and Western Culture* (Grand Rapids Eerdmans, 1986).

If you don't love yourself than you can't love others and you can't love God.

1 John 4:7–5:4

❧

DEAR FRIENDS, LET us love one another, for love comes from God. Everyone who loves has been born of God and knows God. ⁸Whoever does not love does not know God, because God is love. ⁹This is how God showed his love among us: He sent his one and only Son into the world that we might live through him. ¹⁰This is love: not that we loved God, but that he loved us and sent his Son as an atoning sacrifice for our sins. ¹¹Dear friends, since God so loved us, we also ought to love one another. ¹²No one has ever seen God; but if we love one another, God lives in us and his love is made complete in us.

¹³We know that we live in him and he in us, because he has given us of his Spirit. ¹⁴And we have seen and testify that the Father has sent his Son to be the Savior of the world. ¹⁵If anyone acknowledges that Jesus is the Son of God, God lives in him and he in God. ¹⁶And so we know and rely on the love God has for us.

God is love. Whoever lives in love lives in God, and God in him. ¹⁷In this way, love is made complete among us so that we will have confidence on the day of judgment, because in this world we are like him. ¹⁸There is no fear in love. But perfect love drives out fear, because fear has to do with punishment. The one who fears is not made perfect in love.

¹⁹We love because he first loved us. ²⁰If anyone says, "I love God," yet hates his brother, he is a liar. For anyone who does not love his brother, whom he has seen, cannot love God, whom he has not seen. ²¹And he has given us this command: Whoever loves God must also love his brother.

⁵ ¹Everyone who believes that Jesus is the Christ is born of God, and everyone who loves the father loves his child as well. ²This is how we know that we love the

children of God: by loving God and carrying out his commands. ³This is love for God: to obey his commands. And his commands are not burdensome, ⁴for everyone born of God overcomes the world. This is the victory that has overcome the world, even our faith.

AN ABRUPT SHIFT in subject begins at 4:7. Instead of continuing his teaching about discernment in 4:1–6, John provides an extended exhortation on love, echoing ideas found elsewhere in the letter.¹ In 2:3–11 John introduced this subject, underscoring the believer's fidelity to "the light." To love one's fellow believer is to show that one lives "in the light" (2:10). In 3:10–24 John explored practical applications of the love command, connecting it with eternal life. To love is to prove that we have eternal life working in us (3:14–15). According to C. H. Dodd, the links between 4:11–5:4 and 3:10–24 are such that the thought of 3:24 leads directly into 4:7.²

In 4:7ff. John is concerned that we understand fully what inspires our love for one another. As Marshall puts it, "John is here concerned with definition, not exhortation."³ What is the connection between love and God? What is the basis of our love for each other? What effects show up in the lives of men and women who exhibit this kind of love? Hidden in this section is John's famous statement that "God is love" (4:8), corresponding to his other two affirmations: "God is light" (1:5) and "God is Spirit" (John 4:24). However, we must be careful what we do with this affirmation, for it has been the source of breathtaking misuse. If God is love, does that mean all loving people have somehow found God? That all loving people are children of God?

---

1. I have chosen to keep this section together even though it is longer than other units in the commentary It should be seen as a literary whole, moreover, it repeats and reinforces similar themes again and again

2 Dodd, *The Epistles of John*, 95 This has led some critics to suggest a rearrangement for this section

3 Marshall, *The Epistles of John*, 211.

The Origin of Christian Love (4:7–10)

SIX TIMES IN this letter John employs the personal address "beloved" (NIV, "dear friends"),[4] expressing his pastoral, heartfelt concern for the welfare of his followers. The exhortation to love (see also 3:11, 23) he now explains as originating from God himself (4:7a). The coming of Jesus Christ provides a compelling portrait of God's love for us. This theme—the compelling origin of divine love—weaves its way throughout the section (4:7–11, 16, 19). Thus for John, an exhortation to obedience does not come with a threat. Instead, obedience is encouraged through inspiration. God's inspiring love, his generous affection, compels us to obey. If he has done this much for us, how can we do less? Genuine love cannot be exhibited in any community unless it reflects God's love, unless it is empowered by an experience of being loved.

Christians who live out such love are exhibiting much more. They are also giving evidence that they *have been born* from God and *know* him (4:7b; cf. 5:4). The first verb is a perfect tense, suggesting that divine rebirth is past, yet bearing fruit in the present. A person once converted now demonstrates the fruit of that conversion. The second verb is a present tense, implying that love is connected to an ongoing awareness of who God is. Why did John select these particular words? Spiritual rebirth and divine knowledge were no doubt promoted among the secessionists (see 3:9). John therefore gives a test of true spiritual maturity that defeats in a stroke his opponents' spiritual claims; he bases his comments on their unspiritual conduct, that they have been unloving.

John goes on to point out that the reverse is also the case (v. 8). Whoever does not love—in the setting of the Johannine church—cannot possibly know God (also 4:20). Note that the tense of the verb "to know" has changed from the present tense to the aorist (or past) tense. John describes here a person who has never experienced God's love at any time. No doubt our emphasis should be on the positive character of this principle: Since God is love, those who encounter him have the power to become loving persons.

When verse 8 says "God is love" (cf. v. 16), it is important to note what John is not saying. He is not saying that "God is loving" (though this is true). Nor is he saying that one of God's activities is "to love" us

---

4 The Greek word used here is *agapetoi* (2.7, 3:2, 21; 4 1, 7, 11)

(though this is true as well). John is saying that God *is* love, that "all of his activity is loving."[5] Love is the essence of his being. But the reverse is not the case. We cannot say, in other words, that "love is God," as if any display of affection suddenly qualifies as divine. John is carefully defining the character of who God is and what it means to live in relation to him. To genuinely contemplate the true identity of God is to become like him. A true apprehension of the personhood of God should lead us to change how we live and behave.

In verses 9–10 John carries his theological definition further with words strongly reminiscent of 1 John 3:16, "This is how we know what love is: Jesus Christ laid down his life for us" (cf. John 3:16). The ultimate act of God's self-revelation is found in his activity in Jesus Christ. The NIV "showed" in verse 9 translates the Greek word *phaneroo* (lit., "revealed"), a word that refers to the disclosure of things formerly hidden.[6] Never before has God done such a thing in history! Christ is the unveiling of God's heart; he is God, displayed vulnerably before the world.[7]

These verses offer two developments over 1 John 3:16. (1) God's love is what initiated the sending of Jesus. We enjoy not only the love of Christ, but also *God's hidden passion* for humankind, visibly expressed in Jesus Christ. Thus we should see not only Christ as our ally, working to placate an angry God. It is *God himself* who loves us—who is devoted to us. As Paul says in 2 Corinthians 5:19, "*God* was reconciling the world to himself in Christ."

(2) First John 3:16 describes how Christ surrendered his life for us and how this should inspire our sacrifices for one another. Now John adds that the sending of Jesus, this overture of love, is intended that we might live (v. 9b) and that the penalty for our sins might be covered

---

5 Smalley, *The Epistles of John*, 239

6 This revelation takes place "among us " The Greek *en hemin* can mean "in us," or even "to us" in some cases. Since this revealed love affects directly who we are as we love one another, John may be intending the full force of *en*, meaning that this love has "impacted each one of us "

7 In verse 9 the NIV translates the Greek word *monogenes* as "one and only," while the NIV note gives "only begotten" as an alternative The word is used in Greek literature only for children, in the LXX it translates the Hebrew word for "only" or "single " The suggestion "only begotten" understands the latter half of the word as derived from the Greek verb *gennao* ("to give birth") This is incorrect Rather, the word would derive from *genos*, meaning "type" or "kind "

(v. 10b). "To have life" is a favorite Johannine expression (John 5:25; 6:51, 57, 58; 11:25; 14:19).[8] But such life comes about *only* through forgiveness of sins. This is the second time Jesus' death is called "an atoning sacrifice" (see discussion on 2:2). This term and its associated verbs and nouns appear only six times in the entire New Testament.[9] The Greek word *hilasmos* describes an act of "removing" an offense (e.g., through sacrifice), which repairs a relationship with God and is often translated "expiation." Thus, enjoying God's love has a requirement: the renewal of a broken relationship that can only be accomplished by Jesus Christ.

The Inspiration of Christian Love (4:11–16)

VERSE 11 SHIFTS subjects to the immediate concern on the apostle's mind. We are alerted to this change by his use again of "beloved" (see above, v. 7). John is a pastor writing passionately to his followers.

The conditional clause in verse 11 (beginning with Gk. *ei* ["if"], translated "since" in NIV) must be interpreted accurately. It does not express uncertainty (as some translations suggest) but fact: "*since* God so loved us. . . ." There is no condition here—John has already affirmed in no uncertain terms that God's activity in Christ has given us indisputable evidence of the Father's love. Therefore, the exhortation to love springs not from any anxiety about losing this love nor from a threat of God's wrath. Our obligation to love one another is a by-product of God's loving generosity toward us (cf. 3:11, 14, 23; 4:12, 21; 5:2; 2 John 5). John believes that this is the first inspiration of Christian love: It is a reflection of divine love already showered upon us.

Moreover, John goes on to say that as we meet this obligation to love, we experience something unparalleled: God lives within us as his love is made complete through us (vv. 12, 15). This explains John's reference to the invisibility of God in verse 12. Love that is inspired by God, that is a fulfillment of this divine obedience, makes God a tangible reality. In verse 13 we learn of the vehicle that brings this presence of God about, namely, the Holy Spirit. This notion is paralleled

---

8 The *zao/zoe* word group occurs fifty-four times in Johannine literature
9. See Luke 18 13, Romans 3 25, Hebrews 2 17, 9 5; 1 John 2 2, 4 10

in 3:24. Those who obey God's commands live in him and *he lives in them.* "This is how we know that he lives in us: We know it by the Spirit he gave us." Here, then, is the second inspiration of Christian love: God's own Spirit, which is powerfully alive within us as we obey (3:24) and love (4:13).

Finally, John offers a third source of inspiration. We do not simply hear about what God has done in Christ, nor do we simply experience the Spirit. John insists that through our proclamation—our testimony—the reality of God presses itself into our lives (vv. 14–16). We are forced to observe that faithful, loving discipleship is not simply an emotional experience of being loved or a response to an ethical command. It is not even loving conduct, although all of these things are significant. *Such discipleship has theological content.* God's indwelling is mediated to us through the work of Christ ("If anyone acknowledges that Jesus is the Son of God, God lives in him and he in God," v. 15). John's vision of discipleship demands our minds as well as our hearts.

The Results of Christian Love (4:17–19)

IN VERSE 17 John makes the remarkable statement that a life inspired by God, a life shaped by this quality of Christian discipleship—such a life exhibits a *love that is made complete* (cf. 4:12, 18). The NIV misses an important connective with the foregoing verses: *"By this* love is made complete among us."[10] That is, by everything said thus far, by the principles outlined above, God's love is perfected *among us.* Note that in verse 12 John refers to love being perfected *in us.* Now a different emphasis is apparent. God's love is perfected not through our perception of it or our experience of it, *but through our expression of it.* God's love reaches completion by the degree to which it is shared among us. Thus some have suggested that for completion to take place, John has a divine triangle in mind (see illustration, page 190). As C. H. Dodd wrote, "The energy of love discharges itself along lines which form a triangle, whose points are God, self, and neighbor."[11]

---

10. Greek *en touto.* Brown cites John 16:30, 1 John 3:10, 19 as precedents in Johannine grammar for such a clause as pointing back to what precedes. Other interpreters have seen this phrase pointing forward to the subsequent *hina* or *hoti* clauses.

11. C. H. Dodd, as cited in Thompson, *1–3 John,* 126.

The most immediate result of this perfect love is assurance:[12] We will have boldness or confidence on the Day of Judgment. John refers to this boldness four times in his letter (2:28; 3:21; 4:17; 5:14).[13] The use in 3:21 (as well as in the book of Hebrews) defines confident, child-like speech in prayer. Here in 4:17 it evokes vivid images, as Robert Law wrote, of "the judgment-seat before which all must stand, and of the frank confidence with which people turn to their Judge and look upon His face."[14]

Experiencing and expressing the love of God so powerfully, knowing unequivocally that God-in-Spirit resides in our lives, result in unbounded confidence as we approach the day when we meet God. We are not irreverent but assured, not flippant but forthright. Because of his indwelling we know that despite our continued life in the world, we are different: "We are like him" (v. 17b), that is, we are like Jesus.[15] We enjoy a privileged place with God.

The principle John has in mind is the character of God's love. "Perfect love drives out fear" (v. 18a). There can be no apprehensiveness or fear of God when we fully comprehend his love. Fear and love are mutually exclusive. To fear the character of God or to fear the final judgment paralyzes us. It destroys the perfection love offers (v. 18b). But this leaves open the question whether or not there is a place for fear (see application below).

---

12 Note that verse 17b introduces a *hina* clause, indicating result
13. It occurs nine times in the Fourth Gospel
14. Law, *The Tests of Life*, 280
15. Manuscripts indicate the scribal concern to reconcile this verse with 3.2

The Command to Love (4:20–5:4)

JOHN CLOSES THE section with an exhortation. He has been describing two dimensions in our experience: (1) the love we share with God (expressed through Jesus Christ), and (2) the love we share in the community (viewed as a by-product of God's love). To be sure, it is easier to love people we see rather than God, who may seem intangible at times. In 4:20–21 John is not saying that we should practice human love in order to grow into divine love. Nor is he saying that human love is the exclusive way we love God. He is not interested in teaching us about stages of loving God, but about giving us tests by which we can see if we really love God in the first place. The absence of love for one another betrays an absence of love for God. Those who live with this duplicity, saying that they love God but in their hearts hate some human being, are (in John's unyielding words) "liars."[16]

This final exhortation does not rely on experience to fuel our love. For those whose lives require a stronger stimulus, John ushers a divine command: "Whoever loves God must also love his brother." Similar words have occurred elsewhere in this letter (2:9; 3:10, 23). The point bears emphasis since John's community was no doubt struggling with impulses to hate their opponents. Jesus commonly summarized God's view of life with this same double command. When asked by the rich young ruler about the commands of God, for example, he remarked,

> "'You shall love the Lord your God with all your heart, and with all your soul, and with all your mind.' This is the greatest and first commandment. And a second is like it: 'You shall love your neighbor as yourself.' On these two commandments hang all the law and the prophets." (Matt. 22:36–38, NRSV; cf. John 13:34)

It is critical to keep 1 John 5:1–4 as a part of this discussion. John does not change his subject, but here gives it a different nuance. In 5:1a we learn that holding a true confession of faith is evidence of rebirth

---

16. Curiously, the word "liar" (Gk *pseustes*) is a favorite Johannine term. Of ten New Testament uses, John employs seven: two in the Fourth Gospel (8:44, 55) and five in 1 John (1:10; 2:4, 22, 4:20, 5:10). This word underscores the intensity of the struggle within the community for its very life.

(just as in 4:7 it was love and in 2:29 and 3:9 it was obedience). Verse 1b adds a general principle, which unfortunately we often miss:[17] Whoever loves the "one who gave birth" (NIV, "father") loves his offspring. That is, "everyone who loves the parent loves the child" (NRSV). John may have something specific in mind. If you love your own parents, surely you will love their other children. Or again, if you love God (as parent), you will love all his children (including Jesus). Therefore, using a family metaphor, John is broadening the ethical challenge. God has many children. To love him—or to love Jesus—demands that we love other children of God as well.

These arguments now lead to the affirmation in 5:2. Some interpreters view "this is" as referring back to 5:1.[18] Hence: "On the principle that we must love all members of God's family, we know that we must love God's children whenever we love God." Other interpreters (including the NIV) prefer to point the principle forward: "This is how we know that we love the children of God: by loving God and carrying out his commands." Essentially, the question here turns on what fuels Christian love: Is it grounded in moral obligation or in God's love? Perhaps (with Smalley) both should work together. "The two loves are inseparable."[19] The command mentioned in 5:2 is the command to love God's children, but this obligation springs from a profound affection for God in the first place.

In 5:3b–4 John repeats what he said in verse 1. People who understand the true identity of Christ—those who love God and all his children, who obey his commands—these are people who have been born of God. If they have such divine power on their side, the command to love cannot be a burden. No impediment, no temptation from the world, can rob them of moral victory. Stott remarks, "The reason why we do not find the commandments of God burdensome lies not, however, only in their character. It lies also in ourselves, namely, that we have been given the possibility of keeping them."[20] The victory of the Christian life, therefore, is not about us *as we are in*

---

17. The Greek words for "father" and "child" do not occur, thus, the passage is not referring to God as Father. Hence the NRSV helpfully translates "parent" and "child."

18. The debate in John about the direction of the phrase *en touto* has already appeared in 4:17.

19. Smalley, *1, 2, 3 John*, 268

20. Stott, *The Epistles of John*, 174

the world. It is about power—transformation through rebirth—and about how that power defeats the world's impulses that once controlled us.

JOHN'S UNYIELDING INTEREST in love is one well-known hallmark of his letters. Again and again he affirms the importance of love and outlines what might prompt such love. But what inspired such interest? I believe his pastoral context of working in a sorely divided church forced him to ponder deeply how to bring a warring church to unity. Thus, John is doing pastoral theology here, and it is linked entirely to his context of division and controversy. But the question we might ask is whether that context limits the usefulness of his words today. Is it necessary to be in a context of crisis or conflict in order to appreciate John's words? As I look at these verses and strive to bridge them to my own Christian context, I am forced to ask how contextually "bound" these verses may be.

On the one hand, I can answer that conflict is intrinsic to virtually every Christian setting. This view springs from a realistic appraisal of human fallenness. I do not have to go far in my church, my denomination, or my vocation to find tensions parallel to those in the Johannine community. On the other hand, I note that John responds to this crisis without fixing blame or lodging exhortations for particular sins committed. Rather than diagnose the source of the conflict, he concentrates on the remedy. And the remedy is not merely a hollow demand that Christians love one another; instead, John buttresses the demand to love with a theological affirmation of what makes love possible in the first place. In these verses, John seems quite candid that loving reconciliation is not an easy thing (why else does he give so many reminders?). Therefore, he points the way for men and women to be grounded powerfully in God's love and then be able to experience a transformation that will affect community life.

This, then, is my bridge. To simply reconstruct John's struggles for my congregation is to rob the letter of its timeless power. To say that we ought to love one another (while true) says nothing new. But to construct the motive and power that enables love is truly significant. John envisions Christian believers who are so completely healed inwardly that reconciliation within the community is a natural by-product of spiritual maturity.

COLLEGE COMMUNITIES AND churches alike strive to become places of loving reconciliation. The challenge is particularly acute for colleges. At Wheaton College, for example, we have over 2,500 students living together daily, eating meals, attending classes, and pursuing recreational activities. In such a setting the need for Christlike love is pressing. This semester I spoke to the senior class in chapel from Matthew 5:23–25, where Jesus says that if we are worshiping and need to be reconciled to a brother or sister, we should first go, repair the relationship, and then return to the altar. It was a communion service, and I challenged them to interrupt their "time at the altar" (taking bread—but no juice) if they needed to be reconciled to someone. I had no idea what would happen, though there was an abundance of grape juice returned to the chaplain's office.

The need for loving reconciliation is always with our communities. And the Johannine exhortation to love is apt since our college world (like the world of the church) is constantly beset with undisclosed tensions or rivalries. This is a part of what it means to belong to the human community.

These verses pose a central question: What will trigger righteous conduct? What message, what thought process, what experience will trigger activity that can only be described as charitable, gracious, forgiving, and loving? Certainly there must be some antidote, some solution to conduct that is divisive and unloving.

(1) *The grace of God and righteousness.* Not long ago I attended a meeting of faculty and administrators who were discussing the problem of legalism in evangelical colleges. The question at hand was rules of conduct—lifestyle standards—and how these affect spiritual development. Curiously, there was a difference of opinion about what would trigger righteous behavior. "The wrath of God has a place in shaping our conduct," one person contributed. And another: "When God saved Israel in Egypt, the first thing he gave them was the law of Sinai. Law aids our righteousness." Then we heard a quote from C. S. Lewis

(always at the standby for evangelicals!), "Love is that which forgives the most and *condones the least*" (emphasis his). In a word, many were willing to say that *law can trigger righteousness*.

Of course, no one would deny a place for the law, for rules of conduct that place limits on behavior. But the deeper question is whether rules can inspire a life of devotion, service, and worship. Moreover, does a framework of law cultivate the sort of reflex to obey that inspires genuine spiritual maturity?

In these verses, John is promoting a community that will exhibit spiritual maturity, that will lift up high virtues of love and share them enthusiastically. John envisions an obedient community that will devote itself to God completely. How does he do it? First John 4:11 is the answer: Righteousness is only triggered in response to the abundant love of God. "Since God so loved us, we also ought to love one another." Righteous Christian conduct is fueled by the realization that God has devoted himself to us so exhaustively that we can do nothing other than respond.

Last spring I was explaining to an introductory New Testament class Paul's view of grace as it appears in Galatians. Paul shares John's opinion that it was God's love expressed in Christ that inspires the Christian life. In fact, as Paul argued in Romans 7, law by itself simply triggers rebellion. Then I tried an experiment. I asked all forty students to write a one-page essay analyzing whether their lives had been shaped by the threat of law or the wonder of God's grace. I was devastated by the results. Over 90 percent of the class admitted privately that the possibility of God's disfavor and wrath had shaped their Christian outlook since childhood. God's unending love was not foremost in their minds, but his possible displeasure was. Christianity, they reported, was *really about following the rules*. When I told them it was not, you could hear a pin drop. Some privately commented that this was the first time they had heard such "good news."

I do not believe that my student sampling was unusual. These were mature young men and women who came from strong evangelical churches and families. And their reflex was to please God *so that* he would continue to favor them. They had not learned to please God because he already favored them. Because of this reality many Christians are troubled, and many have a genuine fear of God. The following was written by a 21-year-old student who is a strong, knowledgeable evangelical. Her sentences were submitted in a term paper describing the justice of God.

> I feel like God punishes me for sins all of the time. I feel that there is always something I am being punished for. I know that is impossible because there are not enough minutes in the day for God to punish us. I probably should not call it punishment, but that is the way I feel about God's justice. I know of God's love and blessings for me and for that I am eternally grateful and thankful. But I live with this fear that one mess-up and I will be punished again.

I am forced to ask, what is happening in the church? In our families? Who has stolen the good news out of the gospel? As a result, I have built into my syllabi numerous points where I emphasize the loving, abundant generosity of God. And this semester (as I write) it happened again: After one such explanation of God's unmerited love, a mature student told me, "I've never heard anything like this before."

(2) *The risk of generous love.* An immediate reaction among students—and even some colleagues—is the fear that without some disciplinary threat, without law, such generous love could be exploited. No doubt that is true. I am quite sure that Paul's opponents in Galatia were saying the same thing. But it is striking that both John and Paul are willing to endure that risk. John is fully aware of this prospect, for he refers to Christians who fail to live up to their calling. However, like Paul, he never resorts to using fear. He never says that failed Christian discipleship loses the love of God. In 4:19 he quickly and decisively points out the hypocrisy of such unresponsive disciples. But he does not threaten them with the abandonment of God.

Neither does Paul. It is safe to say that the Galatians had fallen from Paul's ideal of discipleship. Yet he exhorts them to "walk in the Spirit" (rather than in the flesh) because it is God who has gifted them so generously (Gal. 5:16–26). Nor does Paul use fear. He underscores the theme of freedom despite the Galatian misbehavior (5:13). And he simply reminds them, "The entire law is summed up in a single command: 'Love your neighbor as yourself'" (5:14). Fear is not a primary pastoral tool.

John does not use fear as a pastoral strategy because "perfect love drives out fear" (1 John 4:18). Whenever our perception of God is shaped by fear and anxiety, worry perhaps over losing his affection, we have not plumbed the depth of his love. We have not experienced his commitment to us. Thus in verse 8 John says it is clear that anyone who does not love another person does not know God because if we have really witnessed God's love in Christ, we will be changed. Love is the essential character of God's being (vv. 8, 16). To fail to express love means that we have not met such powerful divine love ourselves.

(3) *The question of awe.* To imagine God as completely loving runs another risk, that of losing profound respect for him because we have made him too personal, too approachable. Perhaps he becomes a grandparent in our thinking, a wizened relative who is sage and generous. For some, he is a "friend" but hardly a holy, all-powerful Lord.

No doubt this was less of a problem in the first century when audiences with any Jewish heritage held God in high respect. His *distance* and majesty were commonplace in Jewish spiritual life. His grandeur was primary. Thus when the New Testament speaks of God as a loving Father, there is an emotional scandal presented to the hearer: This great, awesome Lord is also interested in profound intimacy with me? When we reclaim this scandalous tension in our preaching and teaching, when we affirm with abandon that God is holy, powerful, and supreme—and at the same time affirm his shocking intimacy with us—good news is found.

An Arab-Christian in the Middle East put it to me this way: "Our problem is that we do not know what it is to live with an absolute monarch." The sheiks, sultans, and kings of Saudi Arabia and the Persian Gulf countries often enjoy absolute power.[21] With a word they can bring economic ruin to anyone. Some can take life simply with a command. Limitless power (within their domain) is characteristic of their lives. Those living in close proximity to such a sultan know that he can be either their greatest benefactor or their greatest enemy. And to be a child, a prince or princess living in the palace, puts one in a breathtaking place of privilege. You are safe alongside the storm, protected next to the lion. The hand that has slain many blesses you.

---

21. For that matter, many modern rulers in the Middle East assume such absolute tyrannical authority based on these old assumptions of power in Arab culture. Consider the rule of Saddam Hussein in Iraq, King Assad in Syria, and the modern royal families in the Persian Gulf countries

When we reclaim the awesomeness and power of God, giving him utmost respect, then his loving-kindness takes on new potency. This is the tension I want my students to feel when they consider the character of God. I want them to feel fear, awe, privilege, and blessing—all at the same moment. This is the good news. The lion's paw is soft, yet powerful. Its growl is deep and loud, yet it utters my name with affection.

(4) *Christian victory and confidence.* John raises an interesting series of questions about spiritual confidence and certainty. The chief thrust of his message is to buttress the average Christian's understanding of God's love and to build a Christian ethic responsive to it. In 5:4 John talks about a victory that overcomes the world. But many in the church have worked hard to win this victory and still feel inadequate. How often I have seen spiritual fatigue on my students' faces—fatigue at trying to generate experiences described in the pulpit! What pastoral strategies are available, what other avenues can enhance our perception of God's presence and shore up our uncertainties? After we announce good news, what then?

John's first suggestion might center on obedience. If I cannot feel God's affection, must I await that feeling before I act? *Or in the course of my activity, might I experience his love for me anew?* I know Christians who have served in desperate situations, and in their serving have tasted for the first time the wonder of divine love. Some have entered urban Chicago to work. Others have gone overseas or worked in our prison system. The point is that they were exhibiting extraordinary love among the loveless, not as a way to make God love them, but as a spiritual exercise, to invigorate their hearts, to touch love itself—because they have felt loveless themselves. Remarkably, loving someone who is unlovely brings into focus the power of God's choice to love us in our unloveliness.

In our passage, therefore, John is quick to charge his followers again and again with an exhortation to obey the command to love regardless of how they feel. First John 4:21 and 5:3 are clear: Those who choose to love God must also choose to love their brothers and sisters and be obedient. Exhortation blends with encouragement time after time as the apostle weaves the delicate fabric of a theology shaped by unmerited love, all the while expecting obedience.

John's second suggestion makes many of us uncomfortable. It is mystical. In 4:13 he tells us that "we know" God lives in us and we in him "because he has given us of his Spirit." This same idea appears in 3:24, "And this is how we know he lives in us: We know it by the Spirit he gave us." John raises this possibility of spiritual reassurance without explaining how it might take place. He assumes that the Holy Spirit is a natural part of his followers' experience and uses this experience as a means of assuring them.

Of course, this forces us to ask the question: Do we refer to the Holy Spirit as an ambiguous "seal" that was placed on our lives at some remote point (when we were baptized or came to faith)? I have clear memories from when I was a teenager, asking my Lutheran pastor about this "Holy Spirit." And my firmest memory is that he could only point to my baptism. "Let's look it up in a concordance," he said weakly. But by then my confidence had evaporated.

I think John has something else in mind. The power to know God's love in reality, the power to love others as he loves us, the reassurance that gives us victory over our doubts—these things may come to us through an experience mediated in the Spirit. A vision perhaps? A Spirit-forged gift? An unexplainable resolve and peace? In any case, this gift is not intellectually obtained, nor is it the fruit of ethical behavior. It is ecstatic, mystical, otherworldly.

But are there other ways we might experience God's mystical love that John has not mentioned? One avenue is the body of Christ. When I am loved *supernaturally* by another Christian, when I am loved *supernaturally* by the body of Christ, I gain a fresh vision of God's love at work through them for me. When God's love feels distant, the body's love is tangible and real, and when I experience it, my own ability to love is quickened. This too, this undramatic, less-than-fantastic, simple experience of love is a working of God's Spirit among us.

1 John 5:5–12

WHO IS IT that overcomes the world? Only he who believes that Jesus is the Son of God. ⁶This is the one who came by water and blood—Jesus Christ. He did not come by water only, but by water and blood. And it is the Spirit who testifies, because the Spirit is the truth. ⁷For there are three that testify: ⁸the Spirit, the water and the blood; and the three are in agreement. ⁹We accept man's testimony, but God's testimony is greater because it is the testimony of God, which he has given about his Son. ¹⁰Anyone who believes in the Son of God has this testimony in his heart. Anyone who does not believe God has made him out to be a liar, because he has not believed the testimony God has given about his Son. ¹¹And this is the testimony: God has given us eternal life, and this life is in his Son. ¹²He who has the Son has life; he who does not have the Son of God does not have life.

JOHN'S INTEREST IN spiritual victory in the previous section leads him to make a specific development about reconciliation. In 4:7ff. John urged that Christian maturity (anchored in a right understanding of God's love and commitment) should result in a loving, reconciled community. Such an experience of God's love results in rebirth and victory, victory even over the world (5:5). But should we pursue such reconciliation at all costs? If there are differences of opinion, should ardently held beliefs be set aside?

As he did in 4:9–10, John refuses in 5:5b–12 to let these affirmations about God and community healing drift free without a Christological mooring. It is only through Christ's incarnation and sacrifice that we gain a clear, undistorted view of God's commitment to us. Therefore, regeneration and ethical inspiration must be theologically informed and Christologically centered.

But there were rival points of view in the Johannine community, and John cannot ignore them. Whose voice, whose witness and testimony do we obey? Of the seventeen uses of the word group for "testify/testimony" in John's letters, ten of them appear in these few verses.[1] Indeed, the question that drives the passage is *what testimony* should be given authority in reconciling these differences.

Therefore John must offer some formula, some method for reconciling theological differences and for weighing the validity of conflicting testimonies. Since the differences in the community were primarily Christological, he does not point to the Old Testament. He cannot even point to the New Testament (since it is unwritten!). Nevertheless, he does have a strategy: The arbiters of truth are the Spirit, traditional theological affirmations, and the trustworthy words of Christian witnesses. Each of these point to one concrete event in history, namely, the incarnation of Jesus Christ.

The Testimony of the Water and the Blood (5:5-6b)

FIRST JOHN 5:6 IS perhaps the most perplexing verse in all of the Johannine letters, "This is the one who came by water and blood—Jesus Christ. He did not come by water only, but by water and blood." Without explanation, John uses a somewhat indecipherable phrase ("water and blood"), which was surely known among his followers. Three views attempt to explain the passage. (1) Some believe "water and blood" refer to the sacraments of baptism and the Eucharist.[2] The chief problem with this view is singular: John's interest is not in church ritual but in historic incarnation. The Johannine schism centers on Christology as it was expressed in history, not on worship.[3]

(2) A second view points to John 19:34, that while Jesus was on the cross, a spear thrust into his side brought forth "blood and water."[4] In this sense John may be saying that the cross is the significant saving

---

1. Words springing from the Greek *martyreo* ("to witness, testify") appear in 5:6, 7, 9 (4x), 10 (3x), and 11. This is about 60 percent of all appearances in John's letters.

2. This view can be found in Luther and Calvin and in sacramental interpreters of John such as O. Cullmann.

3. The view, however, that "blood" cannot refer to the Eucharist in the Johannine literature is mistaken. This is the case in John 6:52-58.

4. This view was supported by Augustine and today has a number of supporters (e.g., Grayston, Kysar, M. Thompson).

event in Jesus' life. This may be important if the secessionists claimed that they were without sin and had no need of ritual cleansing (1 John 1:7). But one difficulty with this view is the closing phrase of verse 6, "not . . . by water only, but by water *and blood.*" John is making a counterpoint to some claim involving only (or primarily) water.[5]

(3) A third view, held by the majority of interpreters, sees water and blood as summing up the totality of Jesus' incarnational ministry on earth.[6] Jesus' baptism (water) and crucifixion (blood) frame his ministry: He was declared Son of God in the Jordan (John 1:34), and he obtained even more power and authority through his glorification at Golgotha. Marshall, for instance, understands that John is refuting a Docetic (or pre-Gnostic) tendency that downplayed a complete incarnation. Some (like Cerinthus, see p. 30) were teaching that the heavenly Christ descended on the man Jesus at baptism but departed before he was crucified. Hence, John says, Jesus came not only by baptismal water, but also through the blood of the cross.

Brown (followed by Smalley) offers a variation of the third view.[7] He doubts whether the denials of Cerinthus should be read back into the Johannine community. But he does think that the secessionists' propaganda (similar to what Cerinthus would teach) emphasized a misreading of the Fourth Gospel in which Jesus' baptism (with its dramatic emphasis on the Spirit) became the salvific feature of his life. Water and Spirit brought saving revelation. Enlightenment, not sacrifice, was the premier avenue to God. Perhaps even John 3:34 was called into service: "The one whom God has sent speaks the words of God, for God gives the Spirit [to Jesus] without limit." John's refutation insists that the life-giving work of Christ is found at the cross. It is Jesus' sacrificial death—not his incarnation alone—that gives life: not by water only, but by water *and blood.*

Either variation of the third view gives a complementary result: John is wrestling with a heresy that demoted the cross. John insists that the testimony of the "water and the blood" upholds a full incarnation. Life and truth can only be found when a complete incarnation embraces a genuine death on the cross.

---

5. Note too that John reverses the order of the terms from John 19:34.

6. This view is supported by Tertullian, Stott, Marshall, and Bruce.

7. Brown, *The Epistles of John,* 594–99; Smalley, *1, 2, 3 John,* 278–80.

The Testimony of the Spirit (5:6c–8)

BUT AS I have urged elsewhere, this is a controversy fueled by pneumatic (or charismatic) impulses. Teachers claiming to bear the Spirit were pressing their views on the community (2:27; 4:1–6). This was the spiritual terrain common to the Johannine churches. John therefore adds yet another component to his list of witnesses: "And it is *the Spirit* who testifies because the Spirit is the truth" (v. 6c).[8] In verse 7 the Spirit is explicitly added to "the water and the blood," and in verse 8 these three are affirmed as sharing one view.[9] What did John have in mind?

A possible background may be Jewish law, where at least two witnesses were required in order to confirm some testimony (Deut. 19:15; John 8:17–18). Jesus' trial illustrates this well. Because the Sanhedrin witnesses could not agree (Mark 14:56, 59), their claims against Jesus failed. John, on the other hand, points to three witnesses (with a fourth to follow), and these three are all in agreement![10]

The present tense of the verb "testifies" in "the Spirit testifies" implies that this testimony is an inner witness of the Spirit that is ongoing. John 15:26 says that the Spirit of truth will testify to Jesus. But verse 27 immediately refers to the testimony of Christ's followers, the church, who will in effect implement the Spirit's work. John's thought here in 1 John 5:6–7 may be similar. The work of the Spirit is evident as the church testifies for Christ.

Since John's chief concern is soteriological, since he is emphasizing the centrality of the cross, he may be thinking of the one whose testimony at the foot of the cross anchors its historicity. John 19:35 describes the Beloved Disciple in this very role: "He who saw this has testified so that you also may believe. His testimony is true, and he knows that he tells the truth" (NRSV). If it is the Spirit who testifies—

---

8 Some commentators believe that "the water and the blood" now joined to the Spirit in verse 8 refer to the sacraments, particularly since the verb "testify" is present It is best, however, to give "water and blood" the same meaning as that found in verse 6.

9 A footnote in the NIV notes that at 5·7–8 the Latin Vulgate and some very late (post-sixteenth century) Greek manuscripts add that three witnesses also testify in heaven. the Father, the Word, and the Holy Spirit. This is a late scribal addition, placed, no doubt, in the margin. It does not appear among early church fathers, who combed the New Testament looking for Trinitarian references It should therefore be given no consideration in any interpretation of 1 John 5

10 Stott, *The Epistles of John*, 181.

and if the Beloved Disciple is the community's premier witness—then indirectly verse 8 is arguing that the Beloved Disciple's eyewitness account is Spirit-inspired. The Spirit conveys the truth; the Beloved Disciple conveys the truth. Therefore, what the Beloved Disciple has said comes from the Spirit.

Thus, John is saying that Spirit-inspired teaching will not dislodge the historic events of salvation witnessed at the cross. This witness began with the Beloved Disciple and has been nurtured within the community of believers.

The Testimony of the Father (5:9–12)

IT IS DIFFICULT to interpret John's next thought (5:9–10) if we think of the Father's testimony as separate from that of the Spirit, the water, and the blood. Indeed, John does not indicate how the Father's testimony is given (he merely refers to the fact of it). John 5:37 is similar, where Jesus, in his roll call of witnesses, includes the Father as supporting his case but does not explicitly say how.[11]

Instead, John simply urges that since we accept human testimonies,[12] we ought to accept a divine testimony all the more. It is God's divine authority that rests behind the testimony of the water and the blood. It is *God's* Spirit that is affirming truths about the gospel of Jesus Christ. It is impossible to avoid thinking about the schism in John's church at this point. Human testimonies were struggling for acceptance. John says that these testimonies must come up against not just other points of view, but against God himself.

God's point of view, expressed in the historic life of Jesus and kept alive in the witness of the church through the Spirit, must now win the day. Indeed, God's witness is exclusively—and exhaustively— about his Son (v. 10). Thus the test of whether or not we accept God's testimony rests here: Do we embrace the truth about Jesus Christ? Do we concur with the apostolic eyewitness? Put in another light (as John is prone to do), to reject the truth about Jesus, to reject the "water and the blood," is to stand opposed to God and contradict his testimony.

---

11 Unless in John 5:37 Jesus is referring to God's voice given at baptism (see 5:37b)

12. The NIV omits translating the first Greek word in verse 9, "if" (Gk. *ei*) The use of this word here does not imply doubt but certainty, as if to say, "Since we accept .. "

But what is really at stake here? Is it merely orthodox belief in Jesus? Does John simply want to preserve the honor of the Son and defend the testimony of God? This is important, but John now says more. The testimony of the Father has to do with life, eternal life (vv. 11–12). Since life comes to us through the death of the Son, to deny "the blood," to deny an incarnation that embraces the cross, to deny the salvific, substitutionary work of Jesus on Calvary, puts our own salvation in jeopardy. Thus, disbelieving the right testimonies has severe consequences. Claiming a divine enlightenment that neglects the Son is eternally perilous.

THESE VERSES REMIND us that the Johannine letters were documents forged in the midst of a desperate theological debate.[13] We have read hints of Christological polemics throughout. Claims of opponents are paraphrased in some cases (1:6–10). We even read accusations (2:4–11; 3:9–10), descriptions of defectors from the church (2:19–21), and warnings about false teachers and prophets (2:26; 3:7; 4:1–3). We also have an idea concerning what they debated (2:22–23; 4:3). Perhaps 2 John 7 crystallizes the intensity and content of this debate: "Many deceivers, who do not acknowledge Jesus Christ as coming in the flesh, have gone out into the world. Any such person is the deceiver and the antichrist."

When we read a phrase like "water and blood," we can be sure that we are entrenched in this very debate. In the first few verses of chapter 5, John has affirmed God's love for us and how it should affect our communities. But in reaching out for the best example of divine love (the life and death of Jesus), he finds himself caught up again in the Christological controversy. "Water and blood," then, is a *literary salvo*, fixed to some degree in the context of John's campaign for the truth. The traditions of the earliest church claimed that one of his opponents was the notorious Cerinthus (so Irenaeus).[14] We can at least be sure that John was battling a controversy that diminished the need for a complete incarnation that stretched from Bethlehem to Golgotha.

---

13. For a full summary of the controversy, see the introduction.
14. Irenaeus, *Against Heresies*, 3.3.4.

My hermeneutical struggle here is to ask to what extent 5:5–12 are completely bound to this historical context. John's original salvo, while potent on one battlefield, may be less so on another. Nevertheless, within that salvo is a concern, a universal concern, that is dynamically relevant today.

Let us return to John's setting for a moment, where we see religious leaders with a keen interest in Jesus Christ. Teachers and prophets were making pronouncements about truth, some of whom claimed to be inspired by the Spirit. But they were reinterpreting Christ's work so that the cross was secondary (or irrelevant), and they were promoting alternate sources of "life" that had no need of Christ's substitutionary death.

What does John do with this? In the framework of this schism, he argues that it is not possible to claim the inspiration of the Spirit, to say one speaks for God, and at the same time deny the incarnational reality of Jesus. To do this is to undercut one's claim to possess the Spirit in the first place. For John, one cannot claim intimacy with God and contradict God's premier revelation of himself. One cannot teach Christian theology and at the same time dismantle incarnational Christology and soteriology.

This is therefore a critical bridge point for us. I need to observe theological trends that dilute the significance of the Incarnation and the salvific works of the cross. While John's theological salvo—water and blood—may possibly be ineffective today, still, I need to unpack its theological center and apply it to my own setting.

CONTEMPORARY THEOLOGICAL TRENDS are often ready to dispense with the sacrifice of Christ while trying to keep Christianity itself. Finding the cross to be an embarrassment, a mythological accretion perhaps, some have sought a Christology emptied of any sacrificial soteriology.

This was most apparent in a conference sponsored by the World Council of Churches and underwritten in large part by the Presbyterian Church (U.S.A.).[15] From November 4–7, 1994, 2,200 people

---

15. A local sponsor was The Greater Minneapolis/St. Paul Council of Churches. The PCUSA contributed $65,000 Additional funding came from the American Baptist Church,

from 49 states and 27 countries filled the Minneapolis Convention Center to "reimage" God. The conference called for a "Second Reformation" that would begin radical theological surgery on the church's belief systems.

Essentially the conference developed a new anchor for truth. The foundation for Christian theology would no longer be in the historic events of salvation recorded in the Bible. The star of the show, instead, was Sophia (*Wisdom*)—a long-suppressed feature of the biblical tradition, which resides principally within the female psyche. To the reimagers, Sophia never takes a historic, particularistic form, but appears in many ways and in many spiritual traditions. South Dakota Indian tribal dances and Zulu rituals are equal contributors for theological reflection. The conference program was explicit: Sophia is the place in us where the entire universe resides. For a multicultural, therapeutic society like ours, this is religion made-to-order. Self-discovery is the platform for divine revelation.

It is most important to note that in this church setting, historic Christology was totally dismantled. The target of the conferees was the cross. Christian soteriology promoted violence, they claimed. A father killing his son is a formula for child abuse. One speaker (Delores Williams) did not disguise her convictions at all, "I don't think we need a theory of atonement at all. I don't think we need folks hanging on crosses and blood dripping and weird stuff. . . . We just need to listen to the god within."

This demands new rituals as well. Alongside dances to Sophia that reminded many of Canaanite fertility rites was born a new Eucharist, fashioned not from bread and wine but from honey and milk. Liturgies joined to this pagan Eucharist shocked even those with minimal theological sensitivities:

> Our maker Sophia, we are women in your image. . . . With the hot blood of our wombs we give form to new life. . . . Sophia, creator God, let your milk and honey flow. . . . With nectar between our thighs we invite a lover, we birth a child; with our warm body fluids we remind the world of its pleasures and sensations. . . . We celebrate the sweat that pours from us during our

---

the United Church of Christ, the Evangelical Lutheran Church of America, and the United Methodist Church.

labors. We celebrate our bodiliness, our physicality, the sensations of pleasure, our oneness with earth and water.

We must be clear about one thing: These were people committed to the church—people whose lives were nurtured in Christian settings—and they were willing to utterly dispense with traditional Christology.

Is this sort of heresy merely orbiting the periphery of the church? Are these theological "eccentrics" simply to be dismissed as irrelevant and thus ignored? On the contrary—and this is why what happened in 1994 is important to us—because of the conference, open discussions about the validity of the pursuit of Sophia and the archaizing of Christian orthodoxy has been taking place in mainline churches throughout the country. "Reimaging" was worthy of debate, worthy of a hearing, and has made its appearance in thoughtful churches everywhere. It has been defended as well not only by mainline church bureaucrats, but also by theologians in Christian colleges and seminaries who see it as one more form of acceptable diversity. *The barbarians are not simply at the gate; they have entered the church narthex.*

(1) *John urges that "the blood"—the cross—must remain central to all we are and preach.* I think here of the scorn that Paul describes in 1 Corinthians 1–4, where he defends the "foolishness" of the cross. "We proclaim Christ crucified, a stumbling block to Jews and foolishness to Gentiles, but to those who are being called, both Jews and Greeks, Christ is the power of God and the *wisdom* of God" (1 Cor. 1:23–24 NRSV). Not only does Paul anchor the meaning of Jesus in the cross, but he locates the wisdom (*sophia*) of God here as well. Therefore, the cross may not be demoted in *any* Christian soteriology. The mystery of what God is doing on our behalf is hidden there in all its particularity and severity. Christ is not simply one example of God's divine wisdom revealed to the world, a wisdom that can stand alongside other religious systems. Christ is *the* wisdom of God, and this wisdom is manifested in his salvific death.

(2) *John points to the custodianship of the Spirit as preserver of the truth.* But John does not make clear how this witness to the truth takes place practically. When does the Spirit testify concerning these matters of orthodox belief?

For many evangelicals this is an inner testimony, a spiritual discernment. No doubt this is true. But I cannot help but wonder if John has more in mind. In these verses John is reciting a traditional formula ("water and blood") and encapsulating in them a symbol of orthodox conviction. This "creedal" recitation has become an anchor that should safeguard Christians from wrong belief. Throughout the letter John does the same thing, pointing believers to a recitation of what "was from the beginning." Concrete foundations, therefore, not personal creativity and innovation, provide us with the substance and strength of our faith.

This means that one avenue of the Spirit's work is the very human institutions that build and protect those foundations. This is undoubtedly one function of the church. The church, through its confessions and traditions, through its recitation of creeds and its defense of councils, lays a foundation from which secure things can be built. But as an evangelical, I fear we have lost our understanding of these anchors. I am surprised at how many of my students do not even know the Apostles' Creed (much less the Creed of Nicea), nor do they respect the enormous importance of councils like Chalcedon. Foundation building through recitation has become a thing of the past.

For a number of years, theologians have been sounding the alarm. The underpinnings of *all* we believe are no longer recognized by many. The validity of belief now seems to be *functional*: Thomas Oden describes this crisis with a telling story:

> A plastic plumbing-fixtures tycoon inherited from his Slavic uncle a baroque, antique, jeweled diadem of spectacular beauty and considerable historical importance. He had been entrusted to take care of it but knew nothing of its actual value and did not lift a finger to protect it. He considered it "just old junk." He hung it on an antelope horn on his mantle. Once in a while he enjoyed spinning it in the air, showing it off at employee parties, bending it, getting laughs. On certain occasions when he was in debt, he had been known to dig a jewel out and pawn it.

> Isn't this much like the relation in which we moderns stand to classical Christianity? As moderns, we feel enormously superior to our Christian heritage. It is of little practical value to us, although we are still willing to keep it around. We should hardly feel good about throwing it away altogether, but it is little more

to us than a mantel decoration or a souvenir of a trip long ago to Atlantic City.[16]

I remember a shocking experience during my last year of seminary. My preaching professor required us to read one sermon per day for ten weeks! In addition to the homiletical insight I gained, I noticed in the older sermons, from 1900–1950, a level of theological sophistication I rarely hear today. Pastors were weighing theological themes seriously.

Most recently David Wells has made a passionate argument for reclaiming theology in the evangelical church.[17] Wells chronicles with dismay the loss of theological substance even among Christian leaders; interest in the certainty, the compelling value, and the relevance of theology are disappearing. The theological soul of the church is being lost. And, Wells remarks, the consequences for the church may be dreadful. In a study of seminarians in 1993, Wells discovered that 66.4 percent said that life would not have much meaning without theology and 74.9 percent said that their most important decisions are based on theology. Yet among these same seminarians, 61.2 percent agreed with this statement: "While evangelical theology is still professed, it is losing its power to define what being an evangelical means and how evangelicalism is practiced." One student commented that theology is losing ground in the church because "evangelicals have lost their pursuit of the truth."[18]

(3) *John also urges that no claim to spirituality is legitimate if it dismantles what God has said in Jesus Christ.* This is what makes the Reimaging Conference in Minneapolis so pernicious. Here teachers became false prophets, claiming a divine voice but departing from what that voice had said in Jesus Christ. Minneapolis provided a theology emptied of biblical Christology. As a result, it built a doctrine of life and salvation that made Jesus superfluous.

John claims that to deny Christ in this manner is also to deny the Father. "Anyone who does not believe God has made him out to be a

---

16. Thomas Oden, *Agenda for Theology Recovering Christian Roots* (New York: Harper & Row, 1979), 1–2.

17. D. Wells, *God in the Wasteland The Reality of Truth in a World of Fading Dreams* (Grand Rapids: Eerdmans, 1994)

18. Ibid., 206.

liar, because he has not believed the testimony God has given about his Son" (5:10). Theological expression today, therefore, must be tested against the bar of incarnational Christology. The implications of this are enormous. It presses us to make hard judgments concerning theological diversity, it forces us to weigh the cost of affiliating the church with other religious movements, and it challenges us to wonder when we have emptied our creeds of Christ in environments that are inhospitable to him.

1 John 5:13–21

I WRITE THESE things to you who believe in the name of the Son of God so that you may know that you have eternal life. ¹⁴This is the confidence we have in approaching God: that if we ask anything according to his will, he hears us. ¹⁵And if we know that he hears us—whatever we ask—we know that we have what we asked of him.

¹⁶If anyone sees his brother commit a sin that does not lead to death, he should pray and God will give him life. I refer to those whose sin does not lead to death. There is a sin that leads to death. I am not saying that he should pray about that. ¹⁷All wrongdoing is sin, and there is sin that does not lead to death.

¹⁸We know that anyone born of God does not continue to sin; the one who was born of God keeps him safe, and the evil one cannot harm him. ¹⁹We know that we are children of God, and that the whole world is under the control of the evil one. ²⁰We know also that the Son of God has come and has given us understanding, so that we may know him who is true. And we are in him who is true—even in his Son Jesus Christ. He is the true God and eternal life.

²¹Dear children, keep yourselves from idols.

Original Meaning

JOHN CONCLUDES HIS letter by reinforcing those themes sounded throughout the previous chapters. His key interests again are assurance and definition. In the struggle within his congregation, he has staked out clear boundaries. He has written unyielding definitions of those who understand the truth about Christ and those who have falsified it. The former have life, the latter have death; the former believe the testimony of God, the latter have made him a liar (5:10).

John has also worked to shore up the confidence of his followers. A mere glance at the distribution of key words gives away his concern. The word groups surrounding the Greek "to know" (*oida* and *ginosko*) occur with surprising frequency in the letters of John and make their strongest appearance here.[1] In fact, 1 John 5 has a greater density of use than almost any other New Testament chapter. In 5:13–21 John repeats again and again that he has written so that his followers might know with certainty the truth of their convictions (vv. 13, 15, 18, 19, 20). Now that his writing is drawing to a close, he wants them to be assured and confident in their faith. Unlike the Gospel of John, whose purpose (given in 20:31) is to bring people to faith ("that you may believe that Jesus is the Christ"), 1 John is written for believers. Having believed, they now need to know, with every fiber of their being, that they possess eternal life.

Prayer and Assurance (5:13–15)

SOME COMMENTATORS PREFER to see verse 13 as connected to the previous section, as a closing statement that concludes the thoughts of 5:11–12. This may be the case. But it is frequently John's style to link sections together by employing a common theme. In the present section he wants to strengthen his followers' resolve and to reassure them of their place with God and the promises that accrue to those who hold fast to the faith. Therefore, he recapitulates what he said earlier and, in so doing, gives a summary of his purposes for the whole letter. Smalley helpfully translates the beginning of the sentence, "I have written *so that you may be sure* that you possess eternal life."[2] Even the grammar of this verse underscores the quality of this possession.[3] This is not just

---

1. To examine frequency of usage rather than merely asking how many times John uses a word in a given book, we can study a ratio of uses (occurrences against, say, 1000 words) to compare with other books. For *oida*, for instance, it is less interesting to know how many times it occurs in John than it is to know *how frequently* a book may use a word group in its vocabulary compared with other books. *Ginosko* occurs 222 times in the New Testament. But here we ask who uses it, how often, and where. For example, while most New Testament books average 1.5 uses of *ginosko* per thousand words, the highest books are John (3.14), 2 John (3 6), and 1 John (10.2) The same is true for *oida*. Its highest ratios of use are found in John (4.6), 1 John (6.1), and 1 Thessalonians (7 7). *These are double the New Testament average!*

2. Smalley, *1, 2, 3 John*, 290.

3. The adjective is separated from its noun for emphasis, *hina eidete hoti zoen echete aionion*.

life God has given, it is "life *eternal.*" And it is a gift to be possessed *now.* His present tense implies the enduring, reassuring effects of knowing our eternal destiny. Life is not just a promise, it is an inheritance enjoyed in the present. In Johannine language, it is having fellowship with God (John 17:3; 1 John 1:3–4).

One of the results of this knowledge is confidence or boldness before God, particularly as we pray (v. 14). Once before John raised the subject of prayer and confidence (see 3:21–23). There he urged that successful prayer must be wed to a life that glorifies God, that conforms to God's desires, and that thereby pleases him. John now adds that prayer must also be in conformity with God's will. Thus the wonder of prayer "consists not in bringing God's will down to us, but in lifting our will up to His."[4]

Jesus perhaps modeled this best. His will was always one with the Father (John 4:34), he always did the Father's works (6:38–40), and he always spoke what the Father wished him to say (3:34; 8:55; 14:10; 17:8). John believes that through this oneness a profound intimacy will result, making prayer a genuine unity of wills. In John 15:7 Jesus says, "If you remain in me and my words remain in you, ask whatever you wish, and it will be given you." Spiritual remaining is the key that unlocks the power of prayer.

To say that God "hears" (Gk. *akouo*) us does not diminish his interest at all. This does not imply that our prayers are merely "audible." John uses this word frequently in his Gospel (fifty-nine times) and letters (sixteen times). It suggests "attentive listening" or "listening favorably" (John 9:31; 11:41–42); in some cases it means "to understand."[5] In other words, God does not simply hear us, but he understands and responds. Moreover, John takes the next step: "We know that we have what we ask for." In other words, our requests are granted. This is a remarkable statement and has led to endless misunderstanding and anguish over the centuries. Any contemporary application demands careful thought (see pp. 219–27). No doubt the condition of verse 14 (abiding in God's will) applies not only to God's hearing but also to our receiving God's gifts. Union with God's will is a prerequisite for each.

---

4. Law, *Tests of Life,* 301

5 This is evident in the many places Jesus says, "He who has ears, let him hear!" (*ho exhon ota akoueto,* e g., Matt. 11:15, 13 9)

Prayer and Sin (5:16–18)

THOUGHTS ON PRAYER lead in a more somber direction in verses 16–18, but there is a link with the foregoing that is important. Christians who are alert to God's will should know with confidence the success of their prayers. But likewise they should know the seriousness of sin and how it impedes spiritual vitality. Moreover, they should know the power of prayer for another person—particularly for one who sins. It is likely that John has been leading up to this all along.[6] In the letter he has marked off clear boundaries between true believers and the secessionists, the orthodox and the heretical, and he has emphasized the importance of sin and righteousness for the church (1:7–10; 2:12; 3:4–5, 8–9; 4:10). Christians acknowledge their sin (1:8; 2:1–3), but they do not persist in sinful habits (3:6–9). Unbelievers, by contrast, sin consistently but often refuse to admit it. Sin (for many of them) is an archaic category.

John has in mind a situation in which one believer sees another committing a sin. The NIV refers to "brother," which literally translates the Greek word but in John's idiom means any fellow believer. In this case, we are told to pray, and God will respond giving him or her life.[7] The chief difficulty in the verse is that John says this intercession should be done for "those whose *sin does not lead to death.*" It is important to note what John is *not* saying. He is not saying that prayer for "sins leading to death" is prohibited or that there is a level of sin beyond which prayer is useless. The NIV translation of verse 16b obscures John's interest to some extent, for he is only making his recommendation for "sin [that] does not lead to death." He is silent about the other.

But what are these two types of sin? The "sin leading to death" could refer to physical illness and death (cf. Num. 18:22; Deut. 22:26; Isa. 22:14; Acts 5:1–11; 1 Cor. 5:5; 11:29–30). But this interpretation seems unlikely in the present passage, particularly since verse 16 says God will give the sinner life. This life must be *eternal* life; if it were physical life, John should extend it to those other "mortal" sins, the very

---

6. I. H Marshall, *The Epistles of John,* 245.

7 In the Greek text the subject of "will give" in verse 16 is ambiguous (Gk. "and he/she will give him/her life"). The NIV is right in supplying God as the subject, making his life-giving act a response to prayer.

thing he does not do. And those with "less deadly sins" do not have their physical lives in jeopardy in the first place.

A more helpful solution comes from the Old Testament distinction between inadvertent sins and intentional sins. In the Old Testament the temple sacrificial rituals only provided forgiveness for accidental or unconscious sins (Lev. 4:2, 13, 22, 27; 5:15–18; Num. 15:27–31; Ps. 19:13). When someone sinned intentionally and willfully, the sinner was either exiled (Num. 15:30–31) or killed (Deut. 17:12). This dual classification of sin persisted into Judaism of the New Testament period (cf. Qumran, 1QS 5:11–12).

But the more difficult exegetical question lies one step further. What type of sin does John have in mind for Christians? We will open this subject below.

Three Certainties (5:19–20)

JOHN CONCLUDES THIS section with three bold statements about Christian certainty. Verses 18, 19, and 20 each begin with the same statement, "We know" (Gk. *oidamen*; cf. 3:2, 14), which gives the verses a rhythmic cadence. And in each case, the verses sound themes that have been dear to John's heart from the first chapter. The first addresses the ongoing righteousness of God's children; the second speaks of the fallenness of the world; the third gives the hope that is in Christ as we live in this world. Sanctification, disintegration, and redemptive hope are John's final words to his readers.

John's earlier reference to sin (vv. 16–17) inspires a sweeping statement about Christians: They do not sin. The NIV translates "continue to sin" in order to reflect the present tense of the Greek verb. The subject of Christian perfection appeared earlier in 3:6–9; there we explained that even though John seems to be saying that Christians never sin (or cannot sin, 3:9), this hardly fits our Christian experience and does not agree with the teaching elsewhere in the letter about sin (1:7–10; 2:1). The Greek present tense suggests ongoing activity; hence, Christians (in John's view) do not have *the habit of sinning*. Christians do not "live in sin."

But more must be said. John may have in mind the distinction already raised in verses 16–17, that Christians do not engage in "sin that leads to death," namely, intentional, willful acts against God.

Why? Because all people[8] who are genuinely Christians have been "born of God."[9] There are no exceptions. Furthermore, Christ himself sustains and protects them from the evil one (v. 18b).[10] Therefore, Christians do not engage in this sort of sustained, willful repudiation of God. Jesus' protection of his followers is a regular Johannine theme (John 10:7–17; 17:12), and John here affirms that the Christian's plight in the world is not solitary. The quest for righteousness is supported and sustained by Jesus himself. Believers keep Jesus' word because Jesus keeps them.

But we also know more (v. 19). This is John's second bold affirmation. The sustenance and protection of Jesus are essential because the world lies (NIV, "is under the control of") in the grip of Satan. John's imagery is striking. The world is not under siege by Satan; it hardly struggles against him at all. *The world rests in Satan's arms.* John's dualistic outlook is once again drawing sharp boundaries between church and world, light and darkness, God and the evil one. Christians reside in the rival camp to Satan, but our security is assured because Jesus resides there with us. The world is used to Satan's embrace, but Christians cannot be held by him.

Finally, John makes clear our hope. If the world is experiencing disintegration and there are many aligned with the forces of evil, what hope is there for us in the world? John's answer (v. 20) is that Jesus Christ has penetrated the world; he has worked as saboteur, undermining the systems of the world and reversing its possibilities. Note that here John describes the work of Christ as bringing knowledge (he "has given us understanding, so that we may know ..."), but this should not be seen as a type of Gnostic enlightenment—the very thing to which John is opposed! Christian knowledge is focused on genuine reality, things that happened in history. Thus in verse 20 John does not say we merely know truth (Gk. *aletheia*); rather, we know "him who is true [or real]" (Gk. *alethinon*). John uses an adjective rather than

---

8 The Greek word *pas* in verse 18 (translated "anyone" in NIV) emphasizes there are no exceptions to John's rule.

9 Stott, *The Epistles of John*, 191, remarks how the Greek perfect participle "indicates that the new birth, far from being a transient phase of religious experience, has an abiding result."

10 There is a debate about the interpretation of "the one who was born of God." Some have argued that it refers to reborn believers (who keep others safe through their prayers) Many others see this as a reference to Jesus Christ

the usual noun to underscore that Christian certainty is not about abstract reason or inspired enlightenment, but about God, the real God, "him who is true," the only true God (cf. 1 Sam. 3:7; Jer. 24:7; 31:34; John 1:9; 15:1; Rev. 3:7).

To be in the truth (v. 20b), then, is not just about being right, but about sharing in true reality (as opposed to falsehood). John's final thought is undoubtedly the most important. The NIV takes verse 20a as referring to Jesus Christ ("He is the true God and eternal life"), and though interpreters differ, "he" can fully refer to the Son rather than the Father. It is fitting that John's letter ends here. Throughout his writing he has promoted and defended the full divinity of Christ. To lose this one conviction is to miss not just Jesus but God himself.

Final Exhortation (5:21)

RATHER THAN CLOSING the letter with a conventional greeting or blessing, John adds a final exhortation, using his now-familiar title "little children" (cf. 2:1, 12, 28; 3:7). It is an abrupt ending, and many have wondered if it launched a new section now lost to us. Nowhere else, for instance, does John refer to idolatry as one of the threats to the community. Nevertheless, the early Christian church living in the Roman empire was constantly surrounded by pagan idols, and the rest of the New Testament gives constant warnings about them (Rom. 1:23; 1 Cor. 8:4–10; 1 Thess. 1:9).

The verb used in verse 21 (NIV "keep") is different from that used in verse 18. This verb (Gk. *phylasso*) actually means "to guard," a sort of defensive activity (see John 12:25; 17:12). John therefore urges that while Jesus keeps or sustains us (v. 18), we must be diligent and alert— never passive—when it comes to taking care of ourselves.

But what are we to look out for? Idols are often viewed symbolically in the Bible as anything that competes with God. Paul gives idolatry an elastic meaning in Ephesians 5:5 and Colossians 3:5. In other words, John is urging his readers to watch out for anything that may become a substitute for God: religious shams, false religion, and even the error-filled words of the secessionists.

JOHN'S FINAL CHORE in his correspondence to his followers is to strengthen their confidence and resolve. They are in the midst of a disheartening struggle! We have to keep in mind that families—men, women, and children—who once were close are now experiencing conflict. Old friends are now new enemies. And despair is everywhere. John, of course, has declared what is right and what is wrong, who has sinned and who has not. But like a coach who has just outlined the strengths of his team's opponents—and his own team's weaknesses—John must now rebuild. This is similar to a pastor whose congregation is suffering the tremors of a threatened split: The crisis of the church can become a crisis of personal faith. Once the theological boundaries of the debate have been marked off, it is vital to turn to "the care of souls," to see what harm the struggle has inflicted on people who cannot see God anymore because of the skirmishes beneath the steeple.

As I bring 1 John 5:13–21 into my context, I am helped through remembering that these words of encouragement about prayer, eternal life, and Christ's nurturing protection form the climax of John's pastoral effort. He wants his people to be confident Christians, not victimized Christians. And not only does he affirm his care for his followers, but he adds that they need to begin to watch out for one another. John cannot be in all places at all times. Pity the pastor who tries! But through their *joint efforts* John envisions a community that is self-sustaining, mutually encouraging, and watchful lest any particular member falls.

If believers today likewise suffer dismay and shattered confidence because of their experiences in the church, these verses have much to say. Such dismay could spring from an internal struggle, much like that in the Johannine church. On the other hand, it could be a personal struggle of some sort that distorts the presence of God and saps their belief. Verses 13–21 are fresh mortar for damaged foundations; they are salve for wounds incurred when Christians hurt one another. And they offer new vision when confusion has made the spiritual world less certain.

Four areas of strengthening that spring from this passage will serve us well in the church today. This section is a practical paragraph, aimed at rebuilding the personal lives of exhausted people. Inasmuch as men and women in John's day were worn down through struggle, as we too can be, these verses offer potent help. (1)The paragraph is brimming with confidence and tries to instill in us that faith does not have to lack assurance. We live in a world of disbelief. Postmodern prophets seem to say that *uncertainty* is all we can be sure about. When the modern church makes an unholy wedding of faith and uncertainty, we would do well to hear John's exhortation.

(2) John's interest in Christian confidence likewise spills over into the subject of prayer. To be confident in God is not merely an intellectual exercise, but is practically experienced in prayer. Yet any application of 5:14–15 must be cautious, lest formulas and unwarranted expectation result.

(3) John envisions a church where men and women nurture, sustain, and even *warn* one another. Depleted Christians are weakened Christians for whom the world and its allure have a stronger gravitational pull. This too has a needed—and courageous—application in the church.

(4) Finally, John understands that the conflicts of life, the woundedness of our leaders, and the frailty of the church make it impossible for us to rest our confidence in human institutions. Our vision must be of Jesus Christ himself, because the vicissitudes of this life will make all human institutions, including the church, disappointing.

All four of these concerns are aimed at one thing we desperately need today: strengthened believers, whose vision of their Lord is so clear that their stamina in faith, in prayer, and in righteousness is tangible.

I AM OFTEN intrigued when I meet a wounded Christian. They are everywhere. I am especially interested if these wounds have come from the church. If I ask a class of college students to tell me about their experiences in the church that have not been helpful, the stories seem endless. Of course, many will eagerly tell about the wonder of their church and thank God for the community back home. But there are also darker stories, and these we need to hear too.

In some cases, a student tells about a parent who is a pastor and who experienced a damaging power struggle. Other stories tell of charismatic Sunday school teachers who undercut the authority of the pastor. But most will describe interpersonal relationships that have simply been ungodly, relationships that have made them cynical. They speak of men and women for whom the church became an arena to perform musically, teach large crowds, control funds, or simply leverage power. Some witnessed the power of money and how it bought undue influence. For others the church had become a social network— a family network perhaps—that was as satisfying for some as it was devastating for others. It is always the viciousness of such stories that disturbs me—how quickly Christians can hurt one another.

These stories of personal harm and devastation are commonplace not just among students, but within the larger population of the church as well. Adults report breathtaking examples of despair in their experience in the pew. William Hendricks took a special interest in people who have been wounded by the church, studying the stories of men and women who left the church as a result.[11] This book makes for difficult and necessary reading.

While the stories are all different, the result always seems the same. Not only do these people deeply question the church, but they question God as well. For them, the church is Christ's body—his visible presence—and the pastor is genuinely a priest, representing God in word and deed. When community and leadership fail, the damage goes far beyond what we imagine.

Such wounded Christians need healing. They need a fresh vision of God aside from what has been going on in their particular church. This is not to say the local church is unimportant, but if the church is in disarray, if it hurts more than it heals, John's words in 5:13–21 will bring help.

(1) *Christian confidence and doubt.* John emphasizes again and again the importance of Christians knowing with assurance essential facts about their relationship with God. We should know, for instance, that Christ has not only worked on our behalf (v. 20), but he also protects us (v. 18). God's commitment is such that he listens to our prayers (v. 14) and has guaranteed to us eternal life (v. 13). John has urged throughout his letter how Christians should believe and

---

11. William D. Hendricks, *Exit Interviews: Revealing Stories of Why People Are Leaving the Church* (Chicago: Moody, 1993).

emphasized how they should live. But believing and living must be wed to knowing.

Christian communities can be terribly honest. We sometimes discuss our doubts and uncertainties as a means of giving one another comfort. In some places, *not knowing* has even become a virtue. One chaplain at a nearby college even changed his school's annual "Festival of Faith" to a "Festival of Doubt" in order to underscore the point. Needless to say, the chapel series was quite depressing! Of course, this cautionary spirit sometimes springs from humility (intellectual or personal). Sometimes it springs from our personal distaste for some fundamentalists who use their theological certainties to bludgeon those different from them. At other times, however, such uncertainty is utterly misplaced.

The church has sometimes confused uncertainty in faith with thinking that faith is holding to something when you have no confidence in the truth. "We'll never know those answers till we get to heaven," was one youth leader's response to questioning junior high students who voiced sincere though answerable doubts. I heard one nine-year-old say to his friend, "I guess you get the facts in school, but here at church you just get opinions." This youth group was cultivating a culture of "uncertainty," even though its personal ministry was strong and caring. While it rightly desired to affirm those who doubt, it inadvertently affirmed doubt as a normative Christian experience.

We need to be bold about those things we know with certainty. We need to speak with conviction and assurance about God and his commitment to us. We need to say from lectern and pulpit, "God desires for us to be confident! God desires for us to be bold! God desires to purge doubt from our souls so that we can live enjoying the assurance of one who is eternally loved." When our assurance is truly anchored and secure, no conflict or disarray in the church can ever unsettle it.

Does this mean that Christians cannot have doubts? John does not answer this question for us because his context is focused on the devastation in his church. All Christians have doubts. But our pastoral goal should be to focus elsewhere, as John has done, and to promote certainty where we can.

(2) *Christian confidence and prayer.* The temptation for younger Christians is to view 5:14–15 as a formula for prayer. If we pray sincerely,

we will get what we want. Of course there are conditions, and most will point to obedience in 3:21–23. The Fourth Gospel contains a number of such promises, which generally add that prayer must always be "in Jesus name:"

- "I will do whatever you ask in my name, so that the Father may be glorified in the Son. If in my name you ask me for anything, I will do it." (John 14:13–14 NRSV)
- "And I will ask the Father, and he will give you another Advocate, to be with you forever." (John 14:16 NRSV)
- "If you abide in me, and my words abide in you, ask for whatever you wish, and it will be done for you." (John 15:7, NRSV)
- "You did not choose me but I chose you. And I appointed you to go and bear fruit, fruit that will last, so that the Father will give you whatever you ask him in my name." (John 15:16 NRSV)
- "On that day you will ask nothing of me. Very truly, I tell you, if you ask anything of the Father in my name, he will give it to you. Until now you have not asked for anything in my name. Ask and you will receive, so that your joy may be complete." (John 16:23–24 NRSV)

Similar confidence in prayer is explained in Mark 11:21–24. After the apostles discovered the fig tree that Jesus had cursed the previous day, Peter exclaimed:

"Rabbi, look! The fig tree you cursed has withered!"

"Have faith in God," Jesus answered. "I tell you the truth, if anyone says to this mountain, 'Go, throw yourself into the sea,' and does not doubt in his heart but believes that what he says will happen, it will be done for him. Therefore I tell you, whatever you ask for in prayer, believe that you have received it, and it will be yours."

Jesus even follows his saying with an example of a spiritual condition that might impede the success of such prayers, namely, that sin against another person leads to dissonance between us and God (11:25). Jesus opens this subject elsewhere in Matthew 7:7–8; 18:19–20. In Luke 11:5–10 Jesus tells an entire parable about confidence in prayer and follows it with poetic lines about God's eagerness to give us generous gifts.

How do we balance the practical realities of prayer with these promises? It will not do simply to say that if we follow these formulas, all prayers will be answered just as they are uttered. God does not serve as our butler. On the other hand, it will not do to reject these promises altogether, as if prayer was anything more than wishful thinking. Rather, John has in mind a union, a mystical union, between our lives and the Spirit of God that will ultimately express itself in one voice. This is what the Johannine language for "in my name" is trying to depict. We become one with Jesus. Our will is then transformed freely to become his will. With God's stepping so deeply inside our lives, we have utter confidence that he knows the quietest thoughts of our hearts.

Some will object that this is no gift at all! Our desires are hijacked, submerged by God's overpowering voice! But in reality God's will is graced by a wisdom far beyond anything we could think or imagine, and trusting him in his goodness is part of our union with him. This means that as Christians we need to develop prayer that listens as well as prayer that speaks. "Listening prayer" has always been commonplace among Christian mystics and spiritual masters, but strangely uncommon among us who are evangelicals.

Nevertheless, it is verses such as 1 John 5:14–15 that can lead to tremendous disappointment. At times it seems that every effort, every attempt to seek some connection with God fails. God's silence—or the circumstances of my life—are unexplainable. The psalmist in Psalm 44:23–24 reflects this frustration:

> Awake, O Lord! Why do you sleep?
>   Rouse yourself! Do not reject us forever.
> Why do you hide your face
>   and forget our misery and oppression?

Job cries out in Job 30:26–27:

> Yet when I hoped for good, evil came;
>   when I looked for light, then came darkness.
> The churning inside me never stops;
>   days of suffering confront me.

Few writers have attempted to address this problem of thoroughgoing disappointment. Philip Yancy's courageous book *Disappointment with God* tells story after story of believers who, because of crushing disappointment with God, have questioned the validity of their faith. Three questions, Yancy argues, are left unaddressed by the church: (1) Is God unfair? Why doesn't he consistently punish evil people and reward good people? Why do awful things happen to people good and bad? (2) Is God silent? If he is so concerned about our doing his will, why doesn't he reveal that will more plainly? (3) Is God hidden? Why doesn't he simply show up sometime, visibly, and dumbfound the skeptics once and for all?[12]

Yancy surveys the biblical stories (particularly the early Old Testament books) and finds clues to patterns in how God relates to his people. And *disappointment* is not an uncommon theme. But there are answers, and Yancy culls these from everywhere: from Leo Tolstoy to Frederick Buechner to a terminally ill twenty-three-year-old woman named Peggy, who wrote, citing William Barclay, "Endurance is not just the ability to bear a hard thing, but to turn it into glory."[13]

Yancy's evidence is clear and compelling. Passages such as 1 John 5:14–15 can present overwhelming personal questions and anguish about the faith. We need to be equipped to hear them and wrestle honestly with them.

(3) *Sin that leads to death.* Today the Roman Catholic Church continues a medieval tradition that distinguished between venial sin and mortal sin. Venial sins are "pardonable" sins that do not exclude one from the kingdom of God (cf. Gal. 5:19–21; Eph. 5:5 with James 3:2; 1 John 1:8). Mortal sins, however, have more severe consequences and lead to spiritual death. Aquinas described these differences as degrees of disorder: Mortal sin violates the basic principle of divine order; venial sin does not touch the principle but simply brings disorder to the soul. Moreover, venial sins may disorder the soul to such a degree that at some point, a person turns from God. It is this turning, this repudiation of God, that introduces mortal sin and eternal death.

I find this clarification instructive. John is urging prayer for individuals whose lives are marked by a degree of sin that has *not* led to their eternal death. He distinguishes these sinners from those whose

---

12. P Yancy, *Disappointment with God: Three Questions No One Asks Aloud* (Grand Rapids: Zondervan, 1988), 44–46.

13. Ibid., 157.

sins are intentional, whose lives have separated them from the community, who no longer have divine life in them. In John's context, this latter group no doubt describes the secessionists, who have allied themselves with darkness and are leaving the community. They are no longer with God; they are with the antichrist. On the other hand, John knows other Christians whose lives are perilously close to danger. Perhaps they are flirting with switching sides; perhaps they have committed sins that could lead to dangerous places. John has hope for them.

What is less clear is how we apply this to our present setting today. Scripture indicates that there are sins so severe that forgiveness is virtually impossible (Matt. 12:31–32; Mark 3:28–30; Luke 12:10; cf. Heb. 6:4–6). Paul even indicates that there are certain sins that exclude people from the kingdom (1 Cor. 6:9; Gal. 5:21; 1 Thess. 4:6). Therefore, we must not take this lightly. Sinners who become engrossed and complacent in their sinning are in genuine jeopardy.

But this is not John's chief interest. John calls for serious involvement in the lives of people whose sins are not leading to death. These may be inadvertent sins (following the Old Testament example) or even minor (venial) sins. Either way, John calls for investment, active participation, mutual ownership of the problem.

What value is this? John says we must be alert to the lives of those living around us in the church. We must hold them up, pray for them, interrupt them, and confront them. Christians must "name" the sinfulness, the brokenness, that is alive in other Christians. We must admit when brokenness is within our ranks. And we must have the courage to do something about it. When Christians are hurting other Christians because of their brokenness (as in the Johannine context), still other Christians must intervene through prayer and words.

(4) *Confidence and the sustaining presence of Christ.* John is trying to repair what the division has broken. He wants his followers to be confident in their knowledge of God, confident in their prayers, and alert to those whose spiritual lives are suffering disintegration. There is, however, a fourth interest in the passage. John wants us to be confident because it is Christ, not the church, who sustains us amidst the disintegration of the world. In 5:18 he talks about Christ's protection; in 5:20 he talks about being "in him" (in Christ) who is true, as if we are hidden within the powers of Jesus' presence.

Christians who are wounded by the disarray of the church and the brokenness of its family need a larger vision of God. They need a vision of Jesus, whose glory and power loom over the fragments of community that warring Christians leave behind. They need a vision that transcends the broken, splintered experience of a local congregation.

Life in the church can be painful. And yet Jesus has not abandoned us. Pastors and mature Christian leaders can and will disappoint. But Jesus still remains committed and invested. I remember once teaching a Wednesday evening class at Willow Creek Community Church outside Chicago. After class a wounded Christian who had departed her church in dismay approached me. She had not gone to church for years. "It is so hard to believe these things about Jesus when his followers act the way they do," she said. The word "hypocrisy" was not far from her lips.

She had been wounded in a skirmish not unlike that in John's church. And I am sure I know what John would have told her: Jesus is true even though all else fails. You are still a child of God even though your family, the church, is broken beyond repair. And you can still discover the light and walk in it, even if those around you are succumbing to the darkness.

2 John

THE ELDER,

To the chosen lady and her children, whom I love in the truth—and not I only, but also all who know the truth—²because of the truth, which lives in us and will be with us forever:

³Grace, mercy and peace from God the Father and from Jesus Christ, the Father's Son, will be with us in truth and love.

⁴It has given me great joy to find some of your children walking in the truth, just as the Father commanded us. ⁵And now, dear lady, I am not writing you a new command but one we have had from the beginning. I ask that we love one another. ⁶And this is love: that we walk in obedience to his commands. As you have heard from the beginning, his command is that you walk in love.

⁷Many deceivers, who do not acknowledge Jesus Christ as coming in the flesh, have gone out into the world. Any such person is the deceiver and the antichrist. ⁸Watch out that you do not lose what you have worked for, but that you may be rewarded fully. ⁹Anyone who runs ahead and does not continue in the teaching of Christ does not have God; whoever continues in the teaching has both the Father and the Son. ¹⁰If anyone comes to you and does not bring this teaching, do not take him into your house or welcome him. ¹¹Anyone who welcomes him shares in his wicked work.

¹²I have much to write to you, but I do not want to use paper and ink. Instead, I hope to visit you and talk with you face to face, so that our joy may be complete.

¹³The children of your chosen sister send their greetings.

I HAVE BEEN suggesting throughout the commentary that the best lens through which to view the letters of John is the spiritual and theological crisis gripping his church in Ephesus and fracturing its unity. The Johannine schism was an internal struggle, fueled perhaps by arguments surrounding the interpretation of the Fourth Gospel and aggravated no doubt by pneumatic/charismatic teachers claiming new authority in the Spirit and new revelations about Christ. In a word, the false teachers were Docetic, denying the full incarnation of Christ and particularly the need or reality of his salvific death (1 John 2:22; 4:1–3; 5:5–8; 2 John 7–8). They also promoted an inspired enlightenment, a new vision, a loftier spirituality that was elitist (1 John 2:9) and perfectionist (1:8).

John sees this as nothing short of an unabashed offense to God himself (1 John 5:10), a challenge to the truth ("truth" occurs twenty times in the letters), and a teaching that jeopardized the very life of the church. Indeed, divisions had already set in. And as we read 1 John, a community of secessionists had already parted company with John's church (1 John 2:19).

The Setting of 2 and 3 John

THE ONGOING HISTORY of the Johannine church is visible in 2 and 3 John. Various theories have been offered for the chronological rearrangement of these three letters. For instance, some have wondered if 2 John is John's original letter and 1 John is his expansion of his ideas—a fulfillment of his wish to say many more things (2 John 12). But such a theory fails to explain how 2 John makes much sense if the recipient has not already read the dense arguments of 1 John. I believe that 2 John is an exhortation—a reminder—of things said before and therefore should *follow* 1 John chronologically. Moreover, 1 John should be read alongside 2 and 3 John, and the shorter letters should be interpreted in light of 1 John.

The Johannine letters show us a community that took its faith seriously. Some have even wondered if it fostered a sectarian outlook in which inner love and cohesion were as absolute as the boundary the community had erected between itself and the world. Christians were taught to reject the world utterly (1 John 2:15–17; 4:4–5), to practice a love within the community that had no natural counterpart (1 John 4:19–21; 2 John 5; 3 John 5–6), and to view themselves as elect, chosen of God (1 John 5:19–20; 2 John 7–9).

Did such a community with its high passion for excellence finally collapse under its own internal pressures? The intensity of its vision armed its critics with an intolerance that finally tore the fabric of the church. When we read 1 John, this group has departed (1 John 2:18–19); yet John still views them from the doorway of the church they left: "former members" might be their title. They are men and women with connections to the church and with influence on the Christians who stayed behind (see 1 John 2:27 and the many denials in 1 John). By the time we read 2 John the rupture seems complete (2 John 7). They are no longer just exiles from the church; they are now "in the world" and allied with the antichrist. And John warns that contact with them is forbidden (2 John 10–11). In 3 John a deeper crisis has developed, in which one circle in the Johannine community (a house church?) seems on the verge of defecting entirely, thanks to the influence of Diotrephes (3 John 9). Is this the same schism of 1 John and 2 John? John's own emissaries cannot even make inroads into this fellowship (3 John 10).

These letters are testimonies to pastoral crises and pastoral heroism. They bear eloquent testimony to the vulnerability of the church when it lives on the frontiers of the world and is subject to the world's influences. And they warn us of the one "who runs ahead and does not continue in the teaching of Christ" (2 John 9)—particularly when such teachers are from within their own ranks. In John's case, the threat must have seemed overwhelming as members left and a few circles of believers split off.

Many have speculated about the fate of the community and tried to reconstruct what happened after 3 John was written. Good evidence suggests that much later the secessionists became fully Gnostic and carried the Fourth Gospel with them into the ranks of heretics.[1] However, those believers who held firm, who did not deny a fully incarnational Christology, soon found support in "The Great Church," those congregations that were nurtured by the writings of Paul and the other Gospels. The gift they brought to these orthodox communities

---

1. Recall that all of the earliest commentaries on John were from Gnostic writers. See the introduction, pp. 17–46

was their apostle-pastor's account of Jesus, namely, the Fourth Gospel. With it came John's three letters—ready refutations of any misuses of that Gospel by later Gnostics.[2]

Fidelity to the Truth: Commitment to Love (1–6)

SECOND JOHN IS A message "from the front lines," much like a scrap of war correspondence discovered long after the battle has passed. The tension implied in 1 John takes on a desperate tone. Therefore, John writes with two purposes in mind: to buttress his followers' commitment to the truth and to warn them about the severity of their opponents and the need to protect themselves.

Because this is a personal letter, it follows conventional first-century epistolary form—unlike 1 John, which is not actually a personal letter but a public theological document. The author identifies himself ("the elder," v. 1), names his addressees ("the chosen lady and her children," v. 2), and gives a salutation ("grace, mercy and peace," v. 3); at the end of his message he appends a closing greeting (vv. 12–13). This letter is one of the smallest in the New Testament, shorter even than Jude and Philemon; but like them it is intense and direct.

Rather than give his name (cf. Paul, 1 Cor. 1:1; 2 Cor. 1:1; Gal. 1:1), the author simply calls himself "the elder" (Gk. *presbyteros*). On the one hand, he seems to know the church well—and is known by them. However, it is his *position* that is now important and the authority that comes with it. "Elder" was used among Jews to indicate religious leaders (Acts 4:5); this practice was adopted by the early Christians (Acts 11:30, 15:6, 22; 1 Tim. 5:17; 1 Peter 5:1). Therefore, the "elder" (in my view, John) was an overseer of some sort, someone with pastoral oversight outside the congregation (see further pp. 17–46).

An ancient tradition has thought "chosen lady" refers to a person. Both words are personal names for women in Greek (Electa, Kyria). But this usage here is unlikely. Not only does the tone of the letter imply a wider audience, but the letter itself lapses into the plural at many points (vv. 5, 6, 8, 10, 12). The New Testament thinks of the church with feminine metaphors (e.g., "the bride of Christ," Eph. 5:22–32) and even calls Christians "the chosen [*or* elect]" (Rom. 8:33;

---

2. On the history of the Johannine community, see R. Brown, *Community of the Beloved Disciple* (1979) and *The Epistles of John*, 103–15. See Brown's bibliography on pp. 140–44.

16:13; Col. 3:12; 1 Peter 1:1). Thus, we should view 2 John as a personal note written by John and sent to a particular congregation (affectionately described as "her children").[3]

Perhaps we should view the Johannine community as a series of small house churches distributed over a distance. These may have been isolated groups of people, few in number, who met in a village home for study and prayer. Or, if a larger urban community is imagined—for example, in Ephesus—these communities may have been houses in the city, each nurturing about twenty-five believers and knit together with informal connections with John as local elder/leader. This letter is addressed to one of these fledgling households of faith, now struggling for life.

John's deep love for his church is expressed in his first sentence, "whom I love in the truth." This phrase could be adverbial ("whom I love truly"), but no doubt John intends more. For him, the truth is not mere sincerity, but a reality belonging to God (1 John 2:4). People who know the truth love each other (v. 2) because they have this truth abiding within them (cf. 1 John 2:21). It is important to remember Johannine vocabulary here. Truth was not only incarnate in Jesus Christ (John 1:17; 14:6), but it also describes the Holy Spirit ("the Spirit of truth," 14:15–17). Therefore, the community of love is a community "in truth," namely, a community that has embraced Jesus Christ (1 John 5:20) and experienced the indwelling power of the Holy Spirit (3:24). Thus, the threefold blessing of verse 3 is announced triumphantly as a promise, not a wish: "grace, mercy and peace *will be* with us." If the truth is with us forever (v. 2) and Jesus is the truth, the gifts of Jesus ("grace, mercy and peace") are likewise certainties.[4]

John's first message actually begins in verse 4, where he celebrates the continuing faithfulness and obedience of these Christians to the truth.[5] All ecclesiastical matters are eclipsed by two critical affirmations of the faith, which he recites here: Christians must embrace and obey

---

3 John uses the Greek word *tekna* frequently for his followers (see 1 John 3:1, 2, 10; 5:2, 2 John 1·1, etc.)

4. This formula, "grace, mercy and peace," occurs in the New Testament in 1 Timothy 1.2; 2 Timothy 1 2, Jude 2 "Mercy and peace" was a Jewish blessing (2ApocBar 78:2; cf. Gal. 6.16), to which the Christians added the Greek term "grace." See Smalley, *1, 2, 3 John*, 321.

5 It was common in ancient letters to report some joy at news concerning the recipient (see Eph. 1·15, Phil. 1·3, Col 1.3, 2 Thess 1.3, 2 Tim 1.3; 3 John 3)

the *truth*, and at the same time *love* those who are brothers and sisters in Christ. "Truth" and "love" are the twin themes that echo throughout 1 John and here appear in summary form. They are the key elements that distinguish Christians from the world, and in this case, the faithful Johannine church from those who have left. The secessionists' unyielding hatred (1 John 2:9), their disobedience before God's word (1 John 2:4), indeed, their departure from the truth (4:6), all show how far they have moved from God.

But this is a bittersweet report. Couriers may have come to John reporting how faithful this remaining house church was.[6] On the other hand, verse 4 may imply something different. John's rejoicing that "some of" the believers here remained faithful may suggest that *others have not.* We can only speculate about the relation of the two groups. Have the secessionists won the upper hand? Are John's faithful barely holding on? The answer to these questions may explain the cautious exhortation that follows (vv. 7–11). It may also explain the exhortation to love in verses 5–6. The authority behind John's exhortation is not new. This love command is old—it comes from Jesus himself (John 13:34; 15:12, 17; 1 John 3:11; 2 John 5–6). John's call is for these believers to consolidate their besieged community and confirm the essence of their beliefs—in other words, to fortify themselves against those who are out to destroy them.

Specific Warnings (7–11)

WITH STUNNING SPECIFICITY, John moves in verse 7 from the truth and love that inspire celebration to the treachery and deception that are lurking just outside the church's doors (vv. 7–11). These defections are numerous (*"many* deceivers ... have gone out"), and John no doubt has in mind those who have split off from the church in the recent past.[7] "Deceivers" (Gk. *planoi*) can also be translated "liars"; Jesus uses the word in Matthew 24:4, 11, and 24 to warn against false prophets and messiahs, who will lead God's people astray. Clearly these people have not only left the church and taken up residence in the world, but they have "gone out" into the world in order to spread their teachings.

---

6 Marshall, *The Epistles of John*, 65; Stott, *The Epistles of John*, 205.

7 The Greek verb in verse 7, *exelthon*, is in the aorist, meaning that the event happened some time ago.

Their description in verse 7b is given fuller treatment in 1 John 2:17–27. Those who departed have become allies with evil. These false prophets have denied the complete incarnation of Christ (see 1 John 4:2) and should now be seen as agents of the antichrist. First John 4:1–3 describes their work in full:

> ... because many false prophets have gone out into the world. This is how you can recognize the Spirit of God: Every spirit that acknowledges [NRSV confesses] that Jesus Christ has come in the flesh is from God, but every spirit that does not acknowledge [NRSV confess] Jesus is not from God. This is the spirit of the antichrist, which you have heard is coming and even now is already in the world.

The confession listed in 1 John 4:1–6 finds a new twist in the present verses. Rather than use a perfect tense (as in 1 John 4:2), John now says that orthodox confession affirms "Jesus Christ as coming in the flesh" (v. 7). Why the present tense? This is likely not a reference to the Second Coming; rather, it is John's way of saying that Jesus Christ came *and still exists* in the flesh. In other words, through his incarnation Jesus swept up our humanity and carried it with him eternally. This contradicts any Gnostic teachers who were saying that "the Christ" descended on Jesus at his baptism and departed just before his crucifixion, thus permanently separating the divine Christ from the earthly Jesus. John demands a "confession" that embraces the *ongoing* reality of the Incarnation even in the present.

To oppose this teaching is to be aligned with "the antichrist" (v. 7b; see on 1 John 2:18). This word appears only in 1 John 2:18, 22; 4:3; and 2 John 7. This figure is the quintessential opponent of Christianity, one who is radically opposed to Christ and who dismantles the very center of the faith, not someone with marginal theological differences. John has two words of exhortation: Do not be deceived yourselves, and do not encourage the deceivers.

Verses 8–9 form John's first firm word to his followers: He does not want them to lose all that they have gained so far. The NIV translates, "Watch out that you do not lose what you have worked for," but the preferred Greek text is first person plural, "Watch out that you do not lose what *we* have worked for." As evangelist and pastor, John has been a participant in the birth and maturation of the faith of the recipients of this letter. In other words, they are not the sole custodians of their church, free to do as they wish. John has been a builder among them, and his contributions and responsibility make him a justified critic of what is happening. The chief pitfall he warns against appears in verse 9. While the debated doctrine is the incarnation of Christ, the root problem is that some have "run ahead" and failed to continue in the teachings about Christ. The word "run ahead" in Greek is a term of superiority and appears only here in the New Testament with a negative connotation.[8] This is not progress *in the faith*, but progress *beyond it*.[9]

Here is the tension described throughout 1 John. The charismatic teacher-prophets have proposed a view of Christ that "runs ahead," that pulls up the ancient moorings of tradition. This is why 1 John again and again repeats the idea, "Let remain in you *what was from the beginning*" (1 John 1:1; 2:7, 13, 14, 24; 3:8, 11; 2 John 5, 6). This is John's appeal to the past, his way of urging that creative theological insights never destroy the groundwork of what we already know about Christ in the Scriptures. The incarnate Christ is the only person through whom we know God. Christ's historical work of redemption and mediation is the basis of our salvation. At this point the apostle is uncompromising: to jettison the premier place of Jesus as the exclusive self-disclosure of God, to deny Jesus' full humanity, is to lose God altogether (see 1 John 2:23–24).

Verses 10–11 describe John's second firm word. The consequence of this false teaching is so serious that it demands a serious remedy: No hospitality should be extended to those people who bear such erroneous doctrine. An instruction like this is striking and peculiar in the New Testament, which generally encourages Christians to be generously hospitable (Matt. 10:11–14; 1 Tim. 5:10; 1 Peter 4:8–10). Romans 12:13 (cf. NRSV) and Hebrews 13:2 urge Christians to show hospitality to strangers, as if in the author's mind, an open door and a ready welcome should be characteristic of Christian community.

These troubling verses should be viewed as "emergency regulations," tied directly to the crisis at hand. They are directives from the battle zone, and they underscore the extreme danger the church is in

---

8 The Greek *proagon* can also mean "advanced" and is likely an appeal to the heretics' elitist attitudes

9. Stott, *The Epistles of John*, 211–12

when it not only tolerates, but actually invites into its ranks those whose teachings undermine traditional Christology. But note that John's warning is aimed not at those who merely believe these doctrines but especially at those who teach them (who "bears this teaching"). John uses the plural in verse 10, "If anyone comes *to you*." John is not referring here to a personal visit of one person with another. Rather, this is an audience with the gathered church. Furthermore, when John refers to receiving them "into your house," he likely has in mind a private residence *used as a primary place of meeting and worship* for the community—a house church. The Greek *oikia* ("house") often refers to such a meeting place (Rom. 16:5; 1 Cor. 16:19; Col. 4:15). As Smalley comments, "John is not therefore forbidding private hospitality, but rather an official welcome into the congregation, with the widespread opportunities which would then be available for the heretics to promote their cause."[10]

A Final Greeting (12–13)

BOTH 2 AND 3 John share similar conclusions. John extends a greeting from his church and expresses his desire to make a personal visit rather than rely on "black ink and papyrus"—as the Greek puts it. We should note his confidence that his readers will receive him and heed his words. The rupture is not complete; they have not fallen into the enemy camp. The situation in 3 John is far more ominous, for there orthodox emissaries have already been rejected. John's visit, then, will bring some risk of rejection too. But this is not the case yet.

John's coming to these believers to speak "face to face"[11] is aimed at renewing their fellowship so that both pastor and congregation will be joyful ("so that *our joy* [plural] may be complete"). When a church suffers or celebrates, its pastor does the same. John will be reassured that they are walking in the truth (v. 4), and they will be comforted to know truth from falsehood. This renewal of fellowship, anchored in a confident relationship in Jesus Christ, is John's image of the Christian life, which he hopes to celebrate with them soon.

In verse 13 John's greeting from "the children of your chosen sister" once again employs the metaphorical language we read in verse 1.

---

10 Smalley, *1, 2, 3 John*, 333, cf Brown, *The Epistles of John*, 692–93
11 The Greek literally says "mouth to mouth" (cf Num 12 8)

Although this is the only place the phrase occurs in the New Testament, we can be reasonably sure that John is building on family imagery for the church (see on v. 1). "Two sisters" are talking with each other about conditions in the family, and their speech swings from expressions of love and intimacy to feelings of worry and concern.

 AS WE CARRY this letter out of the first century and into our own, we find one important interpretive challenge before us. *Unless the original context of 2 John and 3 John in some manner corresponds to our context today, we must apply them very cautiously.* More to the point, 2 John can be greatly misused if its meaning is not defined by its original context. Some of the New Testament literature can neglect its setting with less problem and the message of the text still be brought to modern pulpits successfully. Not so with 2 John, for there original context is *everything*.

I recently visited the Vietnam Memorial in Washington, D.C. It was perhaps my fourth visit to the grassy site beneath the Lincoln Memorial. There I listened as young guides explained to groups of tourists the wall's architectural design with its inscribed names and pointed to the bronze memorials to soldiers and nurses across the field in the trees. But nothing was said about anguish and about how the wall is raw commentary on a devastating national experience. No one interpreted the faces of the statues or the gaze of bronze female medics looking skyward for a medevac to lift them from their jungle hell. No one talked about the 1960s. As a result, the visit of these tourists was an utter loss. They walked past withered flowers and worn letters resting against the wall without a thought. At the Vietnam Memorial on Washington's mall, *original context is everything*.

We must not be such unaffected tourists as we read 2 John. This letter too is an artifact from a war. I have described at length the letters' highly specific setting (see pp. 229–31); to some degree this controls what we can do with them. I have suggested that here we have a house church living on the perimeter of the Johannine community. They have received John's more public document, outlining the temptations and threats stemming from the false teachers (1 John); now John is communicating to them directly through letter and personal emissary. Both seem inadequate. And in the near future he hopes to visit them in person, so that he can rebuild their friendship, talk about true doctrine, and celebrate their union with the orthodox community. But the subtext of these communiqués is clear: The church is in serious danger.

Therefore, when we open 2 John, we must keep in mind that its recipients are under siege. They are having a devastating experience. In some cases, the threats are subtle. In other cases, missionaries from "the enemy" are trying to make inroads into the church. Thus John employs the strongest language he can—"deceivers," "antichrist," do not . . . welcome him"—because the very existence of the church is at stake.

This is a far cry from Christians today as they meet a believer from another faith. This is also a far cry from meeting *an evangelist* from another faith, who poses no genuine threat to the church. Some Christians have used 2 John 11 to rebuff such people. The leading interpretive error is to universalize John's stern warnings while all along neglecting the original context of the letter. Second John demands thoughtful, cautious reflection before it is brought to the pulpit.

What are the building blocks of this original context that we can identify and carry forward? What basic elements from this original context are essential in any application today? Three come to mind. (1) The church's opponents are attacking a theological issue at the center of the church's faith, namely, Christology. This is no peripheral theological speculation, such as a debate about the charismatic gifts, the mode of baptism, or small groups. Jesus Christ himself is "in the dock," and the result of this debate will either spawn a religion centered on his work and words or relegate him to some secondary place. (2) John is warning against teacher-leaders who are out to sabotage the local church. These are not innocent contacts between the Johannine Christians and unbelievers or heretics. Rather, these teachers are trying to gain access to a congregation in order to win an audience and a following. Stott even believes that John may be referring to "official visits" by these teachers, who plan to address the congregation.[12] (3) John's instructions to repel these teachers and refuse them access involves their survival. The result of this struggle will have immense

---

12 Stott, *The Epistles of John*, 213.

consequences for these people's personal salvation—and the survival of the church itself.

IF EVER WE feel overwhelmed by the trivia of church life, by the divisions centered on philosophy of ministry or church maintenance, 2 John serves as exhortation and reminder. Most of us know little of the sort of threat described here. And perhaps when we have no genuine external threats to our survival, we find endless things to quarrel about: youth programs, worship style, carpet, and hymnbooks. In February 1994 I attended a conference on Middle Eastern Christianity in Washington, D.C., and roomed with an Egyptian pastor from Cairo. Each night we compared notes on our national churches. I was sobered. In Egypt the Arab Christian church is struggling for life in an increasingly hostile fundamentalist Muslim world. What are this pastor's concerns? That his people will love each other and remain unified, and that they will stand for the truth about Jesus Christ no matter what the cost. In southern Egypt of late, that price can be high—being a faithful Christian may cost you your life.

These are the twin themes found in 2 John, which distill so much of what it means to be the church. John's formula is simple: that we love one another as an act of obedience to Jesus Christ, and that we live in the truth, which means defending true belief about Jesus Christ. Love and truth are the twin stars by which the Johannine church navigated—all else was secondary. Perhaps being under siege forces a church to purge itself of its dispensable agendas.

But once we say that the essential nature of the church is "love and truth," all our problems are not solved. Would that it were so easy! The ongoing questions that John leaves open here center on whom we love and how much truth we should fight for. Are we obligated to love those who disagree with us concerning the truth?

(1) *Shutting the gates of the church.* John's teaching that Christians should show no hospitality to their opponents has met with severe criticism among some interpreters. C. H. Dodd, for example, rejected this teaching as being at odds with Jesus' words in Matthew 5:46–47:

> If you love those who love you, what reward will you get? Are not even the tax collectors doing that? And if you greet only

your brothers, what are you doing more than others? Do not even the pagans do that?

Similarly, Brown remarks that the type of "fierce exclusiveness" we find in 2 John generally backfires on its practitioners. In 3 John, Brown notes, the apostle gets a taste of his own medicine when his missionaries find the gate locked on them. "In retrospect, the [elder] may have come to wonder whether it would not have been wiser to do unto his adversaries as he would have them do unto him."[13]

We must admit that Dodd and Brown are correct on at least one point: The church has often "shut the gate" in order to justify its intolerance of theological deviation. Jehovah's Witnesses have seen many evangelical doors slam. Mainline liberals have likewise shut the gate on conservatives. Evangelicals have not only shut the gate but mounted a cannon atop, aimed at other conservatives who deny inerrancy, drink alcohol, or refuse some brand of conservative politics. This was the farthest thing from John's mind.

On the other hand, is there a place for "shutting the gate"? Does a time come when fellowship with some group should be denied or when contact should end? Should Christians ever "draw a line in the sand"? We have good evidence from antiquity that the early Christians were obedient to Jesus' words to receive openly the traveling teacher/prophet (Matt. 10:40; Mark 9:37). However, more evidence shows that this hospitality was quickly exploited. The early second-century Christian writing *Didache* teaches, "Whenever someone comes and teaches you all these things we have talked about, receive him. But if the teacher himself has deviated by teaching another doctrine that contradicts these things, do not listen to him" (*Didache* 11:1–2). The same warnings were voiced in Ignatius in the same time period (*Smyrnaeans* 4:1; *Ephesians* 7:1). In his *Letter to the Ephesians* Ignatius tells the Christians to "stop up their ears" so that traveling beguiling teachers will not pollute them (9:1).

Despite what we hear in our popular culture, tolerance is not an ultimate virtue. Strong action is appropriate when individuals jeopardize the very integrity of the church. It is significant that in Matthew 18:17 Jesus describes a church member who sins seriously and yet will not

---

13. Brown, *The Epistles of John*, 693.

accept admonishment. Quite simply, the person is to be shunned: "Treat him as you would a pagan or a tax collector." Paul manifests the same view in 1 Corinthians 5:1–5, 13. In other words, tolerance must have its limits if the church is to have integrity.

It is clear that the pressing issue for John's church had to do with the Incarnation, which is no peripheral subject. But John gives us little guidance concerning what other matters would qualify as "gate-shutting" concerns. It is easy to be glib about this and refer to genuinely peripheral issues like baptism and tobacco. But matters become far more intense—and the questions more difficult—when we wonder about the legitimacy of other divisive issues. What about inerrancy? Homosexuality? Abortion? Catholicism? Women's ordination? Do these justify gate-shutting today? Is it right to exclude from fellowship those who embrace such issues? The answers here are often complex.

(2) *Using the doctrine of the church.* Many of my students have a tangible disdain for doctrine. Their primary arbiter in matters of faith and practice is the Bible. This is excellent and I affirm them. However, I also wonder if they recognize that every heretic marched into exile with a Bible tucked into his or her luggage! John offers a provocative phrase in verse 9 when he describes someone "who runs ahead and does not continue in the teaching of Christ." Note that John is not saying that we ought to merely abide in Christ; we also must abide in the teachings about Christ. What were these teachings?

Admittedly, we can point to a recitation of Bible verses that defend the humanity and divinity of Christ, and no doubt John could do this too (using the Fourth Gospel). But in the fourth century Arius did the same and came to a different result. John implies that Christians would do well to respect and learn from the consensus that has come to us from tradition, from the things passed down from the beginning. In John's world, this meant the traditional teachings that bore apostolic authority. But what does this look like today? What does it means for us to learn from the historic consensus of the church?

All of this suggests a renewed interest in the history of the church. We ought to revive our creeds in which mature men and women of faith struggled to define Christianity. I think, for instance, of the potency of understanding Chalcedon as we read New Testament Christology, or the power of what happened in the Reformation as we study Galatians. Creeds usually disguise stories of challenge to the faith analogous to our own time and place. What better tutor than the Barmen Declaration of 1934 to teach mature Christians to continue to live by the Word of God rather than the demands of nationalism (in that case, the Nazis)!

(3) *Guarding the message of the church.* I am reminded again and again in John's letters that there is one central theological doctrine that overshadows all else. We have life only through Jesus Christ, God's Son, who truly became one of us for our salvation. This much is obvious. But voices constantly arise in our own culture that would like to dilute the exclusive (and offensive) nature of that message. For some, Jesus Christ is one more *problem* that makes genuine union among the religions of the world impossible. For others, the incarnation and death of Jesus is one more *embarrassment* that harks back to an archaic day when crosses and sacrifice meant something. For still others, Jesus Christ is one more *offense* that promotes a patriarchal system of abuse that in the modern world we must purge.

My point is this: We will experience a pressure to dilute the message of Christ that is no different from the pressure faced by the Johannine world. John's followers felt acute pressure from the sophisticated halls of Hellenistic *academe*—not to mention the popular voices of the marketplace—to reduce the person of Christ into someone less than he was. John calls his followers to stand firm, and he would have us do the same.

3 John

T HE ELDER,
To my dear friend Gaius, whom I love in the
truth.

²Dear friend, I pray that you may enjoy good health
and that all may go well with you, even as your soul is
getting along well. ³It gave me great joy to have some
brothers come and tell about your faithfulness to the
truth and how you continue to walk in the truth. ⁴I have
no greater joy than to hear that my children are walking
in the truth.

⁵Dear friend, you are faithful in what you are doing
for the brothers, even though they are strangers to you.
⁶They have told the church about your love. You will do
well to send them on their way in a manner worthy of
God. ⁷It was for the sake of the Name that they went
out, receiving no help from the pagans. ⁸We ought
therefore to show hospitality to such men so that we
may work together for the truth.

⁹I wrote to the church, but Diotrephes, who loves to
be first, will have nothing to do with us. ¹⁰So if I come, I
will call attention to what he is doing, gossiping maliciously about us. Not satisfied with that, he refuses to
welcome the brothers. He also stops those who want to
do so and puts them out of the church.

¹¹Dear friend, do not imitate what is evil but what is
good. Anyone who does what is good is from God. Anyone who does what is evil has not seen God.
¹²Demetrius is well spoken of by everyone—and even
by the truth itself. We also speak well of him, and you
know that our testimony is true.

¹³I have much to write you, but I do not want to do
so with pen and ink. ¹⁴I hope to see you soon, and we
will talk face to face.

Peace to you. The friends here send their greetings.
Greet the friends there by name.

3 John

THE THEOLOGICAL AND historical controversy outlined for 2 John (see the introductory comments in the commentary on 2 John) is likewise applicable to this short letter (the smallest in the New Testament).[1] The entire Johannine community likely knew about the temptations to false doctrine, and this small congregation would have been no exception. Now, however, the challenge to John's leadership is becoming acute.

The literary and historical connection between 2 John and 3 John is almost impossible to establish. Clearly they stem from the same author, who in each case refers to himself as "the elder," uses similar terms (e.g., "truth," "love," "welcome"), and employs identical closing sentences (see 2 John 12; 3 John 13). There is no reason to doubt that this author could be John the apostle (likewise the author of 1 John).

The letter's recipients are more difficult to determine. Was this letter sent to the same church as 2 John? Some think that the earlier correspondence mentioned in 3 John 9 ("I wrote to the church") must be the letter 2 John. If this is true, Diotrephes read John's denunciation of the false teachers in the earlier correspondence, did not like it, and is now retaliating. But this is speculative and remains unproved. It is probably best to see this earlier letter, likely sent to Diotrephes, as lost or even destroyed. This much we know: The church of 3 John belonged to the wider Johannine community, read the publicly circulated 1 John, and lived at some distance from John himself.

Because 3 John is highly personal, it mentions several names that are now only names to us and presupposes a setting now lost to us. In fact, some have viewed it as the most nontheological letter in the New Testament. For instance, it is the only New Testament book that does not mention "Jesus" or "Christ" (but see v. 7). Rather than outlining a number of theological doctrines, 3 John is a brief note dashed off to one heroic Christian who is standing firm while a community near him is struggling under the pressure of a single antagonist. Rather than outline its themes (as we did in 2 John), if we sketch the setting of the letter, its various parts fall into place.

---

1. Second John has 245 words; 3 John has 219 words. By comparison Philemon has 355 words and Jude 457 words. The present letter is short enough to fit onto a single sheet of papyrus.

Rebuilding the Scene

IMAGINE A HOUSE church located some distance from John's primary ministry. It is in the grips of the theological struggle described in 1 John and confronted in 2 John. John himself once wrote to the church, but an influential man named Diotrephes rejected his letter (3 John 9)![2] John then sent emissaries to the church, but Diotrephes stepped forward and refused to acknowledge the traveling ministers (v. 10). He even repudiated John publicly (v. 9), spreading rumors about his character (v. 10). In fact, Diotrephes forcefully stopped anyone who showed sympathy to the visitors or tried to speak with them. "Anyone who sides with these men from John," Diotrephes threatened, "gets thrown out with them" (cf. v. 10).

The missionaries found a courageous host, however, in a man named Gaius. We cannot tell if Gaius belonged to Diotrephes's house church or if he lived some distance from it. Perhaps he was a leader of another house church located nearby. Clearly Gaius knows Diotrephes, but he does not feel threatened by that man's power. It was Gaius's habit to offer hospitality to traveling Christians and help finance their journeys (vv. 5–6). Thus he not only gave these emissaries from John rest and refreshment, but sent them "on their way" (v. 6)—that is, gave them money—and they returned to John with their report about the rebellion of Diotrephes's church and about Gaius's faithfulness (v. 3).

What should John do in response? He wants to visit the church personally but cannot at the present (v. 14). Yet he knows that he must shore up the true believers and encourage their faithfulness—people like Gaius, who still walk in the truth, whom he calls "friends" (v. 5), and whom he loves dearly (v. 1). He must also keep a foothold in the congregation. So John plans a strategy. In verses 5–8 he commends Gaius for his hospitality and encourages him to continue. The practical side of this is clear: When John himself comes for a visit, he will need allies who stand for Christ and against Diotrephes. Gaius will be one of those allies.

It is significant that John does not ask Gaius to intervene in the controversy by confronting Diotrephes himself. Christians are called to different roles, and Gaius has done enough if he stands firm for

---

2 The name Diotrephes is not common, but it does appear in Greek literature in the period

Jesus Christ and provides John and his couriers an entrée into the community.

John therefore writes this letter in anticipation of his upcoming visit. Verse 12 introduces the courier of the letter, a Christian named Demetrius. No doubt, John assumes, the hospitality and financial support shown to other Christian travelers will be extended to Demetrius, who is well known by the Johannine community and a personal friend of John himself. Moreover, John says, even "the truth" speaks well of him! Does this reference to "the truth" mean Jesus, the truth (cf. John 14:6)? Or does it mean that Demetrius's discipleship is in such harmony with the truth that his reputation is well known? We cannot know for sure.

This strong affirmation of Demetrius surely anticipates what Diotrephes will say about him. Demetrius bears the authority of John himself, and since Diotrephes rejects John, he will likewise reject Demetrius. This echoes Jesus' warning in John 15:18–19 about rejection and hatred, particularly by those who have "gone over" to the world (cf. 17:16):

> If the world hates you, keep in mind that it hated me first. If you belonged to the world, it would love you as its own. As it is, you do not belong to the world, but I have chosen you out of the world. That is why the world hates you.

John's testimony should strengthen Gaius's confidence in Demetrius, but the problem will only be resolved when John confronts Diotrephes personally.

Reconstructing John's Struggle with Diotrephes

WHAT WAS THE nature of the problem with Diotrephes? Why was he so antagonistic to John? The tense of the Greek verb in verse 9 translated "will have nothing to do" is present. This construction means that John is not referring to a single event but to an enduring attitude. The verb itself can mean two things, both of which are at work here. (1) Formally, it means "to receive or welcome" someone. Diotrephes was simply refusing to be hospitable to the missionaries. (2) But the verb also has a figurative meaning, carrying the idea "to accept or recognize" someone. Diotrephes was rejecting not merely his obligation to be hospitable, but John himself as elder. This rejection of the missionaries was his way of refusing to acknowledge the authority of John, and this attitude was going to continue.

Scholars have offered much speculation regarding the nature of the tension in 3 John, and this letter has been made to serve theories of what was happening in the late apostolic period when leadership was shifting to a second generation. If we distill these theories, two general orientations emerge.

(1) Some believe that Diotrephes represents an argument centered on church government, authority, and leadership (known as polity). In the period after the apostles, elder-bishops emerged, who enjoyed independent authority over their local congregations.[3] Perhaps Diotrephes was one such leader who coveted control. He may have hosted the house church in his home for some time and now desired more influence.[4] He did not like the extended authority of John and thought that an independent body should go its own way, under his direction.

A variation of this theme suggests that Diotrephes was not trying to rearrange structures of church government, but represents a charismatic leader who enjoyed the freedom promised in the Spirit to be spontaneous and creative. Perhaps he had held an office and was now enjoying a following. Perhaps he had usurped his power. In any case, it was the power of his personality that had won the day and intoxicated this man with dreams of authority. From his side, John represents a controlling ecclesiastical office that sought to limit Diotrephes's dreams.

(2) The problem of Diotrephes had to do with doctrine, not polity. He may have aligned himself with the secessionists mentioned in 1 and 2 John. Or perhaps he was a rival missionary working in the church or a member converted away from Johannine orthodoxy. In any case, he was an intellectual leader who had embraced a movement and a teaching contrary to John's defense of Jesus. On this accounting, he represents the opponents described in 2 John.

These two views are difficult to defend since 3 John gives us so little information about the struggles in this early period. To suggest

---

3 Evidence for this appears in Ignatius (see *Philad.* 7).

4. See Brown, *The Epistles of John*, 734, for this view

that here we have a mutiny against apostolic government presses the evidence too far, and to suggest a formal affiliation between Diotrephes and the secessionists is strained when we find virtually no theological argument in the letter concerning right faith in Jesus or obedience. Diotrephes is not called the "antichrist," a "deceiver," or a "false prophet," nor is he labeled with the criticisms John frequently uses (see 1 John 2:18; 3:10; 4:1; 2 John 7). On the other hand, the literary similarities between 2 and 3 John suggest that these letters are addressing similar contexts. Furthermore, note that 3 John continues to emphasize "the truth," as if orthodox belief is the subject of the struggle. First John also implies that the Christological controversy is widespread. To be sure, the rejected missionaries stood for "the Name" (v. 7), and one wonders if this is the basis of their rejection.

It is best to exclude grandiose schemes for this letter. Diotrephes was simply a powerful lay leader who had gained control and rejected John's authority. Possibly one way to undercut John's influence was to exploit the theological controversy that was circulating in the Johannine community. But there does not seem to be sufficient evidence to say that John viewed Diotrephes as a leading opponent in the secession.

WHEN WE LIFT this letter into the twentieth century, the same concerns that controlled 2 John must dictate our interpretation here. To some degree the context of our setting must parallel that of John in the first century. Third John is private correspondence, and we must be cautious as we seek to apply all of its concerns to our church when this was not John's intention.

An excellent example of a "bridging" of this letter that has gone wrong comes to us from Oral Roberts, the charismatic preacher and founder of Oral Roberts University in Tulsa, Oklahoma. Third John played a pivotal role in his spiritual life. In the midst of personal suffering and agony, Roberts felt that God had spoken to him personally and powerfully through the words of 3 John 2. In this verse, John seemed to be saying that God desired not simply spiritual prosperity—but prosperity in every respect. The following is how this verse is translated in the King James Version, the translation Roberts used:

"Beloved, I wish above all things that thou mayest prosper and be in health, even as thy soul prospereth." Clearly, Roberts thought, God desires spiritual abundance for us; but likewise this verse affirmed that abundance was to be ours *in all things*, particularly in matters of health and material prosperity. David Harrell, Roberts' biographer, chronicles the event carefully:

> Oral had rushed out of his house one morning to catch the bus to class when he realized he had not read his Bible, as was his custom. He returned, hastily grabbed his Bible, opened it "at random," and read 3 John 2. He had read his New Testament, he reported, at least a hundred times, but this verse seemed brand new. He called [his wife] Evelyn and read it to her. "This is not in the Bible," she challenged. "It is," Oral replied. "I just read it." "Evelyn," he said, "we have been wrong. I haven't been preaching that God is good. And Evelyn, if this verse is right, God is a good God." The idea seemed revolutionary, liberating. They had been nurtured in a belief system that insisted "you had to be poor to be a Christian." Perhaps it was not so. They talked excitedly about the verse's implications. Did it mean they could have a new car, a new house, a brand-new ministry? In later years, Evelyn looked back on that morning as the point of embarkation: "I really believe that that very morning was the beginning of this worldwide ministry that [Oral] has had, because it opened up his thinking."[5]

This "discovery" led Roberts to pursue a world-famous healing ministry, and today 3 John 2 has become a favorite verse among Pentecostal and charismatic believers. Those committed to the so-called "prosperity gospel" know it well and use it frequently.

But sadly, this was not John's intention. Good health and success were themes that accompanied personal letters throughout the Greek world (cf. Rom. 1:10). The words found in 3 John 2 were not written as biblical promises, but were mere literary formulas one might use to greet a reader. At the Pentecostal Church of God School of Theology in Cleveland, Tennessee, New Testament scholar Chris

---

5. For a survey of Oral Roberts' life and how this verse played a pivotal role, see David Harrell, *Oral Roberts An American Life* (Bloomington, Ind · Indiana Univ. Press, 1985), 65–66.

Thomas uses this verse as a case study in all of his introductory interpretation classes. According to him, 3 John is the ideal example of an ancient letter, and interpreting it rightly avoids the misuse of verses such as verse 2. A quick examination of the first few verses in Paul's letters shows how that apostle used customary formulas to open his correspondence. Today we greet one another with a formula saying like, "How are you?" but we rarely have in mind receiving an inventory of someone's health. For this reason, "Fine" is the acceptable answer, regardless of how we may feel! For someone to construe John's ancient greeting as a theological affirmation misses his entire point; his serious concerns about the church and its well-being are to follow in subsequent verses.

The elder John is trying to work with a congregation—a house church—that is being led by a man who has rejected his pastoral authority. Because of distance or some other problem we do not know, John is unable visit the church yet and thus is doing his best by sending letters and representatives. This problem of leadership at a distance must have been common among the early apostolic leaders. Paul's churches, for example, were built around the Mediterranean world, and when controversies arose, distance and the inconvenience of travel in that day made correspondence essential. He used letters and emissaries for his churches in Galatia, Colosse, and Thessalonica in the same way. Titus, Timothy, and Silas were all men who no doubt served the apostle in this capacity. Demetrius is one such emissary for John in the current setting.

Third John suggests that the Johannine community was made up of scattered congregations (tradition suggests that they were all in western Asia Minor, near Ephesus). As they grew, they brought in converts who had no knowledge of the history of the church or the importance of apostolic tradition. Imagine young Christians believing in Jesus and not knowing much about his followers or their teachings! The names given in 3 John (Gaius, Diotrephes, and Demetrius) are all Greek; this fact suggests a cultural context far removed from Judea and Galilee. Thus when a traditional source of authority steps forward—an apostolic elder—some chafed at the thought of submission. "Our religion is working for us! It feels right! Why should we conform to a foreigner, someone who represents traditions and people we don't even know?"

Therefore, 3 John raises some interesting questions about conflict resolution and pastoral leadership in the church that have an immediate value for us today. John knows he has a problem here. This letter is evidence of his strategy to solve it. Consequently, I will use 3 John successfully when I can adapt his strategy for my own.

CONFLICT IS NO stranger to the church. Strong persons like Diotrephes often become leaders and teachers. In fact, they are generally invited and encouraged in those roles and quickly enjoy a wide following. But what happens when the views of people like this conflict with pastoral leadership? Perhaps it is not disagreement about views at all but a conflict of personalities, some form of competition, or even a loss of respect for each other. In some cases (rare ones, we hope), such lay leaders pose an overwhelming threat to pastoral authority. I have known cases where a "Diotrephes" has successfully worked to remove a pastor or where such a person has actually split the church in two, sometimes making an irreparable fracture within the congregation and sometimes leading parishioners out to form a second congregation.

(1) *John's first strategy.* I am intrigued by the way John did not let go of this situation. He persisted, first by sending a letter (that was tossed out) and then by sending emissaries (who were rejected). But he did not allow this to discourage him. Third John is his second letter, sent with another emissary, Demetrius. I sense that John is determined not to let this church—or Diotrephes—go.

John's first strategy for resolving this conflict, therefore, is not to retreat but to remain in contact. This should be our strategy too. All too often our impulse when we must confront people of strong will and ambition is to retreat. The prospect of losing or of being shamed is so apparent that it seems better to "wait and see" what will happen, to stay on the sidelines, or to keep away from the perpetrators. Others will muster support against someone like Diotrephes and be passive-aggressive, sabotaging him at every turn and discrediting his standing in the church. Those to take this approach use the very tools criticized in 3 John 10: "I will call attention to what he is doing, gossiping maliciously about us."

Of course, the chief reason for remaining connected to the "Diotrepheses" of our world is to save the church! Many times they are confusing zeal for the body of Christ with personal ambition, and as their power grows, the church itself is harmed. But there is another reason for not giving up. Diotrephes needs to be saved from himself. *Diotrephes needs John*. For John to show weakness by retreating is to posture himself in a way that makes it impossible for Diotrephes to respect him. Diotrephes needs John to be strong and persistent because that is the only strategy that can penetrate his heart. This courageous role is one way in which John can love Diotrephes.

This first strategy seems clear enough, but in today's church it also may seem idealistic. When pastoral leadership is challenged by a confrontive, aggressive Diotrephes, there is a great deal of risk involved. In some cases a pastor's job is at stake. What then? If the balance of power is possessed by his opponents, a pastor can be easily threatened. *And Diotrephes knows it.* Therefore, there must be leverage and support from without, from outside the congregation. There must also be proactive, encouraging support from within the church's lay leadership. Either way, pastors cannot be left alone to slay the Diotrepheses of the world.

(2) *John's second strategy.* But there is more. John has found an ally in Gaius. This man is not called to manipulate the situation or to confront Diotrephes. Gaius knows Diotrephes well and could, of course, play this role. But John chooses not to work indirectly. Gaius is simply an objective foothold in the situation, someone who lives neither in John's camp nor in that of Diotrephes. Gaius knows the situation but is not embroiled in the crisis and certainly is not infected with Diotrephes's peculiar form of rebellion.

When Demetrius (the courier of 3 John) came to stay with Gaius, what did he learn? Did John use this as an opportunity to get an objective "read" on the crisis? And when John himself finally came to the area and Gaius and John could talk "face to face" (v. 14), what did he ask? It will not do to think that John exploited Gaius and his position in order to discredit Diotrephes. Even though the language of verses 9– 10 may sound strong to us, it is mild compared with John's tone for the heretics who were picking off his congregations (see 1 and 2 John). None of the polemical flourishes of John's earlier letters appear here.

Gaius becomes a point of reference that gives John pastoral objectivity in this remote congregation. Gaius no doubt could correct the apostle's notions of the severity of the crisis, much like Titus counseled Paul during his conflict with the Corinthian church (2 Cor. 7:5–13). Wounded pastors—John included—have trouble being objective. *John needs Gaius.* Without him, John can have no confidence that his approach in the situation is correct. Modern crises are no different than those of the first-century world. Pastoral objectivity that is anchored in the counsel of wise elders is always superior.

(3) *John's third strategy.* The final striking dimension of this letter is John's willingness to talk personally with Diotrephes. When he cannot be there, he sends a letter. But when he has opportunity, he will come personally. This pattern is striking because the situation is clearly dangerous. Paul took this same risk when he went to Corinth on his "painful visit" (2 Cor. 2:1). And as the evidence of 2 Corinthians suggests, he was asked to leave the church against his will.[6] Those in charge decided that Paul was not welcome. Fortunately, through the efforts of mediators such as Titus, the church repented and Paul returned. Nevertheless, such confrontations incur high risk.

The temptation to avoid Diotrephes and fall silent must have occurred to John. It is one thing to write a letter or even send a messenger. But it is altogether another matter to go personally and confront your opponent. We can successfully rationalize conflict avoidance in countless ways. I know Christian leaders who as children grew up with so much conflict that confronting a potentially hostile situation is virtually impossible. I know others who have an inherent sense of powerlessness that has been born through the destructive work of tyrannical parents. Such powerlessness often masquerades as Christian piety and meekness, but it is neither of these.

John is confident that he can enter this situation successfully because he is prepared. He has continued to communicate with those in the church; he has counseled with his couriers; he will talk deeply with Gaius when he gets there; and he knows that God is with him and that God's desire is for the truth to win and for his people to walk in its freedom and joy. God wants his church—the Johannine churches and our churches—to grow in love and truth. If all parties—John and Diotrephes alike, pastors and lay leaders alike—fail to stand for the

---

6. On the evidence for Paul's painful visit (not recorded in Acts), see any of the major introductions on the Corinthian correspondence.

truth and to act in sincere, courageous love, the vigor of the church will be compromised.

Of course, this raises countless modern questions. How should the church plan for confrontations? What processes should be in place to make sure that concerns are heard fairly and objectively? Many denominations today have judicial structures in place that help arbitrate such confrontations, but many independent churches do not. Will the pastor then have a solo, head-on confrontation? Will chaos erupt? Moreover, congregations must wrestle with another more troubling question. Second John 10–11 suggest that John is willing to take severe measures against people like Diotrephes. Should he not repent, I feel confident that John would have chosen to remove him from the church. Note how in 1 Corinthians 5 Paul suggested such a tactic regarding an immoral man in that congregation. Should today's church have similar resolve and courage? Are we in theory ready to reject an unrepentant Diotrephes? And would we in practice be able to do it?

Scripture Index

Scripture Index

Scripture Index

Subject Index

Bring ancient truth to modern life with the
NIV Application Commentary *series*

Covering both the Old and New Testaments, the **NIV Application Commentary** series is a staple reference for pastors seeking to bring the Bible's timeless message into a modern context. It explains not only what the Bible means but also how that meaning impacts the lives of believers today.

Genesis
This commentary demonstrates how the text charts a course of theological affirmation that results in a simple but majestic account of an ordered, purposeful cosmos with God at the helm, masterfully guiding it, and what this means to us today.

John H. Walton   ISBN: 978-0-310-20617-0

Exodus
The truth of Christ's resurrection and its resulting impact on our lives mean that to Christians, the application of Exodus is less about how to act than it is about what God has done and what it means to be his children.

Peter Enns   ISBN: 978-0-310-20607-1

Leviticus, Numbers
Roy Gane's commentary on Leviticus and Numbers helps readers understand how the message of these two books, which are replete with what seem to be archaic laws, can have a powerful impact on Christians today.

Roy Gane   ISBN: 978-0-310-21088-7

Judges, Ruth
This commentary helps readers learn how the messages of Judges and Ruth can have the same powerful impact today that they did when they were first written. Judges reveals a God who employs very human deliverers but refuses to gloss over their sins and the consequences of those sins. Ruth demonstrates the far-reaching impact of a righteous character.

K. Lawson Younger Jr.   ISBN: 978-0-310-20636-1

1&2 Samuel

In Samuel, we meet Saul, David, Goliath, Jonathan, Bathsheba, the witch of Endor, and other unforgettable characters. And we encounter ourselves. For while the culture and conditions of Israel under its first kings are vastly different from our own, the basic issues of humans in relation to God, the Great King, have not changed. Sin, repentance, forgiveness, adversity, prayer, faith, and the promises of God—these continue to play out in our lives today.

Bill T. Arnold ISBN: 978-0-310-21086-3

1&2 Chronicles

First and Second Chronicles are a narrative steeped in the best and worst of the human heart—but they are also a revelation of Yahweh at work, forwarding his purposes in the midst of fallible people, but a people who trust in the Lord and his word through the prophets. God has a plan to which he is committed.

Andrew E. Hill ISBN: 978-0-310-20610-1

Esther

Karen H. Jobes shows what a biblical narrative that never mentions God tells Christians about him today.

Karen H. Jobes ISBN: 978-0-310-20672-9

Psalms Volume 1

Gerald Wilson examines Books 1 and 2 of the Psalter. His seminal work on the shaping of the Hebrew Psalter has opened a new avenue of psalms research by shifting focus from exclusive attention to individual psalms to the arrangement of the psalms into groups.

Gerald H. Wilson ISBN: 978-0-310-20635-4

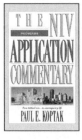

Proverbs

Few people can remember when they last heard a sermon from Proverbs or looked together at its chapters. In this NIV Application Commentary on Proverbs, Paul Koptak gives numerous aids to pastors and church leaders on how to study, reflect on, and apply this book on biblical wisdom as part of the educational ministry of their churches.

Paul Koptak ISBN: 978-0-310-21852-4

Ecclesiastes, Song of Songs

Ecclesiastes and Songs of Songs have always presented particular challenges to their readers, especially if those readers are seeking to understand them as part of Christian Scripture. Revealing the links between the Scriptures and our own times, Iain Provan shows how these wisdom books speak to us today with relevance and conviction.

Iain Provan   ISBN: 978-0-310-21372-7

Isaiah

Isaiah wrestles with the realities of people who are not convicted by the truth but actually hardened by it, and with a God whose actions sometimes seem unintelligible, or even worse, appears to be absent. Yet Isaiah penetrates beyond these experiences to an even greater reality. Isaiah sees God's rule over history and his capacity to take the worst of human actions and use it for good. He declares the truth that even in the darkest hours, the Holy One of Israel is infinitely trustworthy.

John N. Oswalt   ISBN: 978-0-310-20613-2

Jeremiah/Lamentations

These two books cannot be separated from the political conditions of ancient Judah. Beginning with the time of King Josiah, who introduced religious reform, Jeremiah reflects the close link between spiritual and political prosperity or disaster for the nation as a whole.

J. Andrew Dearman   ISBN: 978-0-310-20616-3

Ezekiel

Discover how, properly understood, this mysterious book with its obscure images offers profound comfort to us today.

Iain M. Duguid   ISBN: 978-0-310-21047-4

Daniel

Tremper Longman III reveals how the practical stories and spellbinding apocalyptic imagery of Daniel contain principles that are as relevant now as they were in the days of the Babylonian Captivity.

Tremper Longman III   ISBN: 978-0-310-20608-8

Hosea, Amos, Micah

Scratch beneath the surface of today's culture and you'll find we're not so different from ancient Israel. Revealing the links between Israel eight centuries B.C. and our own times, Gary V. Smith shows how the prophetic writings of Hosea, Amos, and Micah speak to us today with relevance and conviction.

Gary V. Smith   ISBN: 978-0-310-20614-9

Jonah, Nahum, Habakkuk, Zephaniah

James Bruckner shows how the messages of these four Old Testament prophets, who lived during some of Israel and Judah's most turbulent times, are as powerful in today's turbulent times as when first written.

James Bruckner   ISBN: 978-0-310-20637-8

Joel, Obadiah, Malachi

David Baker shows how these three short prophetic books contain both a message of impending judgment (for Israel's enemies and for Israel herself) and a message of great hope — of the outpouring of God's Spirit, of restoration and renewal, and of a coming Messiah. We need to hear that same message today.

David W. Baker   ISBN: 978-0-310-20723-8

Haggai, Zechariah

This commentary on Haggai and Zechariah helps readers learn how the message of these two prophets who challenged and encouraged the people of God after the return from Babylon can have the same powerful impact on the community of faith today.

Mark J. Boda   ISBN: 978-0-310-20615-6

Matthew
Matthew helps readers learn how the message of Matthew's gospel can have the same powerful impact today that it did when the author first wrote it.

Michael J. Wilkins ISBN: 978-0-310-49310-5

Mark
Learn how the challenging gospel of Mark can leave recipients with the same powerful questions and answers it did when it was written.

David E. Garland ISBN: 978-0-310-49350-1

Luke
Focus on the most important application of all: "the person of Jesus and the nature of God's work through him to deliver humanity."

Darrell L. Bock ISBN: 978-0-310-49330-3

John
Learn both halves of the interpretive task. Gary M. Burge shows readers how to bring the ancient message of John into a modern context. He also explains not only what the book of John meant to its original readers but also how it can speak powerfully today.

Gary M. Burge ISBN: 978-0-310-49750-9

Acts
Study the first portraits of the church in action around the world with someone whose ministry mirrors many of the events in Acts. Biblical scholar and worldwide evangelist Ajith Fernando applies the story of the church's early development to the global mission of believers today.

Ajith Fernando ISBN: 978-0-310-49410-2

Romans
Paul's letter to the Romans remains one of the most important expressions of Christian truth ever written. Douglas Moo comments on the text and then explores issues in Paul's culture and in ours that help us understand the ultimate meaning of each paragraph.

Douglas J. Moo   ISBN: 978-0-310-49400-3

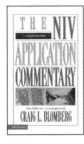

1 Corinthians
Is your church struggling with the problem of divisiveness and fragmentation? See the solution Paul gave the Corinthian Christians over 2,000 years ago. It still works today!

Craig Blomberg   ISBN: 978-0-310-48490-5

2 Corinthians
Often recognized as the most difficult of Paul's letters to understand, 2 Corinthians can have the same powerful impact today that it did when it was first written.

Scott J. Hafemann   ISBN: 978-0-310-49420-1

Galatians
A pastor's message is true not because of his preaching or people-management skills, but because of Christ. Learn how to apply Paul's example of visionary church leadership to your own congregation.

Scot McKnight   ISBN: 978-0-310-48470-7

Ephesians
Explore what the author calls "a surprisingly comprehensive statement about God and his work, about Christ and the gospel, about life with God's Spirit, and about the right way to live."

Klyne Snodgrass   ISBN: 978-0-310-49340-2

Philippians
The best lesson Philippians provides is how to encourage people who actually are doing quite well. Learn why not all the New Testament letters are reactions to theological crises.

Frank Thielman   ISBN: 978-0-310-49300-6

Colossians/Philemon
The temptation to trust in the wrong things has always been strong. Use this commentary to learn the importance of trusting only in Jesus, God's Son, in whom all the fullness of God lives. No message is more important for our post-modern culture.

David E. Garland   ISBN: 978-0-310-48480-6

1&2 Thessalonians
Paul's letters to the Thessalonians say as much to us today about Christ's return and our resurrection as they did in the early church. This volume skillfully reveals Paul's answers to these questions and how they address the needs of contemporary Christians.

Michael W. Holmes   ISBN: 978-0-310-49380-8

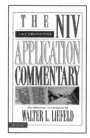

1&2 Timothy, Titus
Reveals the context and meanings of Paul's letters to two leaders in the early Christian Church and explores their present-day implications to help you to accurately apply the principles they contain to contemporary issues.

Walter L. Liefeld   ISBN: 978-0-310-50110-7

Hebrews
The message of Hebrews can be summed up in a single phrase: "God speaks effectively to us through Jesus." Unpack the theological meaning of those seven words and learn why the gospel still demands a hearing today.

George H. Guthrie   ISBN: 978-0-310-49390-7

1 Peter

The issue of the church's relationship to the state hits the news media in some form nearly every day. Learn how Peter answered the question for Christians surviving under Roman rule and how it applies similarly to believers living amid the secular institutions of the modern world.

Scot McKnight

ISBN: 978-0-310-49290-0

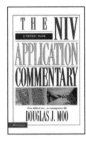

2 Peter, Jude

Introduce your modern audience to letters they may not be familiar with and show why they'll want to get to know them.

Douglas J. Moo

ISBN: 978-0-310-20104-5

Letters of John

Like the community in John's time, which faced disputes over erroneous "secret knowledge," today's church needs discernment in affirming new ideas supported by Scripture and weeding out harmful notions. This volume will help you show today's Christians how to use John's example.

Gary M. Burge

ISBN: 978-0-310-48620-6

Revelation

Craig Keener offers a "new" approach to the book of Revelation by focusing on the "old." He stresses the need for believers to prepare for the possibility of suffering for the sake of Jesus.

Craig S. Keener

ISBN: 978-0-310-23192-9